CHAPTER 1: INTRODUCTION TO NEXT.JS AND ITS ECOSYSTEM

Next.js, a powerful and flexible JavaScript framework, has emerged as a pivotal tool in the realm of modern web development. This introductory chapter delves into the framework's essence, tracing its evolution and elucidating the core principles that define its operation. By providing a thorough overview of Next.js, this chapter sets the foundation for a deeper exploration of its features and the significant role it plays in building scalable, efficient web applications.

Initially released in 2016 by Vercel (formerly Zeit), Next.js was designed to address some of the inherent limitations of traditional single-page applications (SPAs). SPAs, while providing a smooth user experience through client-side rendering, often face challenges with performance, SEO optimization, and initial load times. Next.js sought to overcome these issues by integrating server-side rendering (SSR) capabilities into the framework. This shift allowed for improved page load speeds and better search engine visibility, both crucial aspects for modern web applications.

At its core, Next.js operates on a set of principles that distinguish it from other JavaScript frameworks. One of its foundational principles is the concept of server-side rendering. SSR enables the server to generate the HTML for a page at the request time, rather than relying on the client to build the page dynamically. This results in faster initial page loads and improved SEO, as search engines can index fully rendered pages more effectively. Furthermore, Next.js supports static site generation (SSG), which pre-renders pages at build time, offering additional performance benefits and scalability for sites with static content.

Another fundamental principle of Next.js is its emphasis on simplicity and developer experience. The framework offers a minimalistic setup that allows developers to start building applications quickly without extensive configuration. Its file-based routing system simplifies the creation of new pages and routes, enabling developers to focus on building features rather than managing complex routing logic. This straightforward approach, coupled with built-in support for features such as API routes and dynamic imports, contributes to a streamlined development process.

Next.js also incorporates a powerful set of features designed to enhance application performance and scalability. Automatic code splitting is one such feature, which ensures that only the necessary code for a given page is loaded, reducing the overall bundle size and improving load times. This is achieved through Next.js's built-in support for dynamic imports and its ability to split JavaScript bundles at the page level. Additionally, the framework offers optimized image handling through its Image component, which supports responsive images, lazy loading, and automatic format conversion to ensure optimal performance across different devices.

The framework's integration with React, the library on which it is built, further augments its capabilities. React's component-based architecture aligns seamlessly with Next.js's structure, allowing developers to leverage reusable components and manage application state efficiently. Next.js enhances React with features such as static and server-side rendering, making it a more versatile tool for building complex applications. This synergy between React and Next.js has played a significant role in the widespread adoption of the framework.

In addition to these core principles and features, Next.js is also part of a broader ecosystem that includes a variety of tools and services designed to support modern web development. Vercel, the company behind Next.js, offers a hosting platform optimized for Next.js applications, providing features such as automatic deployments, performance monitoring, and serverless functions. This integration between the framework and its hosting platform ensures that developers can deploy and scale their applications with ease, leveraging the full potential of Next.js.

Moreover, the Next.js ecosystem extends beyond the core framework to include a rich set of plugins, libraries, and community-driven resources. These tools provide additional functionality and enhance the development experience, from state management libraries like Redux and Zustand to UI component libraries such as Material-UI and Tailwind CSS. The active and supportive Next.js community contributes to a vibrant ecosystem, offering tutorials, best practices, and extensions that help developers build and optimize their applications.

As we embark on this exploration of Next.js, it is essential to recognize its impact on modern web development and its role in addressing the challenges faced by traditional frameworks. By integrating server-side rendering, static site generation, and a focus on simplicity and performance, Next.js has established itself as a vital tool for developers seeking to build high-quality, scalable applications. This chapter lays the groundwork for a deeper understanding of Next.js, setting the stage for a comprehensive examination of its features, use cases, and best practices in subsequent chapters.

In summary, Next.js represents a significant advancement in web development, providing a framework that combines the best of server-side rendering and client-side interactivity. Its evolution, core principles, and integration with React position it as a powerful and flexible tool for creating modern web applications. As we continue our exploration, we will delve into the specifics of Next.js's features and capabilities, offering insights into how they can be leveraged to build robust and efficient web solutions.

Next.js's architecture integrates seamlessly with the modern web development landscape, offering a robust solution for a variety of use cases. One of its standout features is the built-in support for static and dynamic rendering strategies, which cater to different application requirements. This flexibility allows developers to choose the most appropriate rendering method based on the specific needs of their project. For instance, static site generation is ideal for content that doesn't change frequently, such as blog posts or documentation. On the other hand, server-side rendering is more suitable for applications requiring real-time data fetching, where the content needs to be updated frequently or personalized for each user.

The framework's support for incremental static regeneration (ISR) further enhances its capabilities. ISR allows developers to update static content without needing to rebuild the entire site. This approach combines the performance benefits of static generation with the dynamic capabilities of server-side rendering, enabling applications to deliver fresh content efficiently while maintaining fast load times. This feature is particularly advantageous for large-scale applications where frequent updates are necessary but rebuilding the entire site would be impractical.

Next.js's ecosystem is enriched by its integration with various tools and libraries that extend its functionality. One such integration is with the popular React framework. As Next.js is built on top of React, it inherits React's component-based architecture, which facilitates the development of modular and reusable UI components. This synergy between Next.js and React simplifies the development process, as developers can leverage their existing knowledge of React while taking advantage of Next.js's additional features.

The framework also provides built-in support for TypeScript, a statically typed superset of JavaScript. TypeScript's inclusion in Next.js ensures type safety and improves code quality by catching potential errors during development. This integration enhances the developer experience by providing clearer and more maintainable code, which is especially beneficial in large projects with complex codebases.

Another crucial aspect of Next.js's ecosystem is its focus on performance optimization. The framework includes various built-in features to ensure that applications run efficiently. For example, the automatic image optimization provided by the Next.js Image component helps manage and deliver high-quality images with minimal impact on page load times. This feature automatically optimizes images based on the device's screen size and resolution, reducing the need for manual image handling and ensuring that users receive the best possible visual experience.

Additionally, Next.js supports API routes, which allow developers to build backend functionality directly within their Next.js application. This feature simplifies the development process by enabling serverless functions to be integrated seamlessly with the frontend. API routes provide a convenient way to handle requests, manage data, and perform server-side operations without the need for a separate backend server.

The framework's emphasis on flexibility and modularity extends to its plugin system as well. Next.js's plugin architecture allows developers to extend the framework's capabilities with custom plugins and integrations. This extensibility is particularly useful for incorporating third-party services, implementing custom configurations, or optimizing specific aspects of an application's performance.

The strong community support surrounding Next.js further contributes to its prominence in the web development ecosystem. A vibrant and active community continuously contributes to the framework's growth, providing valuable resources such as documentation, tutorials, and open-source plugins. This collective effort ensures that developers have access to a wealth of knowledge and tools, facilitating a smoother development process and fostering innovation within the Next.js ecosystem.

Moreover, Next.js benefits from regular updates and improvements, driven by its active maintainers and contributors. These updates often introduce new features, enhance existing functionality, and address any emerging challenges in web development. By staying up-to-date with the latest developments, developers can take advantage of cutting-edge capabilities and maintain the relevance and efficiency of their applications.

In summary, Next.js has established itself as a powerful framework that addresses many of the challenges faced by modern web developers. Its ability to integrate static and dynamic rendering, coupled with its performance optimization features and extensive ecosystem, makes it a versatile and essential tool for building scalable web applications. By leveraging the framework's built-in capabilities and engaging with its supportive community, developers can create high-performance applications that meet the demands of today's digital landscape.

Next.js supports API routes, a feature that significantly simplifies the process of creating serverless functions. These routes enable developers to build backend services and APIs directly within the Next.js application. This capability is particularly beneficial for projects that require server-side logic, such as handling form submissions, authentication, or integrating with external services. By keeping both the frontend and backend components within a single project structure, Next.js streamlines the development workflow and fosters a more cohesive development environment.

The framework's support for custom server configurations also enhances its flexibility. While Next.js comes with a built-in server capable of handling most use cases, developers can opt to use a custom server configuration when more complex server-side logic is needed. This allows for greater control over routing, middleware, and other server-side functionalities, making Next.js adaptable to a wide range of application requirements.

Moreover, the Next.js ecosystem is supported by a vibrant community and a rich set of resources. The framework is backed by extensive documentation, a variety of tutorials, and a thriving community forum. These resources are invaluable for both novice and experienced developers, providing guidance and support as they navigate the intricacies of Next.js development. Additionally, the ecosystem benefits from numerous plugins and integrations that extend its capabilities, offering solutions for common challenges such as authentication, data management, and state handling.

As the web development landscape continues to evolve, Next.js remains at the forefront of innovation by adapting to new trends and technologies. The framework's commitment to embracing modern web standards and practices ensures that it remains a relevant and powerful tool for building contemporary web applications. Whether integrating with GraphQL for advanced data querying, leveraging serverless architectures for scalable backend solutions, or adopting new features from the evolving React ecosystem, Next.js provides a flexible and forward-thinking foundation for developers.

In summary, Next.js represents a significant advancement in the realm of web development, offering a comprehensive solution that balances performance, scalability, and ease of use. Its evolution from a server-side rendering tool to a versatile framework capable of handling static and dynamic content, integrating with modern development tools, and supporting a wide range of use cases highlights its importance in contemporary web development. As we proceed further, we will delve deeper into specific features and best practices for leveraging Next.js to build robust and scalable web applications, exploring how its principles and tools can be effectively applied to real-world scenarios.

CHAPTER 2:
SETTING UP YOUR
DEVELOPMENT
ENVIRONMENT

Establishing a robust development environment is a crucial first step in working with Next.js, as it lays the foundation for a smooth and efficient development process. This chapter provides a comprehensive guide to setting up your environment, covering the installation of essential tools and packages, configuring your local setup, and optimizing your workflow to enhance productivity.

To begin with, the installation of Next.js itself is straightforward, thanks to its compatibility with Node.js, a runtime that allows JavaScript to be executed server-side. Ensure that Node.js is installed on your system; this can be verified by running the `node -v` command in your terminal, which should return the version number of Node.js. If Node.js is not yet installed, it can be downloaded from the official Node.js website and installed according to the instructions provided.

With Node.js in place, you can proceed to install Next.js. This is typically done using a package manager such as npm or yarn. For npm, the command `npx create-next-app@latest my-next-app` initializes a new Next.js project in a directory named `my-next-app`. Alternatively, if you prefer yarn, the command `yarn create next-app my-next-app` achieves the same result. This command sets up a new project with a default configuration, including essential dependencies and project structure.

Once the project is created, navigate to the project directory using `cd my-next-app` and start the development server with `npm run dev` or `yarn dev`. This command launches the Next.js development server, which serves your application locally. Opening your browser and navigating to `http://localhost:3000` should display the default Next.js welcome page, indicating that your environment is correctly set up.

Next, configuring your development environment involves setting up additional tools and preferences to enhance your workflow. One critical aspect is the configuration of a code editor or integrated development environment (IDE). Popular choices for JavaScript development include Visual Studio Code, Sublime Text, and Atom. Among these, Visual Studio Code is highly recommended due to its extensive extension marketplace and robust support for JavaScript and TypeScript development. Extensions such as ESLint, Prettier, and the Next.js Snippets can greatly improve code quality and efficiency.

In addition to configuring your code editor, consider setting up a version control system, such as Git. Git allows you to track changes to your codebase, collaborate with others, and manage different versions of your application. Initialize a Git repository in your Next.js project directory with `git init`, and create an initial commit to begin tracking your project's history. For remote repository management, platforms like GitHub, GitLab, or Bitbucket offer cloud-based repositories that facilitate collaboration and code sharing.

Another important aspect of your development environment

is package management. Both npm and yarn are popular choices for managing project dependencies. npm, which comes bundled with Node.js, provides a straightforward approach to package management. Yarn, an alternative package manager, is known for its speed and reliability, and it can be installed globally using `npm install -g yarn`. Whichever package manager you choose, ensure that your dependencies are consistently managed and updated to avoid potential issues with outdated or incompatible packages.

Configuring your development environment also involves setting up environment variables and configuration files. Next.js supports environment variables through `.env` files, which allow you to define settings specific to different environments, such as development, staging, and production. Create a `.env.local` file in the root of your project to store environment-specific variables, and use the `process.env` object to access these variables in your code. Properly managing environment variables helps maintain a clean and secure configuration, avoiding hard-coded values in your source code.

To further optimize your workflow, consider integrating task runners and build tools. Tools such as Webpack, Babel, and ESLint are commonly used in JavaScript development to streamline the build process, manage module bundling, and enforce coding standards. Next.js includes built-in support for Webpack and Babel, but configuring additional plugins and loaders can tailor the build process to your specific needs. ESLint, a linter for identifying and fixing problems in your code, can be configured to follow best practices and maintain code quality across your project.

Finally, familiarize yourself with the Next.js documentation and community resources. The official Next.js documentation provides detailed information on various features, configuration options, and best practices. Additionally, the

Next.js community, including forums, blogs, and social media channels, offers valuable insights and support. Engaging with the community can help you stay updated on the latest developments and learn from the experiences of other developers.

In conclusion, setting up a robust development environment for Next.js involves installing essential tools and packages, configuring your local setup, and optimizing your workflow. By following these guidelines, you will establish a solid foundation for building efficient and scalable Next.js applications. The steps outlined in this chapter ensure that you are well-prepared to start your development journey, equipped with the tools and knowledge needed to navigate the Next.js ecosystem effectively.

Establishing an efficient development environment extends beyond the initial setup of Next.js and your code editor. It also involves configuring additional tools and practices to streamline your development process and enhance productivity. One important aspect of this configuration is version control, which is critical for managing changes to your codebase and collaborating with other developers. Git, a distributed version control system, is widely used in the industry and integrates seamlessly with Next.js projects.

To begin using Git, initialize a repository in your project directory with the command `git init`. This creates a new Git repository, allowing you to start tracking changes to your code. It is also advisable to create a `.gitignore` file to specify which files and directories should be excluded from version control. For a Next.js project, this file typically includes node_modules, build artifacts, and environment variables. By defining these exclusions, you prevent unnecessary files from cluttering your repository and ensure that only relevant changes are tracked.

In addition to Git, setting up a robust workflow involves

incorporating a task runner or build tool to automate repetitive tasks and improve efficiency. Tools such as npm scripts, Gulp, or Webpack can be configured to handle tasks like linting, testing, and building your application. Next.js comes with built-in support for many of these tasks, but you can extend its functionality by integrating additional tools as needed. For example, setting up a script for code linting with ESLint helps maintain code quality and consistency, while configuring Jest for unit testing ensures that your application's components behave as expected.

Another critical component of your development environment is the management of environment variables. Next.js supports environment variables out of the box, allowing you to define and access configuration settings for different environments, such as development, staging, and production. These variables are typically stored in a `.env.local` file at the root of your project. For example, you might define API keys or database connection strings in this file, ensuring that sensitive information is kept separate from your codebase. By leveraging environment variables, you can manage configuration settings more securely and adapt your application to various deployment scenarios.

As you refine your development environment, consider implementing continuous integration and continuous deployment (CI/CD) practices to automate the build and deployment process. CI/CD tools, such as GitHub Actions, CircleCI, or Travis CI, can be configured to automatically build and deploy your Next.js application whenever changes are pushed to your repository. This automation reduces the risk of errors and ensures that your application is consistently built and deployed according to predefined workflows. For instance, you might configure a CI/CD pipeline to run tests, build the production version of your application, and deploy it to a hosting provider like Vercel or Netlify.

Optimizing your development environment also involves understanding and managing dependencies effectively. Next.js projects rely on various npm packages, some of which may have their own dependencies. It is essential to regularly update these packages to benefit from the latest features, bug fixes, and security patches. The `npm outdated` command can be used to check for outdated packages, while `npm update` updates them to their latest versions. Additionally, using a package lock file, such as `package-lock.json`, helps maintain consistency across different environments by locking the versions of your dependencies.

Lastly, it is important to consider the performance of your development environment. Tools and configurations that enhance performance can significantly impact your productivity. For instance, enabling features like hot module replacement (HMR) in your code editor or development server allows for immediate feedback during development, reducing the time spent waiting for changes to be reflected in your application. Furthermore, optimizing your local environment by managing system resources and using efficient hardware can improve the responsiveness of your development tools and overall workflow.

In conclusion, setting up a development environment for Next.js involves a series of steps that extend beyond the initial installation of the framework. By configuring version control, integrating task runners, managing environment variables, implementing CI/CD practices, and optimizing performance, you create a robust and efficient environment conducive to effective development. This foundation will support your efforts as you delve deeper into building and refining Next.js applications, ensuring that your development process is both productive and sustainable.

integrate testing, build, and deployment workflows into your development cycle. By setting up automated pipelines, you ensure that every change made to the codebase is tested and deployed consistently, reducing the risk of errors and streamlining the release process. For instance, you might configure GitHub Actions to trigger a build whenever code is pushed to the repository. This build process can include steps such as running tests, linting code, and deploying the application to a staging environment. By automating these processes, you can maintain a high level of code quality and expedite the delivery of new features and bug fixes.

Additionally, it is beneficial to configure tools for monitoring and performance optimization. Next.js includes features that inherently support performance optimization, such as automatic code splitting and server-side rendering. However, integrating additional tools for monitoring can provide deeper insights into your application's performance and user experience. Tools like Google Lighthouse or Web Vitals offer valuable metrics on page load times, accessibility, and overall performance, helping you identify areas for improvement. By regularly monitoring these metrics, you can make informed decisions to enhance the performance and reliability of your application.

Another aspect of optimizing your development environment is setting up a staging environment that mirrors your production environment as closely as possible. This allows you to test your application in conditions that are similar to those it will encounter in the real world. Staging environments help catch issues that may not be evident in the local development setup, such as configuration discrepancies or performance bottlenecks. By deploying to a staging environment before production, you can identify and address potential problems, ensuring a smoother deployment process and a more stable application.

As you advance in your development with Next.js, maintaining a well-organized and efficient environment becomes increasingly important. Regularly updating your dependencies and tools is crucial for staying current with the latest features and security patches. Next.js and its ecosystem are actively developed, with frequent updates that introduce new features and improvements. Keeping your development environment up to date ensures compatibility with the latest versions of libraries and tools, reducing the likelihood of encountering issues related to deprecated or outdated components.

Furthermore, consider documenting your development environment setup and configurations. Comprehensive documentation can serve as a valuable reference for your team or future developers working on the project. By documenting the setup process, configuration files, and workflows, you provide clarity and facilitate a smoother onboarding process for new team members. Detailed documentation also helps maintain consistency across different environments and projects, ensuring that best practices are followed and potential issues are avoided.

In conclusion, setting up a robust development environment for Next.js involves more than just installing the framework and tools. It encompasses configuring version control, integrating build and deployment pipelines, implementing monitoring and performance optimization, and maintaining up-to-date dependencies. By focusing on these aspects, you create a solid foundation for efficient development and successful project outcomes. With the right environment in place, you are well-equipped to harness the full potential of Next.js and build scalable, high-performance applications.

CHAPTER 3: UNDERSTANDING THE CORE CONCEPTS OF NEXT.JS

To fully appreciate the capabilities of Next.js, it is essential to grasp its core concepts, which form the foundation of its architecture and development practices. This chapter explores the fundamental elements of Next.js, including its underlying architecture, the file-based routing system, and the approaches to server-side rendering (SSR) and static site generation (SSG). By understanding these core concepts, developers can leverage Next.js to build efficient, scalable web applications that meet a variety of requirements.

At the heart of Next.js is its architecture, designed to offer both flexibility and performance. The framework operates on the principle of universal or isomorphic rendering, which means that it can render applications both on the client side and the server side. This dual rendering approach addresses several common challenges in web development, such as performance optimization and search engine optimization (SEO). By enabling server-side rendering, Next.js allows pages to be pre-rendered on the server before being sent to the client. This results in faster initial page loads and improved SEO, as search engines can index the fully rendered content more effectively.

Next.js's file-based routing system is another core feature that significantly simplifies the development process. Unlike traditional routing methods that require manual configuration, Next.js employs a straightforward approach where the file structure of the `pages` directory determines the routing of the application. Each JavaScript or TypeScript file within the `pages` directory corresponds to a route in the application. For example, a file named `about.js` within this directory automatically maps to the `/about` route. This convention over configuration approach reduces boilerplate code and streamlines the creation and management of routes, allowing developers to focus more on building application features rather than configuring routing logic.

In addition to its routing capabilities, Next.js provides robust support for both server-side rendering and static site generation, each addressing different needs in web development. Server-side rendering allows for the generation of HTML on the server for each request, which is particularly useful for pages that require dynamic content or frequent updates. This approach ensures that users receive fully rendered pages, enhancing the perceived performance and usability of the application. Server-side rendering also facilitates better SEO, as search engines can crawl and index the content before it is rendered on the client side.

Conversely, static site generation pre-renders pages at build time, creating static HTML files that are served to users. This method is ideal for pages with content that does not change frequently, such as marketing pages, blog posts, or documentation. By generating static files, Next.js can deliver content with minimal server processing, resulting in faster load times and reduced server costs. Static site generation also enables incremental static regeneration (ISR), a feature that allows for the updating of static content without rebuilding the entire site. ISR provides a balance between static and dynamic rendering, enabling developers to build applications that can handle a mix of static and frequently updated content efficiently.

The integration of SSR and SSG within Next.js reflects its design philosophy of providing developers with a flexible and powerful toolkit. By supporting both rendering methods, Next.js allows developers to choose the most appropriate strategy for each page based on its content and usage patterns. This flexibility is particularly valuable in modern web applications, where performance, scalability, and SEO are critical considerations.

Furthermore, Next.js's architecture includes support for API routes, which extend its capabilities beyond static and server-rendered pages. API routes enable developers to build serverless functions directly within their Next.js application, handling backend logic and data processing without the need for a separate server setup. This integration of backend and frontend functionalities within a single framework simplifies the development process and promotes a more cohesive application architecture.

As we delve deeper into Next.js, it becomes clear that its core concepts are intricately designed to address common web development challenges. The framework's architecture, file-based routing system, and approaches to rendering provide a comprehensive solution for building modern web applications. By understanding and leveraging these core concepts, developers can create applications that are both performant and adaptable, meeting the diverse needs of users and stakeholders alike.

the build time rather than on each request. This approach is beneficial for pages that do not change frequently or require real-time data. By generating HTML at build time, static site generation ensures that pages are served quickly and efficiently, reducing server load and improving performance.

This method also enhances SEO, as the pre-rendered pages are easily crawled by search engines. Static site generation is particularly useful for content-heavy websites, blogs, and documentation sites, where the content remains relatively static but needs to be delivered swiftly and reliably.

Next.js offers flexibility in how these rendering methods are used, allowing developers to choose the most appropriate approach based on their specific requirements. For instance, a single Next.js application can incorporate both server-side rendered and statically generated pages, enabling a hybrid model that optimizes performance and user experience. This versatility is facilitated by Next.js's data fetching methods, which include `getServerSideProps` for server-side rendering and `getStaticProps` for static site generation. Additionally, the `getStaticPaths` function allows developers to specify dynamic routes for static generation, providing further control over which pages are pre-rendered at build time.

The integration of these rendering approaches with Next.js's file-based routing system creates a seamless development experience. The `pages` directory, as the cornerstone of routing, simplifies the creation and management of routes by mapping file names to URLs. This system eliminates the need for complex routing configurations, making it easier for developers to understand and maintain the application's structure. Furthermore, Next.js supports dynamic routing through file names that include brackets, such as `[id].js`, which allows for the creation of routes with variable parameters. This feature is particularly useful for applications that require dynamic content, such as user profiles or product pages, where the route parameters vary based on user input or external data.

Another key aspect of Next.js's architecture is its support for API routes, which enables the development of serverless functions within the same project. API routes allow developers to build backend logic and handle requests directly within the Next.js application, eliminating the need for a separate backend service. These routes are defined in the `pages/api` directory and can be used for various purposes, such as handling form submissions, interacting with databases, or integrating with third-party services. By incorporating API routes, Next.js provides a unified development environment that encompasses both frontend and backend functionality.

The combination of these core concepts—file-based routing, server-side rendering, static site generation, and API routes—demonstrates the versatility and power of Next.js as a modern web development framework. This integration enables developers to build applications that are both performant and scalable, while also simplifying the development process. The framework's approach to rendering and routing allows for a flexible and efficient workflow, accommodating a wide range of use cases and project requirements.

As we delve deeper into the capabilities of Next.js, it is important to recognize how these core concepts interact to create a cohesive development experience. The seamless integration of routing, rendering, and API functionality not only enhances performance and scalability but also fosters a more streamlined and intuitive development process. By understanding and leveraging these core concepts, developers can effectively harness the power of Next.js to build robust and dynamic web applications that meet the demands of modern web development.

a comprehensive solution for both frontend and backend development needs.

The integration of server-side rendering and static site generation in Next.js is not merely a feature but a reflection of its architectural philosophy aimed at optimizing performance and user experience. Server-side rendering is particularly valuable for dynamic content that changes frequently or relies on real-time data. For instance, pages displaying user-specific data, such as dashboards or personalized recommendations, benefit from server-side rendering as it ensures that users receive the most up-to-date information with each request. On the other hand, static site generation excels for content that remains relatively constant, such as marketing pages, blogs, or documentation, where pre-rendered pages offer immediate load times and reduce the burden on the server.

Next.js's ability to combine both approaches within a single application underscores its versatility. Developers can configure each page or route to use the appropriate rendering method based on its specific requirements, allowing for a tailored balance between performance and dynamic capabilities. This hybrid approach leverages the strengths of both rendering techniques, resulting in a more flexible and efficient development process.

Moreover, Next.js's architectural design extends to its support for incremental static regeneration (ISR), a feature that further enhances the static site generation model. ISR allows developers to update static content incrementally without requiring a full rebuild of the application. By specifying a revalidation period, developers can ensure that static pages are regenerated in the background when new data becomes available, providing users with up-to-date content while maintaining the performance benefits of static generation. This feature is particularly advantageous for applications that experience frequent updates but still require fast response times.

The framework's handling of data fetching is integral to its overall functionality. Next.js provides several methods for fetching data, including `getStaticProps`, `getServerSideProps`, and `getStaticPaths`. Each method serves a specific purpose and aligns with the chosen rendering approach. `getStaticProps` is employed during the build process for static site generation, allowing for the pre-fetching of data required for rendering static pages. `getServerSideProps` is used for server-side rendering, fetching data on each request to ensure that users receive the most current information. `getStaticPaths` complements `getStaticProps` by enabling the dynamic generation of static pages based on external data.

The file-based routing system of Next.js, coupled with its rendering methods, creates a coherent and streamlined development workflow. By relying on a straightforward file structure to manage routes, developers can focus on building features and functionality rather than wrestling with complex routing configurations. This design simplicity, combined with powerful data fetching capabilities, equips developers with the tools needed to create dynamic and high-performance web applications.

In summary, Next.js provides a robust framework that integrates essential web development concepts into a unified environment. Its architecture supports a blend of server-side rendering and static site generation, allowing developers to optimize performance and user experience according to their application's needs. The file-based routing system and data fetching methods streamline development processes, reducing complexity and enhancing productivity. By understanding and leveraging these core concepts, developers can harness the full potential of Next.js to build scalable and efficient web applications.

CHAPTER 4: BUILDING YOUR FIRST NEXT.JS APPLICATION

Having established a solid understanding of Next.js's core concepts, it is time to apply this knowledge by constructing your first Next.js application. This chapter provides a hands-on approach to building a basic project, guiding you through the setup, page creation, and directory structure. By the end of this chapter, you will have a functioning application and an appreciation for the best practices that contribute to efficient development with Next.js.

The journey begins with the initialization of a new Next.js project. This process starts by ensuring that Node.js is installed on your system, as it is required for managing dependencies and running the development server. Once Node.js is set up, the Next.js application can be created using the command line interface. The typical approach involves using the `create-next-app` utility, which scaffolds a new project with a default configuration. Executing the command `npx create-next-app@latest my-next-app` will generate a new directory named `my-next-app`, complete with all the necessary files and dependencies to get started.

Upon completion of the setup, you will find that the newly

created project contains a well-organized directory structure. The `pages` directory is central to this structure, as it dictates the routing of the application. Each file within the `pages` directory corresponds to a route, and the structure of this directory mirrors the routes in the application. For instance, a file named `index.js` within this directory represents the root route of the application, while `about.js` would correspond to `/about`. This file-based routing system simplifies navigation management and eliminates the need for explicit route definitions.

The next step is to start building the application's pages. Begin by modifying the `index.js` file to create a custom homepage. This file, located at `pages/index.js`, is the default entry point for your application. You can edit this file to include basic HTML and React components. For example, replacing the default content with a welcome message and some basic styling will give your homepage a personalized touch. It is also useful to introduce CSS modules at this stage, which are supported out-of-the-box by Next.js. CSS modules allow for scoped styling, meaning that styles defined in a module are applied only to the components in that module, preventing unintended global style changes.

Creating additional pages involves adding new files to the `pages` directory. For instance, to add an 'About' page, create a new file named `about.js` within the `pages` directory. In this file, you can export a React component that will render the content for the `/about` route. Each new file in the `pages` directory automatically corresponds to a new route, so managing the routes of your application becomes a straightforward task of creating and organizing files.

Next, it is important to understand how to handle static assets such as images and stylesheets. The `public` directory serves as the location for these assets. Files placed in the `public` directory are served at the root level of the application, making it easy to reference them in your components. For example, placing an image in the `public/images` directory allows you to access it using the path `/images/image.jpg`. This approach simplifies the management of static resources and ensures that they are efficiently served alongside your application.

As you develop your application, consider incorporating best practices that enhance maintainability and scalability. For instance, organizing your components and styles in a modular fashion can improve the structure of your codebase. Create a `components` directory to house reusable React components and a `styles` directory for CSS modules. This modular approach facilitates easier updates and ensures that components and styles are logically grouped together.

In addition to organizing your project files, it is beneficial to utilize version control systems such as Git. Initializing a Git repository at the beginning of your project allows you to track changes, manage different versions of your code, and collaborate with others. Commit your changes regularly with meaningful messages to maintain a clear history of your development progress. This practice not only helps in managing your codebase but also provides a safety net by allowing you to revert to previous states if needed.

Testing is another crucial aspect of application development. While Next.js provides a solid foundation for building applications, integrating testing frameworks ensures that your code functions as expected and maintains quality throughout the development process. Consider incorporating tools such as Jest for unit testing and React Testing Library for testing React components. Writing tests helps to catch bugs early and ensures that your application remains reliable as you make changes and add new features.

By following these steps and adhering to best practices,

you will successfully build a functional Next.js application. This foundational project will serve as the basis for more advanced features and configurations in future development. As you continue to explore Next.js, you will gain a deeper understanding of its capabilities and how to leverage its features to build sophisticated, high-performance web applications.

creating additional pages involves adding new JavaScript files to the `pages` directory. For instance, to create an "About" page, you would add a file named `about.js` within the `pages` folder. This file will automatically correspond to the `/about` route of your application. In this file, you can define a React component to render the content of the About page. The simplicity of this approach eliminates the need for a separate routing configuration, streamlining the process of expanding your application.

With basic pages set up, attention must turn to the directory structure and how it influences the development process. The `public` directory is another essential part of the Next.js project, designed to hold static assets such as images, fonts, and other files that need to be publicly accessible. Files placed in this directory can be referenced directly via the root URL of the application, which simplifies asset management and ensures that static files are served efficiently.

In addition to the `pages` and `public` directories, the `components` directory is often utilized to organize reusable UI elements. While this directory is not created by default, it is a common convention to create it for managing React components that are used across multiple pages. For example, you might create a `Header` component to be used on every page, providing a consistent navigation experience throughout your application. By placing such components in the `components` directory, you maintain a clean and modular structure that enhances code readability and maintainability.

Next, it is crucial to integrate best practices into your development workflow. One key practice is to maintain a clear separation between components, styles, and logic. This principle ensures that each file and component has a single responsibility, making the codebase easier to understand and modify. Additionally, employing proper naming conventions for files and directories aids in navigating the project and understanding its structure at a glance. For example, using descriptive names for components and pages, such as `HomePage` or `ContactForm`, clarifies their purpose and improves overall project organization.

As you continue building your application, consider leveraging Next.js's built-in support for dynamic routing. Dynamic routes are essential for creating pages that depend on variable data, such as user profiles or product pages. To implement dynamic routing, you create a file in the `pages` directory with a name that includes brackets, such as `[id].js`. This file acts as a template for routes with variable segments, and you can use Next.js's `getStaticPaths` and `getStaticProps` functions to generate and fetch the necessary data for these dynamic routes. This approach allows for the creation of scalable applications that can handle a wide range of use cases.

Another important aspect of development with Next.js is the use of API routes. Located in the `pages/api` directory, these routes allow you to create serverless functions that can handle backend logic and data processing. For example, you might create an API route to handle form submissions or interact with a database. By incorporating API routes into your application, you centralize backend functionality within the same project, simplifying deployment and integration.

To ensure that your application is well-optimized, pay

attention to performance considerations such as code splitting and image optimization. Next.js automatically handles code splitting, which means that only the code necessary for the current page is loaded, reducing the initial load time and improving performance. Additionally, Next.js provides built-in support for image optimization through the `next/image` component, which automatically optimizes and serves images in the most efficient format and size for each user's device.

Finally, continuous testing and refinement are crucial to delivering a high-quality application. Regularly test your application across different devices and browsers to identify and address potential issues. Utilize tools such as linting and formatting to maintain code quality and consistency. By following these best practices and continuously refining your project, you will build a robust and scalable Next.js application that meets both functional and performance requirements.

`[id].js`, where `id` represents a variable parameter in the URL. For instance, if you are building a blog, you might have a dynamic route file named `[postId].js` to handle individual blog posts. Within this file, you can use Next.js's data-fetching methods to retrieve and display content based on the parameter provided in the URL. The `getStaticPaths` function is used to specify which dynamic routes should be pre-rendered at build time, while `getStaticProps` fetches the data required for rendering each page. This capability allows you to efficiently manage dynamic content and ensure that your application remains responsive and scalable.

As you build out your application, consider incorporating error handling and fallback mechanisms to enhance the user experience. Next.js provides built-in error pages that you can customize to fit the design of your application. For example, you can create a custom `404.js` file in the `pages` directory to define the content displayed when a user navigates to a non-existent route. Similarly, you can handle server-side errors by creating a `500.js` file, ensuring that users receive a friendly message rather than a generic error page.

Another critical aspect of developing with Next.js is optimizing your application for performance. Next.js automatically handles code splitting, meaning that only the necessary JavaScript is loaded for each page, reducing initial load times. However, there are additional strategies you can employ to further enhance performance. For instance, leveraging the `Image` component from `next/image` provides automatic image optimization, including resizing and format conversion, which improves load times and visual quality. Similarly, utilizing `React.lazy` and `Suspense` allows for dynamic import of components, ensuring that only the components required for the current view are loaded, thereby reducing the overall bundle size.

Additionally, consider implementing a well-defined CSS strategy to maintain a clean and manageable stylesheet. Next.js supports various styling options, including global CSS, CSS modules, and styled-jsx. Global CSS is useful for defining overarching styles that apply across the entire application, while CSS modules provide scoped styling for individual components. Styled-jsx, on the other hand, allows you to write component-level styles directly within your JavaScript files, offering a more integrated approach. By selecting the appropriate styling method for your needs, you can ensure that your application's appearance is both consistent and adaptable.

Testing is another crucial component of the development process. Next.js does not include built-in testing tools, but it integrates seamlessly with popular testing frameworks such as Jest and React Testing Library. Implementing tests for your components and pages helps identify bugs early in the development cycle and ensures that your application behaves as expected. Writing unit tests for individual components and integration tests for page interactions can significantly improve the reliability and maintainability of your codebase.

As you conclude the development of your first Next.js application, it is essential to review and refine your code. Conducting a thorough code review, optimizing performance, and addressing any issues identified during testing will contribute to a polished and production-ready application. This iterative process of refinement and optimization is vital for delivering high-quality software that meets both functional and user experience standards.

In summary, building your first Next.js application involves a comprehensive understanding of the framework's architecture, file-based routing system, and rendering methods. By following best practices for file organization, dynamic routing, error handling, performance optimization, and testing, you can create a robust and scalable application. This hands-on experience not only solidifies your knowledge of Next.js but also prepares you for more advanced development challenges and opportunities.

CHAPTER 5: EXPLORING STATIC SITE GENERATION (SSG)

In the realm of modern web development, the need for fast, scalable, and SEO-friendly websites has led to the widespread adoption of Static Site Generation (SSG). This chapter explores SSG, particularly within the context of Next.js, and elucidates how this approach can significantly enhance performance and search engine optimization. By leveraging Next.js's static generation features, developers can create highly efficient static websites that serve content quickly and effectively.

Static Site Generation is a method of pre-rendering web pages at build time, producing static HTML files that are then served to users. Unlike server-side rendering, which generates HTML on each request, SSG builds the entire website's pages once and deploys them as static files. This results in faster load times because static files can be served directly from a Content Delivery Network (CDN) or static hosting services, bypassing the need for server-side computations on each request.

One of the primary benefits of SSG is its impact on performance. Since the pages are pre-rendered, users receive the fully constructed HTML immediately, reducing the time required to display content. This is particularly advantageous for websites with high traffic, as static files are easier to cache and distribute globally, ensuring that users around the world experience minimal latency. Additionally, static pages load faster compared to dynamic pages that rely on real-time data fetching and server-side rendering, which can improve user engagement and satisfaction.

Search Engine Optimization (SEO) is another area where SSG excels. Search engines prefer content that is readily accessible and indexable. Static pages, being pre-rendered and served as complete HTML documents, are easily crawled and indexed by search engines. This contrasts with client-side rendered applications, where content might be generated dynamically and might require additional effort to ensure it is properly indexed. By utilizing SSG, developers can ensure that their content is accessible to search engines from the moment it is deployed, potentially improving search engine rankings and visibility.

Next.js provides robust support for Static Site Generation through its `getStaticProps` and `getStaticPaths` functions. The `getStaticProps` function enables developers to fetch data at build time and pass it as props to the page component. This function is used within pages to generate static HTML that includes the pre-fetched data. For instance, if you are building a blog, `getStaticProps` can be used to retrieve posts from a database or an external API, which are then rendered into static HTML files during the build process.

To illustrate the use of `getStaticProps`, consider a scenario where you need to build a static page that displays a list of blog posts. In your `pages/posts.js` file, you would define the page component and include the `getStaticProps` function to fetch the list of posts. This function will be called at build time, allowing the page to be pre-rendered with the list of posts before deployment. As a result, users will receive the complete list of posts as static HTML, ensuring quick load times and improved performance.

For pages that require dynamic content, Next.js's `getStaticPaths` function complements `getStaticProps` by enabling the generation of static pages based on dynamic routes. When working with dynamic routes, such as individual blog posts or product pages, `getStaticPaths` defines which paths should be pre-rendered during the build process. This function returns an object with a `paths` property that lists the dynamic routes to be generated, and a `fallback` property that determines how to handle requests for paths not pre-rendered at build time.

In the context of the blog example, `getStaticPaths` would be used to specify the paths for individual blog posts. For each post, `getStaticPaths` generates a static HTML page using the post's unique identifier. This approach ensures that each blog post is pre-rendered and available as a static page, providing users with immediate access to the content without delays. The `fallback` property can be set to `true`, `false`, or `'blocking'`, depending on whether you want to serve a fallback page while new pages are being generated, or wait until the page is ready.

The flexibility of SSG in Next.js extends beyond simple pages to include complex, data-driven sites. By combining `getStaticProps` and `getStaticPaths`, developers can build sophisticated static websites that offer both performance and scalability. This approach is particularly well-suited for websites with content that does not change frequently or where performance is a critical factor.

In summary, Static Site Generation represents a powerful tool in the modern web development toolkit, offering significant benefits in terms of performance and SEO. Next.js's implementation of SSG provides developers with the means to build fast, static websites efficiently. By understanding and utilizing these features, you can create web applications that deliver exceptional user experiences and achieve optimal search engine visibility.

the `getStaticProps` function could be employed to fetch and render a blog post's content at build time. By returning the fetched data in the props, Next.js generates static HTML for each blog post, ensuring that users access pre-rendered content quickly. This approach is highly efficient for content that does not change frequently or for sites where speed and SEO are critical considerations.

To illustrate this with a practical example, consider a scenario where a website features a list of products. By utilizing `getStaticProps`, the developer can fetch the list of products from a headless CMS or an API at build time. This results in the creation of static pages for each product, which are then served to users with minimal delay. This method ensures that the website is not only fast but also consistently provides up-to-date information, assuming the content is re-fetched and rebuilt at regular intervals.

In addition to `getStaticProps`, Next.js also supports dynamic routes with SSG through the `getStaticPaths` function. This function is used to generate static pages for dynamic routes based on the parameters provided. For example, if the application includes a product detail page with a dynamic route `[productId].js`, the `getStaticPaths` function allows Next.js to determine which paths should be pre-rendered at build time. By specifying the list of paths that need to be generated, developers can ensure that all necessary pages are created and served as static files.

An important consideration when using SSG is managing content updates. Since static pages are built once and served as is, any changes to the content require a rebuild of the site. This can be addressed through various strategies, such as incremental static regeneration or periodic rebuilds.

Incremental static regeneration, introduced in Next.js 10, allows developers to update static content without a full rebuild. By setting revalidation intervals, pages can be regenerated on-demand and served with updated content, balancing the benefits of static generation with the need for fresh data.

To implement incremental static regeneration, you specify the `revalidate` property in the `getStaticProps` function. This property defines the time in seconds after which a page re-generation can occur. For instance, setting `revalidate: 60` allows a page to be regenerated every 60 seconds if new requests come in. This feature combines the performance advantages of SSG with the flexibility to handle dynamic content changes efficiently.

Understanding the integration of Static Site Generation within the broader Next.js framework also involves exploring how SSG interacts with other features of the framework. For example, Next.js's support for API routes allows developers to build serverless functions directly within the application. This integration enables the creation of dynamic content and interactions that complement the static pages generated by SSG. By utilizing API routes for handling form submissions, user authentication, or other dynamic operations, developers can enhance the functionality of their static sites while retaining the performance benefits of static generation.

Furthermore, Next.js's static export capability extends the benefits of SSG to non-Node.js environments. The `next export` command allows developers to export the application as a set of static files that can be deployed to any static hosting provider. This feature is particularly useful for deploying Next.js applications to platforms that do not natively support server-side rendering or API routes, broadening the deployment options and ensuring compatibility with various hosting environments.

In summary, Static Site Generation in Next.js offers a powerful approach to building fast, SEO-friendly websites by pre-rendering pages at build time. Through the use of `getStaticProps` and `getStaticPaths`, developers can generate static HTML for both static and dynamic routes, ensuring quick load times and efficient content delivery. Incremental static regeneration further enhances the flexibility of SSG by allowing updates to static content without requiring a full rebuild. By leveraging these features, developers can create high-performance applications that deliver an optimal user experience while maintaining the advantages of static generation.

of static site generation with the flexibility to keep content current, making it an ideal solution for dynamic content that does not require real-time updates. This hybrid approach ensures that static pages benefit from both the performance advantages of pre-rendering and the ability to incorporate fresh content.

When employing Static Site Generation in Next.js, it is crucial to understand its integration with other features of the framework. For instance, Next.js's support for incremental static regeneration complements SSG by allowing developers to manage content updates efficiently. This synergy provides a robust mechanism to deliver static sites that remain performant and responsive to changes over time.

Furthermore, Next.js's static generation capabilities can be combined with other data-fetching strategies to enhance the development process. For example, a site that uses both static generation and client-side rendering can offer an optimal user experience by leveraging the strengths of each approach. Static pages can be pre-rendered for initial loads and then supplemented with client-side fetching for interactive elements or frequently updated data.

The directory structure of a Next.js application plays a significant role in facilitating SSG. The `pages` directory, where each file corresponds to a route, directly impacts how static pages are generated. By organizing files and creating dynamic routes within this directory, developers can control the paths that are pre-rendered and optimize their site structure accordingly. This organization not only aids in managing content but also contributes to the overall maintainability and scalability of the application.

In addition to structural considerations, developers should also be aware of performance optimization techniques when building static sites. Utilizing features such as image optimization, code splitting, and caching can further enhance the efficiency of static pages. Next.js provides built-in support for image optimization, ensuring that images are served in the most appropriate format and size. Code splitting allows for smaller, more manageable JavaScript bundles, which can reduce load times and improve the overall performance of static sites.

Caching strategies are another critical aspect of optimizing static sites. By leveraging caching mechanisms at various levels—such as browser caching, CDN caching, and server-side caching—developers can ensure that static pages are delivered quickly and efficiently. Implementing appropriate cache headers and configuring CDN settings can significantly reduce latency and enhance the user experience.

Despite the numerous advantages of Static Site Generation, it is essential to recognize scenarios where it may not be the ideal choice. Sites that require real-time data, complex user interactions, or highly dynamic content may benefit more from other rendering strategies, such as server-side rendering or client-side rendering. In such cases, Next.js's flexibility allows for a combination of rendering techniques to meet specific requirements and provide an optimal user experience.

Ultimately, the decision to use Static Site Generation should be guided by the needs of the application and its content. Understanding the trade-offs and benefits of SSG, alongside Next.js's capabilities, empowers developers to make informed choices that align with their project goals. By harnessing the power of static generation, developers can build fast, efficient, and SEO-friendly websites that deliver a superior user experience.

In summary, Static Site Generation in Next.js offers a compelling solution for creating high-performance websites with excellent SEO characteristics. By pre-rendering pages at build time and leveraging features like incremental static regeneration, developers can build static sites that are both fast and capable of reflecting content updates. Next.js's robust static generation features, combined with thoughtful optimization strategies, provide a powerful framework for developing modern web applications that meet the demands of today's digital landscape.

CHAPTER 6: IMPLEMENTING SERVER-SIDE RENDERING (SSR)

Server-Side Rendering (SSR) is a pivotal feature in modern web development frameworks, and Next.js offers a robust implementation of SSR that significantly enhances both performance and Search Engine Optimization (SEO) for web applications. This chapter delves into the mechanics of SSR, illustrating how it operates in contrast to static site generation (SSG) and providing practical examples to guide the implementation of SSR within Next.js projects.

At its core, Server-Side Rendering involves generating HTML content on the server for each request made by the client. Unlike static site generation, which pre-renders pages at build time and serves them as static files, SSR dynamically generates the HTML on the server when a request is received. This approach ensures that the content is always up-to-date and tailored to the specific request, enhancing the user experience by delivering relevant data and reducing the time to first meaningful paint.

The fundamental advantage of SSR is its ability to deliver fully rendered pages to clients, which improves initial load times and provides a more seamless experience for users. This is particularly beneficial for applications where content changes frequently or where the user's request includes dynamic parameters that impact the content. For example, an e-commerce site with product listings that depend on real-time inventory levels would benefit from SSR, as it ensures that users see the most current product information as soon as they land on the page.

Next.js facilitates SSR through its built-in data-fetching methods. The primary function used for this purpose is `getServerSideProps`. This function allows developers to fetch data server-side and pass it as props to the page component before the page is rendered. When a request is made to a page that uses `getServerSideProps`, Next.js executes this function on the server, fetches the necessary data, and then renders the HTML before sending it to the client. This process ensures that the page is served with the most current data, improving both the freshness of content and the SEO performance.

To implement SSR in a Next.js application, you first need to define the `getServerSideProps` function within the page component. This function should handle data retrieval, perform any necessary transformations, and return the data as props. Here is a simplified example:

```javascript
// pages/product/[id].js
import { useRouter } from 'next/router';

export default function ProductPage({ product }) {
 const router useRouter();

 if (router.isFallback) {
  return <div>Loading...</div>;
 }

 return (
```

```
  <div>
   <h1>{product.name}</h1>
   <p>{product.description}</p>
   </div>
 );
}

export async function getServerSideProps(context) {
 const { id } context.params;
  const res  await fetch(`https://api.example.com/products/$
{id}`);
 const product  await res.json();

 return {
  props: { product }, // will be passed to the page component as
props
 };
}
 ` ` `
```

In this example, the `getServerSideProps` function fetches data for a specific product based on the `id` parameter from the request. The fetched data is then passed to the `ProductPage` component, which is rendered server-side and delivered to the client with the product details included.

While SSR offers substantial benefits for dynamic content and SEO, it also introduces certain trade-offs. Unlike static site generation, where pages are pre-rendered and served as static files, SSR requires server-side computation for each request. This can impact server performance and increase response times if not managed properly. Consequently, careful consideration should be given to the complexity of the data-fetching logic and the potential load on the server.

To mitigate performance concerns, developers should leverage caching strategies and optimize data-fetching processes. Implementing server-side caching can help reduce the load on the server by storing pre-rendered pages and serving cached content for repeated requests. Additionally, optimizing database queries and leveraging efficient data retrieval methods can enhance the overall performance of SSR.

The choice between SSR and SSG depends on the specific needs of the application. While SSR excels in scenarios where content is highly dynamic or personalized, SSG is more suitable for static content that does not change frequently. By understanding the strengths and limitations of each approach, developers can make informed decisions and apply the most appropriate rendering strategy to meet their project requirements.

In conclusion, Server-Side Rendering is a powerful feature in Next.js that can enhance performance and SEO by generating HTML content on the server for each client request. By utilizing `getServerSideProps`, developers can ensure that their applications deliver up-to-date content and provide a better user experience. However, it is essential to balance the benefits of SSR with considerations for server performance and response times, ensuring that the application remains responsive and efficient.

When implementing Server-Side Rendering (SSR) in Next.js, it is essential to grasp how this feature can be strategically used to enhance performance and SEO. One of the primary benefits of SSR is its ability to serve up-to-date content quickly, which is crucial for applications that rely on dynamic data or have user-specific content. This is achieved by generating the HTML on the server for each request, ensuring that the content is current and relevant at the moment of delivery.

Unlike static site generation, where pages are built once during the build process and served as static files, SSR provides a dynamic approach by rendering the page for each request. This means that when a user requests a page, the server processes the request, fetches the necessary data, and then sends back the fully rendered HTML. This can significantly reduce the time to first meaningful paint, as users receive a fully rendered page rather than a blank or loading screen.

The implementation of SSR in Next.js involves utilizing the `getServerSideProps` function. This function is unique to SSR and operates on a per-request basis. It allows developers to fetch data on the server before rendering the page and pass that data as props to the page component. This ensures that the page is rendered with the most up-to-date data, which is particularly useful for applications where content changes frequently or where real-time information is required.

For instance, consider an application that displays live sports scores. Using SSR, you can fetch the latest scores on the server and ensure that users receive the most recent data as soon as they access the page. Here's how you might use `getServerSideProps` in such a scenario:

```javascript
// pages/scores.js
import React from 'react';

const Scores ({ scores }) > {
 return (
  <div>
   <h1>Live Sports Scores</h1>
   <ul>
    {scores.map(score > (
     <li key{score.id}>{score.team}: {score.points}</li>
    ))}
   </ul>
  </div>
 );
};

export async function getServerSideProps() {
 // Fetching live scores from an API
```

```
const res  await fetch('https://api.sportsdata.io/v4/scores');
const scores  await res.json();

 return {
 props: {
  scores,
 },
 };
}

export default Scores;
` ` `
```

In this example, the `getServerSideProps` function fetches the latest scores from an API, ensuring that users see the most recent updates every time they access the page. This dynamic fetching and rendering ensure that the content is always current, providing a more engaging and relevant experience for users.

However, while SSR offers substantial benefits, it is important to consider its impact on server performance and scalability. Since SSR involves generating HTML for each request on the server, it can place additional load on the server, especially for high-traffic applications. To mitigate this, it is advisable to combine SSR with caching strategies. Caching can reduce the number of times data needs to be fetched and HTML needs to be generated, thereby improving performance and reducing server load.

Implementing caching strategies effectively involves setting up server-side caching mechanisms and configuring appropriate cache headers. This can include caching the rendered HTML of frequently accessed pages, utilizing Content Delivery Networks (CDNs) to cache static assets, and employing caching layers to manage dynamic content efficiently.

In addition to caching, another approach to managing server load is to use SSR selectively. Not every page needs to be server-rendered, and leveraging a combination of SSR and static site generation (SSG) can optimize performance. For instance, pages with frequently changing data or personalized content can benefit from SSR, while pages with static content can be pre-rendered using SSG. This hybrid approach allows for efficient use of server resources and improved performance across different types of content.

Furthermore, it is crucial to test and monitor the performance of SSR implementations to ensure that they meet the desired performance goals. Tools and practices such as load testing, performance profiling, and real-time monitoring can help identify potential bottlenecks and areas for optimization.

In summary, Server-Side Rendering in Next.js is a powerful feature that enhances performance and SEO by delivering fully rendered HTML pages on a per-request basis. By using `getServerSideProps`, developers can ensure that pages are served with the most up-to-date data, improving the relevance and responsiveness of web applications. Combining SSR with caching strategies and a hybrid approach to rendering can help manage server load and optimize performance, providing a scalable and efficient solution for dynamic web applications.

When integrating Server-Side Rendering (SSR) into your Next.js application, it is essential to consider how this approach fits within the broader architecture of your project. SSR provides significant benefits in terms of performance and search engine optimization (SEO), but it also introduces certain complexities that require careful management. Understanding these complexities will help you make informed decisions about when and how to use SSR effectively.

One of the primary advantages of SSR is its impact on SEO. Search engines, particularly those that rely on indexing content from rendered HTML, benefit from SSR because it delivers a fully rendered page directly from the server. This contrasts with client-side rendering, where the initial HTML response is often a minimal skeleton, with the bulk of the content loaded and rendered via JavaScript. SSR ensures that crawlers and search engines receive the complete content of a page, which can improve indexing and potentially lead to better search rankings.

Another critical aspect to consider is the performance of SSR. Although SSR can deliver faster initial page loads compared to client-side rendering, it does come with its own set of performance considerations. Since each request triggers server-side processing, it is essential to optimize your server's response time and manage server load effectively. Techniques such as caching, efficient data fetching, and reducing server-side computation can help mitigate these concerns. For instance, using in-memory caching to store frequently requested data can reduce the need for repeated database queries, thus improving response times and reducing server load.

It is also important to handle user-specific data appropriately when using SSR. Since SSR involves generating a new HTML page for each request, incorporating user-specific content requires careful management to ensure that the correct data is fetched and displayed for each user. This is particularly relevant for applications with user authentication and personalized content. To maintain security and privacy, ensure that sensitive data is processed securely on the server and that any user-specific information is handled in accordance with best practices.

In addition to these considerations, managing the development and deployment process for an SSR-based application requires a clear understanding of how server-side code interacts with the client-side application. The Next.js framework simplifies this process by allowing developers to focus on defining their pages and data fetching logic, while the underlying system handles the complexities of server-side rendering. However, it is crucial to ensure that your development environment is configured to support SSR effectively, including proper server setup and deployment strategies.

Finally, it is beneficial to continuously monitor and test your application's performance and SEO impact. Tools such as Lighthouse for performance audits and various SEO analysis tools can provide valuable insights into how well your SSR implementation is functioning. Regular testing and monitoring will help you identify potential issues and optimize your application to provide the best possible experience for users and search engines alike.

By understanding the mechanics of SSR and its implications for performance and SEO, you can leverage this powerful feature of Next.js to build robust, high-performing web applications. Balancing the benefits of server-side rendering with its associated complexities will enable you to create applications that deliver both speed and relevance, ensuring an optimal user experience and improved visibility in search engine results.

CHAPTER 7: MANAGING DATA FETCHING IN NEXT.JS

Data fetching is a fundamental aspect of modern web development, particularly when working with frameworks like Next.js that emphasize server-side rendering (SSR) and static site generation (SSG). Effective data management ensures that applications deliver dynamic and up-to-date content while maintaining performance and scalability. This chapter explores the various methods for data fetching in Next.js, specifically focusing on `getStaticProps`, `getServerSideProps`, and SWR. Understanding when and how to use each of these methods is crucial for building robust and efficient applications.

Next.js provides several built-in methods for data fetching that align with its SSR and SSG capabilities. These methods are designed to optimize the delivery of content, whether it is static, dynamic, or fetched on-demand. Each method has its use cases, strengths, and trade-offs, which will be discussed in detail to help you choose the best approach for your specific needs.

`getStaticProps` is one of the key methods for data fetching in Next.js. It is used in conjunction with static site generation (SSG) to pre-render a page at build time. This method allows you to fetch data from external sources, such as APIs or databases, and include it in the HTML output generated during the build process. The primary benefit of `getStaticProps` is that it produces static HTML files, which can be served quickly to users and are highly cacheable. This approach is particularly advantageous for pages with content that does not change frequently or where real-time data is not critical.

To use `getStaticProps`, you define an asynchronous function in your page component file. This function is executed at build time, and the data returned from it is passed as props to the page component. For example, if you are building a blog, you might use `getStaticProps` to fetch a list of blog posts and render them statically. This results in fast load times and improved SEO, as the content is pre-rendered and ready to be served to users.

In contrast, `getServerSideProps` is used for server-side rendering and is ideal for scenarios where the data must be fetched on each request. Unlike `getStaticProps`, which runs only at build time, `getServerSideProps` runs on the server for every request made to the page. This ensures that users always receive the most current data, making it suitable for dynamic content that changes frequently or depends on user-specific information.

The use of `getServerSideProps` requires defining an asynchronous function that retrieves the necessary data before rendering the page. This function is executed on the server for each request, allowing for up-to-date data to be included in the rendered HTML. For example, if you are developing a user dashboard that displays real-time data specific to each user, `getServerSideProps` would be the appropriate method to ensure that the content is accurate and up-to-date.

In addition to these built-in methods, Next.js also supports client-side data fetching through libraries such as SWR (stale-while-revalidate). SWR is a React hook library that provides a powerful mechanism for handling data fetching, caching, and revalidation. It is designed to work seamlessly with Next.js and offers an alternative approach to data fetching that complements `getStaticProps` and `getServerSideProps`.

SWR leverages a caching strategy where data is initially fetched from the cache, and then a request is made to the server to revalidate and update the cache with fresh data. This approach ensures that users see cached data instantly while the application fetches the latest information in the background. SWR is particularly useful for pages with frequently updated data or interactive components where client-side fetching is required.

Using SWR involves integrating the `useSWR` hook into your React components. This hook manages the data fetching process, handles caching, and provides an intuitive API for managing server requests. For instance, if you have a component that displays live statistics or user interactions, SWR can be employed to ensure that the data is always current without requiring a full page reload.

Each method of data fetching in Next.js has its own set of advantages and is suited to different scenarios. `getStaticProps` is ideal for static content that can be pre-rendered at build time, offering speed and performance benefits. `getServerSideProps` caters to dynamic content that needs to be fetched on every request, ensuring real-time data accuracy. SWR complements these methods by providing an efficient way to handle client-side data fetching and caching.

In summary, managing data fetching in Next.js involves understanding the strengths and appropriate use cases of `getStaticProps`, `getServerSideProps`, and SWR. By leveraging these methods effectively, you can build applications that are both performant and capable of delivering dynamic, up-to-date content.

In contrast to static generation, server-side rendering with `getServerSideProps` is essential for scenarios where data needs to be dynamically generated on each request. This method allows developers to fetch data on the server for every incoming request, ensuring that the content is always up-to-date. The primary advantage of `getServerSideProps` is its ability to handle data that changes frequently or depends on user-specific information, such as personalized content or real-time data.

To implement `getServerSideProps`, you define an asynchronous function within your page component file. This function executes on the server each time a request is made to the page. The data returned from this function is passed as props to the page component, similar to `getStaticProps`, but with the crucial difference that it provides up-to-date data for every request. This method is particularly useful for pages that require dynamic content, such as dashboards or user profiles, where the data is subject to frequent updates or depends on the context of the request.

The choice between `getStaticProps` and `getServerSideProps` largely depends on the nature of the content and the performance requirements of the application. `getStaticProps` is well-suited for static content that does not change often and benefits from faster load times and improved SEO through static generation. On the other hand, `getServerSideProps` is ideal for dynamic content that must reflect real-time data or user-specific information, even though it might incur a slightly higher latency due to server-side processing.

Another method for handling data in Next.js is SWR (Stale-While-Revalidate), a data fetching library that provides a powerful approach to client-side data management. SWR is designed to work seamlessly with React and Next.js, offering a way to fetch data on the client side while keeping it synchronized with the server. The name SWR reflects its core principle: serve stale data while revalidating it in the background.

SWR is particularly useful for applications that require frequent updates or need to fetch data on the client side after the initial page load. It supports features such as caching, automatic revalidation, and request deduplication, which enhance the performance and user experience of your application. SWR provides a hook, `useSWR`, that can be used to fetch and cache data in functional components. This hook manages the fetching, caching, and updating of data transparently, allowing developers to focus on the business logic rather than the complexities of data management.

The use of SWR complements the server-side and static data fetching methods by providing a client-side solution that works well with dynamic content and real-time updates. For instance, after an initial static or server-side rendered page load, SWR can be used to fetch and update data dynamically without requiring a full page reload. This approach ensures that users see the most recent data while maintaining a responsive and interactive interface.

When integrating these data fetching methods into your Next.js applications, it is important to consider the specific needs of your project and choose the appropriate method for each use case. By leveraging `getStaticProps` for static content, `getServerSideProps` for dynamic content, and SWR for client-side data fetching, you can build applications that are both performant and capable of delivering rich, dynamic user experiences.

The integration of SWR into a Next.js application provides a client-side data fetching approach that complements server-side rendering techniques. SWR's strength lies in its ability to handle data fetching, caching, and updating without the need for complex state management solutions. By leveraging SWR, developers can achieve a balance between static and dynamic content, optimizing both performance and user experience.

One of the significant advantages of SWR is its built-in support for automatic revalidation. When using SWR, data is initially fetched and cached, allowing the application to quickly serve the stale data while asynchronously revalidating it in the background. This ensures that users always see the most current data while benefiting from the fast response times of cached content. This mechanism is especially useful for applications that display frequently updated data, such as news feeds or stock prices, where users need real-time information but also expect a responsive interface.

SWR also provides features like request deduplication, which prevents multiple requests for the same data from being sent simultaneously. This is particularly valuable in scenarios where multiple components may need to fetch the same data independently. By consolidating these requests, SWR reduces unnecessary network traffic and improves overall application efficiency. Additionally, SWR offers built-in support for optimistic UI updates, allowing applications to provide a more fluid and responsive experience by predicting the outcome of data mutations before the server responds.

To use SWR effectively, developers need to integrate it within the React component lifecycle. The `useSWR` hook allows for declarative data fetching within functional components, simplifying the process of fetching, caching, and updating data. The hook accepts a key that uniquely identifies the data and a fetcher function that defines how to retrieve it. For example, a simple `useSWR` call might look like this:

```javascript
import useSWR from 'swr';
import axios from 'axios';
```

```
const fetcher  url > axios.get(url).then(res > res.data);

function DataFetchingComponent() {
 const { data, error }  useSWR('/api/data', fetcher);

  if (error) return <div>Failed to load</div>;
  if (!data) return <div>Loading...</div>;

  return <div>Data: {data.someField}</div>;
}
` ` `
```

In this example, `useSWR` fetches data from the `/api/data` endpoint using the provided `fetcher` function. The hook returns an object containing the `data`, `error`, and other states, allowing developers to handle loading and error states gracefully.

The choice of data fetching methods in Next.js should align with the specific needs of the application and its performance requirements. `getStaticProps` is ideal for static sites where content does not frequently change and SEO is a priority. `getServerSideProps` provides the flexibility needed for dynamic, user-specific content, ensuring that every page request receives the most up-to-date data. SWR complements these server-side methods by offering a robust solution for client-side data fetching, particularly useful for interactive and dynamic applications.

As applications grow and data requirements become more complex, developers may need to combine these methods to achieve the desired balance between performance, scalability, and user experience. Understanding when and how to use each approach effectively will enable developers to build high-performing Next.js applications that meet the diverse needs of modern web development.

CHAPTER 8: LEVERAGING API ROUTES IN NEXT.JS

In the realm of web development, the ability to seamlessly integrate server-side functionality with client-side applications is crucial for building robust and interactive web applications. Next.js, a popular React framework, offers an elegant solution for this need through its support for API routes. These routes enable developers to create backend functionalities directly within their Next.js application, streamlining the development process and enhancing the overall architecture of their projects.

API routes in Next.js provide a way to build serverless functions that can handle various HTTP methods, such as GET, POST, PUT, and DELETE. This feature allows developers to manage backend logic and interactions with databases or third-party services without requiring a separate backend server. Instead, the API routes are defined within the same project structure as the frontend components, simplifying deployment and maintenance.

To create an API route in Next.js, developers need to define a JavaScript file within the `pages/api` directory of their project. Each file in this directory represents an individual API endpoint. The file exports an asynchronous function that receives a `request` and `response` object, allowing for the handling of incoming requests and sending responses back to the client. For example, a basic API route for fetching user data might look like this:

```javascript
// pages/api/users.js

export default async function handler(req, res) {
 if (req.method 'GET') {
   // Fetch user data from a database or external service
   const users  await fetchUsersFromDatabase();
   res.status(200).json(users);
 } else {
   res.setHeader('Allow', ['GET']);
   res.status(405).end(`Method ${req.method} Not Allowed`);
 }
}
```

In this example, the API route responds to GET requests by fetching user data from a database and sending it as a JSON response. If the request method is not GET, the route returns a 405 Method Not Allowed error, indicating that only GET requests are supported for this endpoint.

One of the key advantages of using API routes in Next.js is the ability to handle server-side logic within the same codebase as the client-side components. This integrated approach simplifies the process of data fetching and state management, as frontend components can interact with backend routes using standard fetch or Axios calls. For instance, a React component that consumes the API route might look like this:

```javascript
// components/UserList.js

import { useEffect, useState } from 'react';

function UserList() {
```

```
const [users, setUsers] useState([]);
const [error, setError] useState(null);

 useEffect(() > {
  async function fetchUsers() {
   try {
    const response  await fetch('/api/users');
    if (!response.ok) {
     throw new Error('Network response was not ok');
    }
    const data  await response.json();
    setUsers(data);
   } catch (error) {
    setError(error.message);
   }
  }

   fetchUsers();
 }, []);

 if (error) return <div>Error: {error}</div>;
 if (users.length  0) return <div>Loading...</div>;

 return (
  <ul>
   {users.map(user > (
    <li key{user.id}>{user.name}</li>
   ))}
  </ul>
 );
}

export default UserList;
```
` ` `

Here, the `UserList` component fetches user data from the
`/api/users` endpoint and displays it in a list. This approach
keeps the data-fetching logic within the component while

leveraging the API route to manage server-side data retrieval.

API routes in Next.js can also be used to handle form submissions, authentication, and integration with external services. For example, handling a POST request for a contact form might involve validating user input, storing data in a database, and sending a confirmation email. An API route for such a form might look like this:

```javascript
// pages/api/contact.js

import { sendContactEmail } from '../../lib/email';

export default async function handler(req, res) {
 if (req.method 'POST') {
  const { name, email, message } req.body;

   // Perform validation and error handling
   if (!name || !email || !message) {
    return res.status(400).json({ error: 'All fields are required' });
   }

   try {
    await sendContactEmail(name, email, message);
            res.status(200).json({ message: 'Message sent successfully' });
   } catch (error) {
    res.status(500).json({ error: 'Failed to send message' });
   }
 } else {
  res.setHeader('Allow', ['POST']);
  res.status(405).end(`Method ${req.method} Not Allowed`);
 }
}
```

This API route processes POST requests by validating the input, sending an email, and returning an appropriate response. It demonstrates how Next.js API routes can be utilized to handle various backend operations within the context of a Next.js application.

By integrating API routes into a Next.js project, developers gain the ability to build full-stack applications with a unified codebase. This approach not only simplifies development and deployment but also enhances the maintainability of the application by keeping frontend and backend code closely related. As the application scales, API routes provide a flexible and efficient means of managing server-side logic while leveraging the powerful features of Next.js.

When integrating API routes within a Next.js application, it's important to understand the underlying mechanisms that facilitate communication between the frontend and backend. API routes in Next.js are essentially serverless functions that are invoked via HTTP requests. These functions run in a Node.js environment, allowing developers to write server-side code that can process data, handle user authentication, or perform other backend tasks.

A critical aspect of API routes is their ability to support various HTTP methods, which allows for flexible interaction with the application's data. Each API route file can handle different types of requests by examining the `req.method` property. For example, a single API route can be designed to manage multiple operations such as fetching data with GET requests, updating data with POST requests, or deleting data with DELETE requests. This versatility is achieved by implementing conditional logic within the route handler function, as shown in the earlier example.

For more advanced use cases, API routes can interact with external services or databases to manage complex data operations. When working with databases, developers often use libraries such as Prisma or Mongoose to handle database queries and schema management. These libraries can be integrated directly into API routes, allowing for efficient data retrieval and manipulation. For instance, in an application that requires user authentication, an API route might verify user credentials by querying a database and issuing JSON Web Tokens (JWT) upon successful authentication.

In addition to handling CRUD (Create, Read, Update, Delete) operations, API routes in Next.js can also be used to implement middleware functions that execute before reaching the main request handler. Middleware can be employed for tasks such as logging, request validation, or authentication checks. By encapsulating these functionalities in middleware, developers can maintain a cleaner and more modular codebase. Middleware functions can be applied either globally across all API routes or specifically to individual routes depending on the application's requirements.

When building API routes, security considerations are paramount. Given that these routes can handle sensitive data and perform critical operations, implementing security best practices is essential. This includes validating and sanitizing user input to prevent injection attacks, using secure methods for handling authentication tokens, and setting appropriate HTTP headers to mitigate security vulnerabilities. For example, using environment variables to store sensitive information like API keys and database credentials is a common practice to ensure that these details are not exposed in the codebase.

Testing API routes is another important aspect of development. Since API routes often handle business logic and data processing, it is crucial to ensure their reliability and correctness. Unit testing frameworks such as Jest or Mocha can be used to write test cases that validate the functionality of individual API routes. These tests can simulate different request scenarios and verify that the responses meet the expected outcomes. Additionally, integration tests can be employed to assess how well API routes interact with other components of the application, such as frontend pages or external services.

To further streamline development, Next.js provides a feature for creating dynamic API routes. Dynamic routes are particularly useful for scenarios where the API endpoint must handle variable parameters, such as user IDs or product slugs. By using file names with brackets (e.g., `[id].js`), developers can define routes that capture dynamic segments of the URL and process them within the API handler. This capability allows for more flexible and scalable API designs.

For example, an API route to fetch details for a specific user might be defined as follows:

```javascript
// pages/api/users/[id].js

export default async function handler(req, res) {
 const { id } req.query;

  if (req.method 'GET') {
  // Fetch user data by ID from a database
  const user  await fetchUserById(id);
  if (user) {
   res.status(200).json(user);
  } else {
   res.status(404).json({ message: 'User not found' });
  }
 } else {
  res.setHeader('Allow', ['GET']);
  res.status(405).end(`Method ${req.method} Not Allowed`);
 }
}
```

In this case, the `[id].js` file captures the `id` parameter from the URL, allowing the route to fetch and return data for a specific user.

Integrating API routes with client-side components involves using standard data-fetching techniques. For instance, client-side code can use the `fetch` API or Axios to make HTTP requests to the API routes, handle responses, and update the UI accordingly. This interaction ensures that data flows seamlessly between the frontend and backend, enabling dynamic and responsive user experiences.

Overall, Next.js's API routes offer a powerful mechanism for building full-stack applications within a unified framework. By understanding the nuances of API route creation, handling different HTTP methods, implementing middleware, ensuring security, and testing thoroughly, developers can leverage this feature to enhance their applications' functionality and performance. This integration of server-side capabilities with client-side rendering epitomizes the flexibility and efficiency that Next.js brings to modern web development.

Testing API routes is another critical aspect of development that ensures your endpoints work correctly and handle edge cases effectively. Implementing thorough tests for API routes involves creating unit tests to verify individual functionalities and integration tests to validate interactions between components. Tools such as Jest, combined with libraries like Supertest, provide a robust environment for testing API routes. These tools enable you to simulate HTTP requests and assert responses, which helps in catching bugs early and ensuring that your API behaves as expected under various conditions.

For unit testing, each API route can be isolated and tested to check if it performs its designated function correctly. This means ensuring that the route returns the expected status codes, handles input validation properly, and processes data as intended. Integration tests, on the other hand, focus on the interaction between the API route and other parts of your application, such as databases or external services. These tests help in verifying that the entire data flow from request to response is functioning smoothly and that all components integrate seamlessly.

In addition to testing, documenting your API routes is a crucial practice that facilitates collaboration and maintenance. Well-documented APIs make it easier for other developers to understand the available endpoints, the required parameters, and the expected responses. Tools like Swagger or Postman can be used to generate interactive documentation for your API routes. These tools allow you to create comprehensive documentation that includes details on request methods, query parameters, and response formats, enhancing the clarity and usability of your API.

As your application grows, managing and organizing API routes becomes increasingly important. Next.js allows you to structure API routes effectively by leveraging a directory-based approach. Each file within the `pages/api` directory corresponds to a separate API route. By following this structure, you can maintain a clear and organized codebase, making it easier to navigate and manage your routes as the application evolves. Additionally, using TypeScript with API routes can further enhance development by providing type safety and reducing runtime errors.

The integration of API routes with frontend components is another key consideration. Next.js applications often require communication between client-side components and server-side logic. API routes provide a straightforward mechanism for this communication, allowing frontend components to make HTTP requests to your backend logic. For instance, you might use the `fetch` API or libraries like Axios to send requests to your API routes from within React components. Handling responses and updating the UI based on the data received from these routes is essential for creating dynamic and interactive user experiences.

Moreover, optimizing the performance of API routes is crucial for ensuring a responsive and efficient application. Performance optimizations can include implementing caching strategies to reduce server load, leveraging database indexes to speed up query execution, and minimizing the payload size of responses. Next.js provides built-in support for incremental static regeneration (ISR), which allows you to update static content on a per-page basis without rebuilding the entire site. This feature can be combined with API routes to enhance performance and deliver fresh content to users with minimal delay.

Lastly, consider the deployment and scaling aspects of your API routes. When deploying a Next.js application, your API routes are typically deployed as serverless functions, which offer scalability and cost efficiency. Serverless functions automatically scale based on demand, handling varying levels of traffic without manual intervention. However, it is important to monitor the performance and costs associated with these functions to ensure they meet your application's requirements and budget.

In summary, API routes in Next.js offer a powerful and flexible way to build backend functionality directly within your application. By understanding how to create, manage, and test these routes, you can effectively handle dynamic content and integrate full-stack features into your projects. Emphasizing best practices in security, documentation, and performance optimization will further enhance the robustness and maintainability of your API routes, providing a solid foundation for building scalable and high-quality web applications.

CHAPTER 9:
WORKING WITH
DYNAMIC ROUTES
AND ROUTING

Dynamic routing in Next.js offers a versatile mechanism for handling flexible URL structures, making it possible to build applications with intricate routing requirements efficiently. This chapter delves into the nuances of dynamic routing, providing an in-depth examination of how to create and manage dynamic routes, handle route parameters, and construct complex routing scenarios to suit diverse application needs.

At the core of dynamic routing in Next.js is the ability to create routes that are not predefined but rather determined at runtime. This is facilitated through the use of file-based routing combined with dynamic segments. The Next.js framework leverages the file system as the primary means of defining routes. By using square brackets in file names, developers can create dynamic segments that are matched at runtime. For instance, a file named `[id].js` in the `pages` directory corresponds to a route that can handle any value in place of `id`, such as `/post/1` or `/post/abc`.

Creating a dynamic route involves defining a file with the desired dynamic parameter in the file name. For example, to handle routes for individual blog posts, you might create a file named `[slug].js` inside the `pages/posts` directory. This setup would map to routes like `/posts/first-post` or `/posts/second-post`. Within this file, you can use the Next.js `useRouter` hook to access the route parameters. This hook provides the parameter values, which can then be used to fetch data or render content specific to the route.

Handling dynamic routes also entails understanding how to manage route parameters effectively. The parameters extracted from dynamic routes are accessible through the `query` object of the router. For instance, in the `[slug].js` file, you can access the parameter by destructuring it from `router.query`. This allows you to fetch content based on the parameter and dynamically render the corresponding page content. To ensure that the application can handle various route parameters smoothly, you should also incorporate error handling and validation mechanisms.

In scenarios where multiple dynamic segments are required within a single route, Next.js supports nested dynamic routes. For example, if your application needs to handle routes like `/users/[userId]/posts/[postId]`, you would create a nested directory structure with files named `[userId]` and `[postId]` accordingly. This hierarchical approach enables you to capture and manage multiple dynamic parameters in a single route. Each segment of the URL can be accessed through the router's `query` object, and the data can be fetched or processed based on these parameters.

Next.js also supports catch-all routes, which provide a powerful means of handling routes with an arbitrary number of segments. Catch-all routes are defined by using three dots inside square brackets, such as `[...params].js`. This approach is particularly useful for applications requiring flexible URL structures, where the number of segments may vary. In the `[...params].js` file, the `params` array contains all segments of the URL, allowing you to handle complex routing scenarios where the structure of the URL is not fixed.

For applications that require more control over routing behavior, Next.js offers the `getServerSideProps` and `getStaticProps` functions. These data-fetching methods can be utilized within dynamic routes to pre-render content based on the route parameters. `getServerSideProps` allows for server-side rendering, fetching data on each request, while `getStaticProps` enables static generation at build time. Both methods can be used in conjunction with dynamic routes to provide a tailored experience based on the parameters.

To further enhance routing capabilities, Next.js includes support for custom server configurations. By extending the default server behavior, developers can implement advanced routing patterns, such as URL rewrites and redirects. Custom server configurations allow for more granular control over routing logic, enabling the implementation of complex routing rules that go beyond the standard capabilities provided by file-based routing.

Effective management of dynamic routes and routing scenarios involves a combination of understanding the routing system, leveraging the dynamic segment capabilities, and integrating data-fetching methods to ensure that pages are rendered correctly. By mastering these aspects, developers can build robust and flexible applications that accommodate a wide range of routing requirements.

Building on the fundamental concepts of dynamic routing, Next.js provides robust tools to handle more complex routing scenarios, including nested dynamic routes and custom route handling. The framework's flexibility allows developers to construct sophisticated URL structures that align with diverse application needs.

When working with nested dynamic routes, the file system-based routing in Next.js becomes particularly powerful. For instance, if an application needs to support routes such as `/users/[userId]/posts/[postId]`, where both `userId` and `postId` are dynamic, the directory structure under the `pages` folder needs to reflect this hierarchy. This involves creating nested directories and files that correspond to the dynamic segments. Within the `pages/users/[userId]/posts/[postId].js` file, the route parameters can be accessed similarly through the `useRouter` hook, allowing you to fetch data related to both the user and the specific post.

Handling these nested dynamic routes efficiently requires a clear understanding of how data fetching and component rendering interact. You might need to perform data fetching based on multiple parameters. For instance, retrieving user-specific posts may involve making API calls that use both `userId` and `postId` to fetch the necessary content. In such cases, the `getServerSideProps` or `getStaticProps` functions can be utilized to handle server-side or static generation data fetching based on the route parameters. This approach ensures that the data is pre-fetched and available when the page is rendered, improving both performance and SEO.

Custom route handling in Next.js extends the flexibility of dynamic routing by allowing for advanced scenarios where you need to manipulate or override default routing behavior. This is achieved through the use of custom server setups. Next.js supports custom servers using Node.js, which enables you to define custom routing logic beyond the file-based system. For example, if you need to implement redirects, rewrite rules, or handle requests that do not fit into the standard dynamic routing model, you can set up a custom server using frameworks like Express.js or Fastify.

In a custom server setup, you define your routing logic directly within the server configuration. This might involve creating routes that handle specific URL patterns or performing server-side operations before passing control to Next.js. For instance, you could set up a custom route that redirects old URLs to their new counterparts or implements conditional logic to serve different content based on headers or other request properties. This custom routing capability is particularly useful for legacy systems or complex applications that require bespoke routing rules.

Next.js also provides an API for managing routing at a granular level through its `next.config.js` file. This configuration file allows you to define redirects, rewrites, and headers that can be applied globally across the application. Redirects can be set up to automatically send users from one URL to another, which is helpful for handling changes in URL structures or implementing SEO best practices. Rewrites enable you to map incoming requests to different URLs internally, which can be used for various purposes, including proxying requests or changing URL patterns without altering the user-facing URLs.

In summary, Next.js's dynamic routing capabilities offer a high degree of flexibility for managing complex URL structures and routing scenarios. By leveraging nested dynamic routes, custom servers, and configuration options, developers can build applications that handle a wide range of routing needs efficiently. Understanding and utilizing these features allows for the creation of sophisticated, performant, and maintainable web applications that can meet various user and business requirements.

Incorporating dynamic routes within Next.js necessitates careful attention to URL parameter handling and efficient data management. A crucial aspect of working with dynamic routes is understanding how to utilize route parameters to dynamically render content and manage application state.

When a route contains dynamic segments, such as `[userId]` or `[postId]`, these segments are extracted and made available through the `useRouter` hook provided by Next.js. This hook is part of the `next/router` module and facilitates the retrieval of route parameters, enabling the dynamic rendering of components based on these parameters. For example, when a user navigates to `/posts/[postId]`, the `useRouter` hook will provide access to `postId`, which can then be used to fetch and display the relevant content.

Handling these parameters effectively involves integrating them with data fetching methods. If a page is designed to fetch data dynamically based on route parameters, Next.js offers `getServerSideProps` for server-side rendering and `getStaticProps` combined with `getStaticPaths` for static site generation. Each method has its use cases. `getServerSideProps` is ideal for scenarios where the data must be fetched at request time, ensuring that the content is up-to-date. Conversely, `getStaticProps` and `getStaticPaths` work well for static generation, where the data is fetched at build time, and paths are pre-defined.

An essential aspect of working with dynamic routes is ensuring that route parameters are properly validated and handled. This involves checking whether the parameters are valid before proceeding with data fetching or rendering. For example, if a route parameter is expected to be a number, you should implement validation logic to handle cases where the parameter might be missing or malformed. This helps to avoid runtime errors and ensures a smoother user experience.

Beyond the basic usage of dynamic routes, Next.js also supports advanced routing features that enhance flexibility. For instance, nested dynamic routes allow developers to create complex URL structures. In such scenarios, you can nest dynamic segments within directories to match more intricate URL patterns. When building a blog application, for example, you might have a structure where posts are categorized by tags, and each tag has multiple posts. This necessitates a routing setup where routes like `/tags/[tag]/posts/[postId]` can be managed effectively. This approach ensures that the application can handle a diverse range of URLs and dynamic content requirements.

Additionally, Next.js allows for custom route handling through API routes. These routes can be used to handle specific server-side logic and data processing. By creating API endpoints within the `pages/api` directory, developers can build a comprehensive backend directly within their Next.js application. For example, an API route might be used to handle form submissions, perform server-side calculations, or interact with external services. These API routes can then be integrated with dynamic routes to provide a seamless end-to-end experience.

Custom route handling is further extended through the use of Next.js's rewrite and redirect features. Rewrites allow you to modify the URL path of incoming requests, effectively serving different content without changing the URL visible to the user. This can be useful for scenarios such as URL normalization or serving content from different sources based on the request. Redirects, on the other hand, enable you to redirect users from one URL to another, which can be valuable for managing deprecated routes or providing user-friendly URLs.

In summary, working with dynamic routes in Next.js provides a powerful framework for building flexible and scalable applications. By leveraging dynamic route parameters, integrating data fetching methods, and utilizing advanced routing features, developers can create sophisticated applications that cater to a wide range of user needs and content structures. The ability to manage nested routes, handle API requests, and implement custom routing logic ensures that Next.js remains a versatile tool in modern web development. As you continue to explore Next.js, these routing capabilities will enable you to build applications that are both robust and adaptable to complex scenarios.

CHAPTER 10:
STYLING NEXT.JS
APPLICATIONS

Effective styling is an essential aspect of developing visually engaging and user-friendly applications. In Next.js, various approaches to styling are available, each catering to different needs and preferences. Understanding these options enables developers to select the most suitable method for their projects, ensuring both aesthetic appeal and maintainability.

Next.js offers built-in support for CSS, allowing developers to apply styles globally or locally. The global styles can be defined in a CSS file and imported into the `_app.js` file, which serves as the top-level component for all pages. This approach is straightforward and integrates well with traditional CSS practices. By importing a CSS file in `_app.js`, the styles are applied globally across the entire application, providing a consistent look and feel.

For localized styling, Next.js supports CSS modules. CSS modules are a powerful feature that scopes CSS classes to individual components, preventing style conflicts and unintended side effects. When using CSS modules, each CSS file is associated with a specific component, and class names are automatically generated to ensure they are unique. This modular approach enhances maintainability by keeping styles encapsulated and reducing the risk of unintended style overlaps.

In addition to built-in CSS support, Next.js seamlessly integrates with CSS-in-JS libraries, such as styled-components and Emotion. CSS-in-JS libraries offer dynamic styling capabilities, allowing developers to define styles directly within their JavaScript code. This method provides greater flexibility, as styles can be altered based on component state or props. Styled-components, for example, enable developers to create styled components with a syntax that closely resembles traditional CSS, while also supporting advanced features like theming and nested styles.

Emotion, another popular CSS-in-JS library, offers similar capabilities with its own set of features. It provides a powerful API for defining styles within JavaScript and supports both styled components and the use of class names. Emotion is known for its performance optimizations and ease of use, making it a strong choice for developers seeking a flexible and high-performance styling solution.

For applications requiring comprehensive design systems or theming, third-party styling solutions such as Tailwind CSS or Material-UI can be highly beneficial. Tailwind CSS is a utility-first CSS framework that promotes a highly composable approach to styling. Instead of writing custom CSS, developers apply utility classes directly in their HTML or JSX. This approach enables rapid development and consistent styling across components, reducing the need for custom CSS rules and fostering a more maintainable codebase.

Material-UI, on the other hand, provides a rich set of pre-designed components that adhere to Google's Material Design principles. This component library offers a wide range of customizable and accessible UI elements, facilitating the rapid development of visually consistent and user-friendly applications. Material-UI components come with built-in styling capabilities and can be customized using a theming system to align with the specific design requirements of a project.

When selecting a styling approach, it is essential to consider the project's requirements, the team's familiarity with different tools, and the overall maintainability of the codebase. Each method—whether built-in CSS, CSS-in-JS, or third-party libraries—has its advantages and trade-offs. Built-in CSS and CSS modules offer simplicity and familiarity, while CSS-in-JS libraries provide dynamic styling options and better integration with JavaScript logic. Third-party libraries like Tailwind CSS and Material-UI offer comprehensive design systems and ready-to-use components that can accelerate development and ensure consistency.

Ultimately, the choice of styling approach depends on the specific needs of the application and the preferences of the development team. By understanding the strengths and limitations of each method, developers can make informed decisions that enhance both the visual appeal and functionality of their Next.js applications. As styling is a critical aspect of user experience, selecting the appropriate method is crucial for creating applications that are not only functional but also engaging and aesthetically pleasing.

Tailwind CSS is a utility-first CSS framework that allows developers to build custom designs directly in their HTML or JSX by applying pre-defined utility classes. This approach contrasts with traditional CSS methodologies by emphasizing composition over customization. Tailwind CSS encourages developers to use its utility classes to construct layouts and design elements without writing custom CSS, thus promoting consistency and reducing the need for repetitive styles. It is particularly advantageous for rapid prototyping and ensures that design systems are both scalable and maintainable.

Material-UI, on the other hand, provides a comprehensive

set of pre-designed components that adhere to the Material Design guidelines established by Google. This framework offers a robust library of UI components, including buttons, forms, and navigation elements, which are designed to be easily customizable. Material-UI allows developers to apply themes and styles at a global level, providing a cohesive design language across the application. It supports advanced theming capabilities, enabling developers to adjust styles dynamically based on the application's context or user preferences.

In addition to choosing a styling method, it is essential to consider the integration of these techniques within the Next.js ecosystem. For example, when using CSS modules or CSS-in-JS libraries, Next.js's build process optimizes and scopes styles automatically, ensuring that the final application performs efficiently and maintains style encapsulation. Next.js also supports server-side rendering, which means that styles are applied during server-side rendering, contributing to faster page loads and improved SEO.

In practice, integrating multiple styling solutions can be beneficial. For instance, developers may use Tailwind CSS for utility-based layout and spacing while leveraging CSS-in-JS libraries for component-specific styles and dynamic theming. This hybrid approach allows for the flexibility of utility-first styling combined with the dynamic capabilities of CSS-in-JS.

When selecting a styling approach, consider factors such as project requirements, team familiarity with the technology, and long-term maintainability. For projects with complex and varied design needs, combining different methods might provide the best balance between flexibility and control. Conversely, simpler projects may benefit from sticking to one styling approach to maintain clarity and reduce complexity.

Practical implementation involves setting up the chosen styling method within a Next.js project. For CSS modules, create a `.module.css` file for each component and import it accordingly. This ensures that styles are scoped to the component and avoids conflicts with other styles. For CSS-in-JS solutions like styled-components or Emotion, install the appropriate library and configure it in your project. These libraries usually require additional setup, such as adding a Babel plugin or configuring the Next.js build process.

For Tailwind CSS, integrate it by installing the library and configuring it through a `tailwind.config.js` file. Tailwind CSS requires defining a theme and custom configurations that align with your design requirements. Once set up, you can start applying utility classes directly in your JSX, which simplifies the process of styling components and building responsive layouts.

Material-UI integration involves installing the library and setting up a theme provider to apply global styles and themes. Material-UI's components can then be used throughout the application, with custom styles applied through its styling solution. This method ensures that your application maintains a consistent look and feel while leveraging Material Design principles.

In conclusion, Next.js provides a flexible environment for styling applications, accommodating various methodologies from traditional CSS to modern CSS-in-JS solutions and third-party frameworks. By understanding and implementing these styling approaches effectively, developers can enhance the visual appeal and usability of their applications while maintaining a manageable and scalable codebase. Each method offers unique advantages, and the choice of which to use will depend on project-specific requirements and personal or team preferences.

When it comes to integrating third-party styling solutions with Next.js, it's important to ensure that these solutions are compatible with the framework's architecture. For instance, while integrating a CSS framework such as Bootstrap or Bulma, it's crucial to manage CSS imports and ensure they do not conflict with other styles in your application. Bootstrap, for example, can be imported into the global `styles/globals.css` file or included via a CDN link in the custom `_app.js` file. This approach allows you to leverage Bootstrap's extensive set of pre-defined classes and components while maintaining consistency across your application.

For more dynamic and customizable styling needs, consider using libraries like Styled Components or Emotion. These CSS-in-JS libraries offer a powerful way to style your components by allowing you to write actual CSS syntax within your JavaScript files. Styled Components, for instance, enables you to create styled components with encapsulated styles, providing a clean and modular approach to component design. Emotion offers similar capabilities but with additional flexibility and performance optimizations, allowing for both styled components and traditional CSS class names.

When using these libraries, the integration with Next.js is relatively straightforward. You can configure Styled Components with a custom Babel configuration to ensure server-side rendering works correctly and styles are properly rendered. Emotion also provides similar setup instructions for Next.js, including configuring Babel for optimal performance and integration.

Furthermore, it's essential to address the issue of global styles and their impact on your Next.js application. Global styles can be managed through the `styles/globals.css` file, which is imported in the custom `_app.js` file. This approach allows you to apply universal styles and maintain a consistent design across all pages and components. For example, setting up base styles such as typography, color schemes, and layout grids can be efficiently managed through this global CSS file.

Another crucial aspect of styling in Next.js is responsive design. Ensuring that your application is visually appealing and functional across various devices and screen sizes is fundamental. Modern CSS frameworks and libraries often include responsive design utilities, such as media queries and flexbox/grid systems, which can be utilized to achieve responsive layouts. Tailwind CSS, for instance, provides a range of utility classes that facilitate responsive design, allowing you to apply different styles based on breakpoints.

Incorporating best practices for responsive design includes using relative units (e.g., percentages, ems) rather than fixed units (e.g., pixels) and designing with a mobile-first approach. This ensures that your application adapts seamlessly to different screen sizes and provides a positive user experience across devices.

Additionally, consider the performance implications of your chosen styling approach. While CSS-in-JS libraries offer a powerful way to handle component-specific styles, they may introduce additional runtime overhead. Ensure that your application is optimized by minimizing the amount of CSS generated and leveraging techniques such as CSS tree-shaking and code splitting.

Overall, the choice of styling method in Next.js depends on the specific needs of your project, including design requirements, team preferences, and performance considerations. Whether you opt for traditional CSS, utility-first frameworks like Tailwind CSS, or CSS-in-JS libraries like Styled Components or Emotion, it's important to understand how these methods integrate with Next.js and how they impact the overall development and performance of your application.

By carefully evaluating these factors and applying best practices, you can effectively manage styles in your Next.js applications, ensuring that they are not only visually appealing but also performant and maintainable.

CHAPTER 11: IMPLEMENTING AUTHENTICATION AND AUTHORIZATION

In the realm of web development, securing applications through effective authentication and authorization is paramount. Authentication confirms the identity of users, while authorization determines their access rights within the application. Next.js, being a powerful framework for building React applications, provides various mechanisms to implement these critical features. This chapter delves into the methods of integrating authentication and authorization into a Next.js application, covering session management, user roles, and integration with third-party authentication providers.

To begin with, understanding session management is crucial. In a Next.js application, session management involves maintaining the state of user authentication across different pages and requests. Typically, sessions are managed using cookies, which store a session token or identifier that persists across page reloads and browser sessions. To handle cookies effectively, libraries like `cookie` and `js-cookie` can be utilized. The `cookie` library helps parse and serialize cookies on the server side, while `js-cookie` provides a simple API for managing cookies on the client side.

For managing user sessions, Next.js applications often integrate with server-side session libraries such as `next-auth`. This library simplifies the process of managing authentication and sessions by providing built-in support for various authentication providers, including OAuth and email-based logins. `next-auth` handles the complexity of session management, such as creating and storing session tokens, handling user sign-ins, and managing session expiration. Its flexible configuration allows for integration with different authentication providers and databases, enabling developers to tailor the authentication process to their specific needs.

Implementing authorization involves defining and enforcing user roles and permissions to control access to different parts of the application. In Next.js, this can be achieved through a combination of server-side logic and client-side checks. On the server side, middleware functions can be employed to verify user roles before granting access to certain API routes or pages. For instance, Next.js API routes can include middleware that checks the user's role before proceeding with request handling. This ensures that only authorized users can access protected endpoints.

On the client side, Next.js applications can utilize React context or state management libraries such as Redux to manage user roles and permissions. By storing user information and role data in the application's state, components can conditionally render content based on the user's role. For example, a component might display admin-only features only if the user has an admin role. This approach ensures that unauthorized users cannot access restricted areas of the application, enhancing security.

In addition to session management and user roles, integrating with third-party authentication providers is a common practice in modern web applications. Next.js supports integration with various authentication services, such as Google, Facebook, and GitHub, through the `next-auth` library or custom OAuth implementations. Integrating with these providers allows users to authenticate using their existing social media or email accounts, streamlining the login process and improving user experience.

To implement third-party authentication, developers need to configure OAuth providers in their Next.js application. This involves registering the application with the chosen provider, obtaining client credentials, and configuring authentication routes. The `next-auth` library provides built-in support for many popular providers, simplifying the process of connecting to these services. Developers can configure provider settings in the `next-auth` configuration file, specifying client IDs, secrets, and callback URLs. Once configured, users can authenticate using the provider's interface, and the application will handle token exchange and user information retrieval.

Moreover, security considerations must be addressed to ensure the integrity of the authentication and authorization mechanisms. For instance, it is essential to use secure connections (HTTPS) to protect sensitive data during transmission. Implementing secure cookie settings, such as HttpOnly and SameSite attributes, further mitigates risks related to session hijacking and cross-site request forgery (CSRF) attacks. Additionally, adopting practices such as password hashing and salting for user credentials enhances the security of stored authentication data.

Handling authentication and authorization in Next.js requires a thorough understanding of both server-side and client-side techniques. By effectively managing sessions, defining user roles, integrating third-party authentication providers, and adhering to security best practices, developers can build robust and secure applications. The combination of Next.js's powerful features and thoughtful implementation of authentication and authorization mechanisms ensures that web applications remain both user-friendly and protected against unauthorized access.

To implement authentication effectively in a Next.js application, it is crucial to handle various aspects, including secure storage of user credentials, session management, and integration with authentication providers. This section expands on these elements, focusing on how they interact within the Next.js ecosystem.

One of the foundational steps in authentication is secure storage of user credentials. When implementing authentication, sensitive information such as passwords must be handled with care. Passwords should never be stored in plaintext; instead, they should be hashed using robust algorithms such as bcrypt. Hashing passwords ensures that even if a database is compromised, the actual passwords are not exposed. Libraries such as `bcryptjs` or `bcrypt` in Node.js facilitate this process. By using these libraries, developers can hash passwords during user registration and then compare the hashed passwords during login attempts.

Beyond hashing, secure session management is a key component of authentication. Sessions are used to maintain user state across multiple requests and interactions. In Next.js, this involves managing cookies that store session tokens or identifiers. These cookies should be secure, HttpOnly, and have appropriate expiration settings to mitigate the risk of session hijacking or cross-site scripting (XSS) attacks. Secure cookies are transmitted over HTTPS, and HttpOnly cookies are inaccessible to JavaScript running in the browser, providing an additional layer of protection.

Next.js applications can use middleware functions to manage sessions. Middleware can intercept requests and check for valid session tokens before allowing access to certain routes or pages. For example, middleware might verify the presence and validity of a session token stored in a cookie. If the token is valid, the middleware allows the request to proceed; otherwise, it might redirect the user to a login page or return an error message.

In addition to session management, integrating with third-party authentication providers is a common practice. Providers such as Google, Facebook, and GitHub offer OAuth-based authentication services that streamline the login process for users. Next.js supports integration with these providers through libraries like `next-auth`. This library abstracts much of the complexity involved in OAuth authentication, offering a straightforward configuration for various providers. By configuring `next-auth`, developers can quickly add social login options to their applications, enhancing user experience and simplifying the authentication process.

`next-auth` manages the entire authentication flow, including redirecting users to the provider's login page, handling authentication callbacks, and storing session information. Developers need to configure `next-auth` with appropriate provider settings and credentials, which can often be obtained from the provider's developer console. The library also supports additional features like email-based authentication, allowing users to sign in using one-time passwords sent to their email addresses.

Once authentication is implemented, managing user roles and permissions becomes essential. Authorization controls access based on user roles, ensuring that only users with specific roles can access certain parts of the application. Next.js allows for flexible role-based access control through both server-side and client-side mechanisms. On the server side, API routes can be protected using middleware that checks user roles before allowing access. This involves validating the user's role from session data and verifying whether it matches the required permissions for a given API route.

On the client side, React context or state management libraries such as Redux can be employed to manage and access user role information. By storing user roles in the application's state, components can conditionally render content based on the user's role. For instance, an admin dashboard might only be visible to users with an "admin" role, while regular users see a standard interface. This dynamic rendering ensures that users have access only to the features and data that are appropriate for their role.

Handling authorization also involves ensuring that routes and components properly enforce access controls. For instance, Next.js provides mechanisms to protect pages and components based on user roles. Higher-order components (HOCs) or custom hooks can be used to wrap protected components, checking the user's role before rendering content. These methods help maintain clean and manageable code, centralizing authorization logic and making it easier to enforce consistent access controls across the application.

Overall, implementing authentication and authorization in a Next.js application requires a combination of secure practices, effective session management, and proper integration with third-party services. By following best practices for password security, utilizing libraries like `next-auth` for third-party authentication, and managing user roles through both server-side and client-side techniques, developers can create secure and well-structured authentication and authorization systems. This comprehensive approach ensures that web applications remain both functional and secure, providing users with a seamless and protected experience.

Building on the integration of third-party authentication providers, managing user roles and permissions is another critical aspect of authentication and authorization. Once users are authenticated, it's essential to define what actions they are permitted to perform based on their roles within the application. This aspect ensures that users have access only to the features and data that they are authorized to use, thus protecting sensitive information and maintaining the integrity of the application.

In Next.js, user roles can be managed through server-side logic and client-side checks. Server-side role management typically involves defining user roles and permissions in your database and enforcing these roles in your API routes and server-side functions. For instance, a route handler can check the user's role before processing a request. If a user attempts to access a resource they are not authorized for, the server can return a forbidden status code or redirect the user to an appropriate page.

On the client side, role-based access control can be implemented by conditionally rendering components based on the user's role. This involves checking the user's role information, which can be stored in state or retrieved from the server, and rendering the UI elements accordingly. While client-side checks are helpful for user experience, they should not be solely relied upon for security, as they can be bypassed. Therefore, server-side enforcement remains the primary method for ensuring authorization.

For managing authentication and authorization flows effectively, developers should consider implementing centralized authentication logic. This involves creating a service or utility that handles all authentication-related tasks, such as login, logout, and session validation. By centralizing this logic, the application becomes easier to maintain and the risk of introducing security vulnerabilities is reduced. A common approach is to use context providers in React, which allow the authentication state to be accessible throughout the application without prop drilling.

Session validation is another crucial aspect. When a user interacts with the application, their session needs to be verified to ensure it is still valid. This verification typically involves checking the expiration of session tokens and refreshing them if necessary. Many authentication libraries and frameworks provide built-in mechanisms for session management and token refresh, simplifying the implementation of these features.

Furthermore, implementing a robust logging and monitoring system is essential for tracking authentication and authorization activities. Logs can provide valuable insights into login attempts, role changes, and access control violations. Monitoring tools can alert administrators to suspicious activities, such as multiple failed login attempts or unauthorized access attempts. This proactive approach helps in identifying and addressing security issues before they become significant problems.

Lastly, it is important to consider the security implications of authentication and authorization strategies. Employing HTTPS to encrypt data in transit, implementing strong password policies, and using multi-factor authentication (MFA) can significantly enhance the security of your application. MFA, in particular, adds an additional layer of security by requiring users to provide a second form of verification, such as a code sent to their mobile device, in addition to their password.

In summary, implementing authentication and authorization in a Next.js application involves a multifaceted approach that includes secure handling of user credentials, effective session management, integration with third-party providers, role-based access control, centralized authentication logic, session validation, and robust logging and monitoring. By carefully designing and implementing these components, developers can create a secure and user-friendly authentication system that meets the needs of their application and protects sensitive data.

CHAPTER 12: OPTIMIZING PERFORMANCE AND SEO

In the realm of web development, optimizing performance and SEO is crucial for delivering a superior user experience and achieving higher search engine rankings. Next.js, with its robust set of features, provides several mechanisms to enhance both the performance and SEO of web applications. This chapter delves into these strategies, offering practical insights into code splitting, lazy loading, image optimization, and SEO best practices.

Performance optimization in Next.js begins with understanding the concept of code splitting. Code splitting is a technique that involves breaking down your application's JavaScript bundle into smaller, more manageable chunks. This process ensures that users only download the code necessary for the current page, leading to faster load times and a more responsive application. Next.js simplifies code splitting by leveraging dynamic imports, which allow components to be loaded on demand rather than including them in the initial bundle. This not only reduces the size of the initial load but also improves the overall user experience by minimizing the amount of code that needs to be parsed and executed upfront.

Another key performance optimization strategy is lazy loading. Lazy loading defers the loading of non-essential resources until they are needed. This approach is particularly useful for loading images and other media assets that are not immediately visible on the page. Next.js provides built-in support for lazy loading images through its `next/image` component, which optimizes images by automatically applying responsive sizing and lazy loading. This not only improves page load times but also reduces the amount of data transferred, which is beneficial for users on slower connections or mobile devices.

Image optimization is another critical aspect of performance enhancement. Large images can significantly slow down page load times and negatively impact the user experience. Next.js's `next/image` component offers several features to address this issue, including automatic resizing, format conversion, and compression. By leveraging these features, developers can ensure that images are served in the most efficient format and size for each device, further enhancing the performance of their applications.

Beyond performance optimization, search engine optimization (SEO) is equally important for ensuring that your application is discoverable and ranks well in search engine results. Next.js provides several features to help developers implement SEO best practices. One of the most fundamental aspects of SEO is ensuring that your application has well-structured metadata. This includes defining relevant meta tags such as the title, description, and Open Graph tags, which provide important information to search engines and social media platforms. Next.js allows for easy management of these tags through its `next/head` component, which can be used to dynamically set the metadata for each page.

Furthermore, Next.js supports server-side rendering (SSR) and static site generation (SSG), both of which play a crucial role in SEO. SSR generates HTML on the server for each request, ensuring that search engines receive fully rendered pages that can be easily indexed. SSG, on the other hand, pre-renders pages at build time, providing a static HTML file for each page. Both approaches enhance SEO by ensuring that content is readily available for search engine crawlers, improving the likelihood of better search rankings.

Additionally, implementing a well-structured and accessible navigation system contributes to better SEO. A clear and logical site structure, with properly defined headings and a well-organized URL structure, allows search engines to understand the hierarchy and relevance of your content. Next.js's file-based routing system inherently supports this by creating routes based on the file structure within the `pages` directory, which aligns with best practices for URL structuring.

In summary, optimizing performance and SEO in Next.js involves a combination of strategies and best practices. Code splitting and lazy loading improve performance by reducing the initial load time and deferring the loading of non-essential resources. Image optimization ensures that media assets are served efficiently, further enhancing performance. On the SEO front, managing metadata, leveraging SSR and SSG, and maintaining a well-structured navigation system are key to improving search engine visibility. By implementing these strategies, developers can build Next.js applications that not only perform efficiently but also rank well in search engine results, providing a better experience for users and achieving greater reach.

In addition to metadata management, optimizing the structure and content of your pages is essential for SEO. This includes ensuring that your pages have a clear and logical hierarchy, with meaningful and descriptive headings. Next.js allows for the use of `Head` from `next/head` to manage the HTML head tags on a per-page basis, which is crucial for setting up meta tags that search engines use to index your pages. Proper use of heading tags (from `<h1>` to `<h6>`) not only helps search engines understand the structure of your content but also improves accessibility for users relying on screen readers.

Another significant factor in SEO is the implementation of a sitemap and robots.txt file. A sitemap is an XML file that lists all the pages of your website, helping search engines crawl and index your content more effectively. Next.js does not provide built-in support for sitemaps, but you can easily generate one using external libraries or custom scripts. Similarly, the `robots.txt` file directs search engine bots on which pages should be crawled or ignored, helping to manage which parts of your site are indexed.

Implementing structured data is also a powerful way to enhance your application's visibility in search engine results. Structured data, often implemented using JSON-LD, provides search engines with additional context about your content, which can improve how your pages are represented in search results. For example, adding schema markup to your product pages can enable rich snippets, such as product ratings and prices, to appear in search results, making your listings more attractive to users.

Page speed is another crucial aspect of both performance and SEO. Search engines, particularly Google, consider page speed as a ranking factor, so optimizing it can have a direct impact on your search visibility. Beyond the basic optimizations already discussed, tools like Next.js's built-in analytics can provide valuable insights into performance bottlenecks. Additionally, employing a content delivery network (CDN) to serve your static assets can further reduce load times by distributing content geographically closer to users.

For dynamic content, Next.js offers incremental static regeneration (ISR), which allows you to update static content without rebuilding the entire site. ISR is particularly useful for content that changes frequently but does not require real-time updates. By setting up ISR, you can ensure that your site remains fresh and up-to-date while still benefiting from the performance advantages of static generation.

When it comes to SEO, optimizing your URLs and ensuring they are descriptive and keyword-rich can also enhance your search engine rankings. Next.js supports dynamic routing, which enables you to create clean, readable URLs that reflect the content of your pages. Implementing human-readable URLs not only benefits SEO but also improves user experience by making your site easier to navigate and understand.

Finally, monitoring and analyzing your performance and SEO efforts are critical to ongoing success. Tools such as Google Analytics and Google Search Console provide valuable feedback on how your site is performing, how users are interacting with it, and how well it is ranking in search engines. Regularly reviewing this data allows you to make informed adjustments and continue optimizing your site for both performance and search engine visibility.

In summary, optimizing performance and SEO in a Next.js application involves a combination of strategies that address both technical and content aspects. From implementing code splitting and lazy loading to managing metadata and structured data, each optimization technique contributes to a faster, more accessible, and better-ranked web application. By leveraging the built-in features of Next.js and following best practices, you can ensure that your application not only performs well but also achieves the visibility needed to reach your target audience effectively.

Beyond the core strategies for performance and SEO discussed, it's important to consider ongoing optimization practices that help maintain and enhance your application's effectiveness over time. Regularly auditing your site for performance issues using tools like Google Lighthouse or WebPageTest can help you stay on top of potential slowdowns or inefficiencies. These tools provide detailed insights into various aspects of your application, such as accessibility, best practices, and progressive web app (PWA) features, which can inform your optimization efforts.

Another aspect to explore is the use of dynamic imports in Next.js to improve the performance of your application. Dynamic imports allow you to load components only when they are needed, which can significantly reduce the initial load time of your application. By leveraging this feature, you can implement code splitting to ensure that only the necessary code is sent to the client initially, with additional code loaded as the user interacts with the application.

It is also worth considering the implementation of caching strategies to further enhance performance. Caching can be applied at various levels, including server-side caching, client-side caching, and CDN caching. On the server side, you can use HTTP caching headers to control how long responses are cached by browsers and intermediate proxies. On the client side, libraries like `swr` (stale-while-revalidate) provide built-in caching mechanisms for fetching data, which can reduce the number of requests made to your server and improve user experience.

Additionally, optimizing your images and media assets is crucial for maintaining fast load times. Next.js provides built-in support for image optimization through the `next/image` component, which automatically optimizes images by resizing, compressing, and serving them in modern formats such as WebP. This built-in feature reduces the need for manual optimization and helps ensure that images are delivered in the most efficient way possible.

To maximize the SEO impact of your Next.js application, consider implementing advanced techniques such as dynamic meta tags. By using server-side rendering or static generation with dynamic values, you can ensure that meta tags are tailored to the content of each page. This practice helps search engines accurately index and rank your pages based on their specific content, improving visibility and relevance in search results.

Another important consideration is the handling of JavaScript and CSS assets. Next.js optimizes these assets by default, but understanding how to fine-tune their delivery can further enhance performance. For example, minimizing and bundling JavaScript and CSS files can reduce the overall size of your assets, which contributes to faster load times. Tools like Webpack, which is used by Next.js under the hood, support various optimization techniques that you can leverage for better performance.

Lastly, maintaining an effective SEO strategy involves staying informed about updates to search engine algorithms and best practices. Search engines frequently update their ranking criteria, and keeping your application aligned with the latest SEO guidelines can help you retain and improve your search rankings. Regularly reviewing and updating your SEO strategy ensures that your Next.js application remains competitive and continues to deliver excellent performance and visibility.

In conclusion, optimizing performance and SEO in a Next.js application requires a multifaceted approach that includes leveraging built-in features, implementing advanced techniques, and continuously monitoring and adjusting strategies. By combining effective performance optimization practices with robust SEO techniques, you can build a high-performing, search-engine-friendly application that delivers a superior user experience and achieves greater visibility in search results.

CHAPTER 13: INTEGRATING WITH DATABASES AND BACKEND SERVICES

Connecting a Next.js application to databases and backend services is crucial for building dynamic, data-driven web applications. This chapter delves into the various methods of integration, from traditional databases to modern backend services, and provides a comprehensive guide on how to handle CRUD (Create, Read, Update, Delete) operations effectively. By the end of this chapter, you will have a clear understanding of how to establish these connections and manage data within your Next.js application.

To begin, it's important to understand the different types of databases and backend services that can be integrated with Next.js. Next.js does not impose any specific constraints on the backend technologies you use, allowing for a flexible choice depending on your project's requirements. You can connect to SQL databases like PostgreSQL or MySQL, NoSQL databases like MongoDB, or utilize backend-as-a-service (BaaS) platforms such as Firebase or Supabase.

When working with SQL databases, you can use an Object-Relational Mapping (ORM) tool such as Prisma or Sequelize. ORMs simplify database operations by abstracting SQL queries into high-level JavaScript methods. For instance, Prisma provides a powerful schema-based approach to define and interact with your database models. You define your data model using Prisma's schema language, generate a client, and then use this client to perform operations such as querying and mutating data. This approach not only streamlines database interactions but also offers type safety and autocompletion, enhancing development efficiency.

In contrast, NoSQL databases like MongoDB offer a schema-less approach, making them ideal for applications with evolving data structures. Libraries such as Mongoose provide an ODM (Object Data Modeling) layer for MongoDB, allowing you to define schemas and interact with your data in a more structured manner. Mongoose also includes features for validation, middleware, and query building, which can greatly simplify working with MongoDB in your Next.js application.

For integrating backend services, Next.js's API routes can act as a bridge between your frontend and external APIs or services. By creating API routes within your Next.js application, you can handle requests and responses, process data, and interact with third-party services directly. For example, you can create an API route to handle user authentication, interact with an external payment gateway, or fetch data from a third-party REST API. This approach allows you to centralize your data fetching and processing logic, ensuring a cohesive and manageable codebase.

When dealing with CRUD operations, the process generally involves setting up routes or endpoints to handle different types of requests. In Next.js, API routes are created under the `/pages/api` directory. Each file within this directory corresponds to an endpoint, and you can use methods like `GET`, `POST`, `PUT`, and `DELETE` to handle various operations. For instance, a `POST` request to an endpoint could be used to create new data entries, while a

`GET` request retrieves data from the database. Handling these operations involves parsing request data, performing necessary validations, and interacting with the database or external services to execute the requested actions.

In addition to direct integration, you may also want to consider the use of serverless functions to manage data operations. Serverless functions, provided by platforms such as Vercel or AWS Lambda, offer a scalable solution for handling backend logic without maintaining a dedicated server. You can deploy serverless functions to handle specific tasks, such as processing form submissions or executing background jobs. This approach reduces the overhead of managing server infrastructure and allows you to focus on writing the application logic.

Security is a paramount concern when integrating databases and backend services. Always ensure that sensitive information, such as database credentials or API keys, is stored securely and not exposed in your application code. Utilize environment variables to manage these credentials and employ secure practices for data access and handling. Additionally, implement proper authorization and authentication mechanisms to protect your endpoints and ensure that only authorized users can access or modify data.

In summary, integrating databases and backend services with a Next.js application involves selecting the appropriate technologies, setting up routes or endpoints to handle data operations, and ensuring secure and efficient data management. Whether you are using SQL or NoSQL databases, leveraging ORMs or ODMs, or integrating with external services, a clear understanding of these concepts will enable you to build robust and dynamic web applications. As you proceed, consider best practices for security and performance to ensure that your application remains secure and efficient as it scales.

When integrating a Next.js application with databases and backend services, a significant aspect to address is managing CRUD operations effectively. These operations—Create, Read, Update, and Delete—are foundational for interacting with data and ensuring that your application can handle user inputs and data modifications seamlessly.

For SQL databases, executing CRUD operations typically involves creating models, setting up queries, and executing transactions. Using an ORM like Prisma, you can define your data models in a schema file, which then translates into database tables. For example, if you're managing a blog, you might define models for posts and comments. Prisma's client API allows you to perform CRUD operations with methods like `create`, `findMany`, `update`, and `delete`. These methods simplify data manipulation, as they abstract the underlying SQL queries into more intuitive JavaScript functions.

In the case of NoSQL databases, such as MongoDB, the approach is somewhat different. MongoDB stores data in JSON-like documents, which can be queried and manipulated using a variety of methods. With Mongoose, you define schemas that outline the structure of your data, then use model methods to handle CRUD operations. For instance, to create a new document, you would use the `save` method on a Mongoose model instance. To read data, you might use `find` or `findById` methods, and for updates, you can use methods like `updateOne` or `findByIdAndUpdate`. Each of these operations is designed to be straightforward, allowing for efficient data management even as your application scales.

Beyond traditional databases, integrating with backend services often involves connecting to external APIs or services that provide additional functionality or data sources. This might include integrating with payment processors, third-party authentication providers, or content management systems. Next.js API routes serve as an effective mechanism for managing such integrations. By creating API routes within your application, you can centralize backend logic and expose endpoints that interact with external services.

For instance, if you need to integrate with a payment gateway, you would typically create an API route to handle transactions. This route would interact with the payment provider's API, process payments, and handle responses. Within this route, you can implement necessary logic for validating requests, handling errors, and managing transaction states. By keeping this logic in API routes, you ensure that your frontend remains focused on user interactions and presentation, while the backend routes manage the complexities of external service interactions.

Similarly, for authentication, you might use an API route to handle login and registration processes. This route could interact with an authentication service or database to validate user credentials, create sessions, and manage authentication tokens. By handling authentication through API routes, you maintain a separation of concerns, ensuring that security-sensitive operations are managed on the server side.

Additionally, integrating with external services often requires handling asynchronous operations and managing responses. For example, when fetching data from a third-party API, you need to handle potential delays and errors in the response. Next.js provides several features to manage asynchronous data fetching and ensure a smooth user experience. Using async/await syntax, you can manage asynchronous operations more effectively, while handling errors through try/catch blocks or error boundaries ensures that your application remains robust and user-friendly.

Another crucial consideration in integrating databases and backend services is securing your application. Ensuring that your API routes and database connections are secure is vital for protecting sensitive data and maintaining the integrity of your application. This involves implementing proper authentication and authorization mechanisms, validating user inputs, and safeguarding against common security vulnerabilities such as SQL injection and cross-site scripting (XSS).

In Next.js, you can enhance security by utilizing environment variables to store sensitive credentials and configuration settings, ensuring that these are not exposed in your codebase. Additionally, employing HTTPS for secure communication between your application and external services is a fundamental practice to protect data in transit. Regularly updating dependencies and monitoring security advisories are also important practices to maintain a secure application environment.

In conclusion, integrating databases and backend services with Next.js involves a combination of establishing connections, managing CRUD operations, and handling interactions with external APIs. By leveraging tools such as ORMs and ODMs, implementing effective API routes, and maintaining a focus on security, you can build a robust and scalable application capable of managing dynamic data and interacting with diverse backend services. This integration not only enhances the functionality of your application but also ensures a seamless and secure experience for users.

To effectively connect a Next.js application with backend services and databases, it's important to consider the security and scalability of your integration. Proper authentication and authorization mechanisms should be implemented to ensure that data interactions are secure and compliant with best practices.

When connecting to databases, securing database credentials and managing user access is paramount. Environment variables should be used to store sensitive information, such as database URLs and credentials, to prevent hardcoding these details in your codebase. In a production environment, secure storage solutions like secret management services or environment configuration tools provided by cloud platforms can further safeguard sensitive information.

Similarly, when integrating with external APIs, ensuring that API keys and access tokens are protected is crucial. These keys should also be stored in environment variables and not exposed directly in your client-side code. Next.js's API routes can act as intermediaries, handling requests to external APIs on the server side. This approach allows you to keep sensitive keys and tokens hidden from client-side exposure while still utilizing external services.

Scalability considerations come into play as your application grows. For databases, you might need to address concerns such as database indexing, query optimization, and efficient data access patterns to handle increased load. Using a well-structured database schema, indexing frequently queried fields, and leveraging caching strategies can enhance performance and scalability. Additionally, employing database replication and sharding strategies can distribute load and improve resilience.

For backend services, rate limiting and throttling strategies can help manage traffic and prevent abuse. Many external services provide rate limiting as a feature, but if you are implementing your own backend services, incorporating rate limiting and retry mechanisms can help maintain service stability. Caching responses from external APIs or databases can also reduce the load on your backend and improve response times.

When handling CRUD operations, it's also important to manage data consistency and integrity. Implementing validation and error handling mechanisms ensures that only valid data is processed and stored. For instance, when accepting user inputs, you should validate the data on both the client and server sides to prevent malformed or malicious data from being processed. Similarly, employing transactions for operations involving multiple database actions can help maintain data consistency by ensuring that all actions complete successfully or none do.

As you integrate with databases and backend services, monitoring and logging are vital for maintaining and troubleshooting your application. Implementing logging mechanisms to capture errors, performance metrics, and operational data can provide insights into how your application is performing and help you quickly address issues. Tools like Prometheus, Grafana, and various logging services can be integrated to collect and visualize metrics from your application.

In conclusion, integrating a Next.js application with databases and backend services involves several key aspects, including handling CRUD operations, ensuring security, and planning for scalability. By employing best practices for managing data interactions, securing sensitive information, and optimizing performance, you can build a robust, functional, and secure web application. Leveraging Next.js's capabilities, such as API routes, and combining them with effective database and service integration strategies, enables you to create applications that are both feature-rich and reliable.

CHAPTER 14: TESTING NEXT.JS APPLICATIONS

Testing is a fundamental practice in software development that ensures applications operate as intended and maintain reliability throughout their lifecycle. In the context of Next.js applications, implementing a comprehensive testing strategy involves several methodologies, each serving distinct purposes. This chapter explores the key aspects of testing Next.js applications, including unit tests, integration tests, and end-to-end tests. It also provides guidance on setting up testing environments, writing effective test cases, and utilizing testing libraries to validate code.

Unit tests are the most granular form of testing, focusing on individual components or functions to ensure they perform as expected in isolation. In Next.js applications, unit testing typically involves testing React components and utility functions. Tools such as Jest and React Testing Library are commonly used for this purpose. Jest, a popular JavaScript testing framework, provides a robust suite of features for writing and running tests, including assertions, mocking, and snapshot testing. React Testing Library complements Jest by providing utilities for rendering components and simulating user interactions, enabling developers to test component behavior in a way that mirrors how users interact with the application.

When writing unit tests for Next.js components, it is essential to isolate the component from its dependencies. This isolation can be achieved by mocking external modules, such as API calls or global state management tools. Mocking helps ensure that tests are focused on the component's logic rather than being affected by external factors. For instance, when testing a component that fetches data from an API, you can mock the API call to return predefined data, allowing you to test how the component handles this data without making actual network requests.

Integration tests, on the other hand, focus on the interactions between multiple components or systems within the application. These tests verify that different parts of the application work together as expected. In a Next.js application, integration testing might involve testing how components integrate with data-fetching methods like `getStaticProps` or `getServerSideProps`. Additionally, integration tests can validate the interaction between UI components and their corresponding API routes. Jest, in combination with testing libraries like React Testing Library, can also be employed for integration testing. By rendering components in a simulated environment and performing user interactions, integration tests help identify issues that may arise from component interactions or data handling.

End-to-end tests provide a higher-level perspective by testing the application as a whole, simulating user interactions across various parts of the application. These tests are designed to ensure that the application functions correctly from the user's perspective, covering scenarios such as navigating between pages, filling out forms, and submitting data. For end-to-end testing in Next.js applications, tools like Cypress or Puppeteer are commonly used. Cypress offers an intuitive interface for writing and running end-to-end tests, with built-in support for handling asynchronous actions and network requests.

Puppeteer, a Node library providing a high-level API to control Chrome or Chromium, can be used for browser automation and testing complex user interactions.

Setting up a testing environment involves configuring the necessary tools and dependencies to facilitate test execution. In a Next.js application, this includes installing testing libraries, configuring Jest, and setting up test scripts. Jest can be configured through a `jest.config.js` file, where you can define test environment settings, module mappings, and test coverage thresholds. Additionally, creating test scripts in the `package.json` file allows you to run tests using npm or yarn commands. For example, a script to run unit tests might look like `"test:unit": "jest"`.

Writing effective test cases is crucial for ensuring comprehensive test coverage and identifying potential issues early in the development process. Test cases should be designed to cover various scenarios, including edge cases and error conditions. When writing test cases for Next.js components, it is important to consider different states and props that the component may receive. For example, if a component renders a loading state while data is being fetched, a test case should verify that the loading indicator appears as expected during this state. Similarly, if a component handles user input, test cases should validate that the input is processed correctly and any resulting actions are performed as intended.

Incorporating testing into the development workflow involves running tests regularly and integrating them into continuous integration (CI) pipelines. Automated testing helps catch regressions and issues early, ensuring that code changes do not introduce new bugs. Setting up CI/CD pipelines with tools like GitHub Actions, Travis CI, or CircleCI allows you to automate the testing process, running tests on each code push or pull request.

Overall, a robust testing strategy for Next.js applications involves a combination of unit tests, integration tests, and end-to-end tests, each addressing different aspects of the application. By setting up a well-defined testing environment, writing comprehensive test cases, and integrating testing into the development workflow, you can ensure the reliability and stability of your Next.js applications, ultimately delivering a higher-quality user experience.

End-to-end tests provide a comprehensive approach by evaluating the entire application flow from the user's perspective. This type of testing ensures that all components and systems work together seamlessly to provide the desired user experience. For Next.js applications, end-to-end testing typically involves scenarios where the application is tested in a real browser environment. Tools such as Cypress and Playwright are well-suited for this purpose. Cypress offers an intuitive interface for writing and running end-to-end tests, while Playwright supports multiple browser contexts and is known for its speed and flexibility.

When setting up end-to-end tests, it is important to create realistic scenarios that reflect actual user interactions. This might include testing user login flows, form submissions, or navigation between different pages. By simulating these interactions, end-to-end tests help uncover issues that might not be evident during unit or integration testing. For instance, a test might simulate a user logging in, navigating through different pages, and interacting with various components to ensure that the application behaves as expected under real-world conditions.

Setting up a testing environment is a crucial step in the testing process. A well-configured environment ensures that tests run consistently and reliably. In Next.js applications, this involves setting up both development and production-like environments. For unit and integration tests, a testing environment can be configured to use in-memory databases or mock data to isolate tests from external dependencies. This isolation helps achieve more accurate test results and speeds up the testing process. For end-to-end tests, setting up a staging environment that mirrors the production environment as closely as possible helps identify issues that might arise when the application is deployed.

Writing effective test cases requires a clear understanding of the application's functionality and user requirements. Test cases should be designed to cover a range of scenarios, including edge cases and potential error conditions. In unit testing, this means verifying that individual functions or components handle various inputs and states correctly. Integration tests should focus on interactions between components and data flow, while end-to-end tests should simulate complete user journeys through the application. It is essential to keep test cases well-organized and maintainable, as this facilitates easier updates and debugging.

Using testing libraries effectively is key to writing robust and reliable tests. Jest is a widely-used testing framework that provides features such as test runners, assertions, and mocking utilities. For React components, React Testing Library offers utilities to render components and interact with them in a way that simulates real user behavior. Combining these tools allows developers to write comprehensive test suites that cover various aspects of their Next.js applications. In addition, using tools like Cypress or Playwright for end-to-end testing ensures that the application's entire functionality is validated from the user's perspective.

As testing practices evolve, integrating automated testing into the development workflow becomes increasingly important. Continuous integration (CI) systems can automatically run tests whenever code is pushed or merged into the repository, providing immediate feedback on code changes.

This integration helps identify and address issues early in the development cycle, reducing the likelihood of bugs reaching production. By incorporating automated testing into the development process, teams can maintain high code quality and ensure that their Next.js applications are both reliable and performant.

In summary, effective testing strategies are crucial for maintaining the stability and functionality of Next.js applications. Unit tests focus on individual components and functions, integration tests validate the interactions between different parts of the application, and end-to-end tests ensure that the application works correctly from the user's perspective. Setting up a reliable testing environment, writing comprehensive test cases, and using appropriate testing libraries are key steps in the process. By implementing these practices, developers can build robust applications that deliver a consistent and high-quality user experience.

When integrating testing libraries, it is important to leverage their capabilities fully to enhance test reliability and coverage. React Testing Library, for example, emphasizes testing components from the user's perspective rather than focusing on their internal implementation details. This approach encourages tests that are more resilient to changes in the component's internal structure, thereby making them more maintainable. The library provides utilities to render components, interact with them, and assert their behavior in a way that closely aligns with how users will interact with the application.

Testing React components with React Testing Library involves rendering components within a testing environment, simulating user interactions such as clicks and form submissions, and then asserting that the component behaves as expected. This method helps ensure that components are not only functional but also provide a positive user experience.

For instance, a test case might render a form component, simulate user input, and verify that the form handles the data correctly and displays appropriate feedback.

Additionally, when testing Next.js applications, it's crucial to address potential issues that may arise from server-side rendering and client-side hydration. Tests should ensure that server-rendered content matches what is rendered on the client side, as discrepancies can lead to confusing behavior or visual inconsistencies. This can be particularly challenging due to the asynchronous nature of data fetching and rendering in Next.js. Testing frameworks like Jest, combined with utilities for handling asynchronous code, can help manage these complexities by providing tools to wait for promises to resolve and validate rendered output.

Mocking is another important aspect of testing, especially when dealing with external dependencies such as APIs or databases. Mocking allows you to simulate interactions with these dependencies without relying on actual implementations, which can be slow or unreliable. Jest's mocking utilities provide mechanisms to create mock functions and modules, allowing you to control the behavior of these dependencies and isolate the functionality being tested. This approach not only speeds up the testing process but also helps in testing components and functions in isolation.

For integration tests, you will often need to test how multiple components and services work together. This might involve setting up a test database, configuring APIs, or mocking external services. Integration tests ensure that these pieces interact correctly, and they are crucial for validating that the application functions as expected in more complex scenarios. For instance, an integration test might involve submitting a form that interacts with a mock API, checking if the API responds correctly, and then verifying that the UI updates accordingly.

End-to-end tests, as previously mentioned, simulate real user interactions with the full application. These tests are typically run in environments that closely resemble production, ensuring that they capture real-world issues. Tools like Cypress and Playwright offer powerful features for end-to-end testing, including capabilities for handling complex user interactions, navigating through pages, and verifying the application's behavior across different scenarios. These tests are essential for catching issues that might not be apparent in unit or integration tests, such as performance bottlenecks or usability problems.

Incorporating continuous integration (CI) into your development workflow can further enhance the effectiveness of your testing strategy. CI systems automatically run your test suite whenever changes are made to the codebase, ensuring that any new changes are validated against your existing tests. This practice helps catch issues early in the development process, reducing the risk of introducing bugs or regressions. Configuring a CI pipeline to run your unit, integration, and end-to-end tests can provide valuable feedback and maintain a high standard of code quality.

Ultimately, a comprehensive testing strategy for Next.js applications involves a balanced approach that includes unit tests for individual components, integration tests for interactions between components, and end-to-end tests for complete user journeys. By carefully setting up your testing environment, writing effective test cases, and utilizing appropriate testing libraries, you can ensure that your Next.js applications are robust, reliable, and ready to deliver a seamless user experience.

CHAPTER 15: HANDLING STATE MANAGEMENT

State management is a crucial aspect of modern web applications, as it directly influences how data is handled and synchronized across the user interface. In Next.js applications, managing state efficiently can lead to improved performance and a more seamless user experience. This chapter delves into various approaches for state management in Next.js, focusing on both client-side solutions and third-party libraries. By exploring the React Context API and Redux, among other tools, this discussion aims to equip developers with the knowledge to integrate these state management solutions effectively into their projects.

The React Context API is a built-in mechanism provided by React for managing state across a component tree. It allows developers to pass data through the component hierarchy without the need for props drilling, where props are passed down manually through every intermediate component. Context is ideal for scenarios where state needs to be shared across many components, such as user authentication status or theme preferences.

To utilize the Context API, developers start by creating a context object using `React.createContext()`. This object provides a Provider and a Consumer component. The

Provider component is used to wrap parts of the application where the context is needed, supplying the context value to all components within its subtree. Conversely, the Consumer component allows access to the context value within components that need it. This setup simplifies state management for global data that does not require complex interactions.

While the Context API is effective for simpler state management tasks, it may not be sufficient for more complex applications involving intricate state logic or performance considerations. In such cases, third-party libraries like Redux offer more robust solutions. Redux is a predictable state container for JavaScript applications, designed to manage and centralize application state in a consistent and predictable manner.

Redux operates on the principle of a single source of truth, where the application state is stored in a single JavaScript object. This object is referred to as the store. To interact with the store, Redux relies on three core principles: actions, reducers, and dispatchers. Actions are plain JavaScript objects that describe events that have occurred in the application. Reducers are pure functions that specify how the state changes in response to an action. Dispatchers are functions that send actions to the store, triggering state updates.

Integrating Redux into a Next.js application involves several steps. First, a Redux store is created using `createStore` from the Redux library. This store is then provided to the application using the `Provider` component from the `react-redux` library, which makes the Redux store accessible to all components. To connect components to the Redux store, the `connect` function is used, allowing components to access state and dispatch actions.

One of the advantages of using Redux is its middleware

support, which enables the handling of asynchronous actions and side effects. Middleware such as Redux Thunk or Redux Saga can be employed to manage complex asynchronous operations, allowing actions to be dispatched before and after asynchronous requests. This capability is particularly useful for managing API calls and other asynchronous tasks within a Next.js application.

In addition to Redux, other state management libraries, such as MobX or Zustand, offer alternative approaches for handling state. MobX, for instance, utilizes observables and reactions to manage state in a more declarative manner. Zustand provides a minimalistic approach with a focus on simplicity and performance. Choosing the right state management solution depends on the specific needs of the application and the preferences of the development team.

State management is not solely about managing application state but also about ensuring that the state is handled efficiently and predictably. Techniques such as state normalization, where state is structured in a flat format rather than nested objects, can help improve performance and simplify state updates. Additionally, leveraging memoization and optimizing component re-renders can enhance the performance of applications that rely on complex state management.

Ultimately, the choice of state management solution should align with the application's requirements and the complexity of its state logic. The React Context API is suitable for simpler use cases with less frequent state updates, while Redux and other third-party libraries offer advanced features for more complex scenarios. By understanding the strengths and limitations of each approach, developers can select and implement the most appropriate state management strategy for their Next.js applications, ensuring a scalable and maintainable solution.

The integration of Redux into a Next.js application requires setting up a Redux store and integrating it with the Next.js app's rendering process. To begin, a Redux store is configured using the `createStore` function from the Redux library. This store needs to be populated with initial state and reducers, which are functions that specify how the state should change in response to actions. For server-side rendering in Next.js, it's also important to ensure that the Redux store can be properly hydrated with initial state on both the server and the client.

In a Next.js application, the `next-redux-wrapper` library simplifies this integration by providing utilities to manage the Redux store with server-side rendering. This library helps in creating a Redux store that is compatible with Next.js's rendering lifecycle. It offers a `createWrapper` function that initializes the Redux store and manages its state during the server-side and client-side rendering phases.

Once the store is created, it needs to be integrated into the Next.js application. This is typically achieved by using a custom `_app.js` file. This file allows you to override the default App component and provides a location to wrap your application with the Redux provider. The `Provider` component from `react-redux` is used to pass the Redux store down the component tree, making the store accessible to all connected components.

In addition to the Redux Provider, the `next-redux-wrapper` library helps in server-side data fetching and synchronizing the Redux state between the server and the client. This ensures that the initial state is correctly rendered on the server and is available to the client when the page is loaded, thus avoiding mismatches or unnecessary re-fetching of data.

Apart from Redux, other third-party libraries and tools can be employed for state management in Next.js applications. MobX is an alternative to Redux that offers a more flexible and less boilerplate-intensive approach to managing state. MobX relies on observable state and computed values to automatically update components when data changes, which can simplify state management for certain applications. MobX also provides tools to create and manage stores, and integrate them with Next.js, similar to Redux, but with a different set of APIs and conventions.

Another notable approach to state management is the use of React Query, which focuses on data fetching and synchronization rather than managing application state per se. React Query simplifies server-side state management by providing hooks to fetch, cache, and synchronize data from remote sources. It automatically handles the fetching and caching of data, and provides hooks to access and manipulate that data in a way that integrates seamlessly with React components. This approach can be particularly effective when dealing with complex data-fetching scenarios and when optimizing performance by reducing redundant network requests.

When choosing a state management solution, it is important to consider the specific needs and complexity of your application. For simpler use cases, React's built-in Context API might suffice. For applications with complex state interactions or extensive data management requirements, Redux or MobX may offer more robust solutions. In scenarios where server-side data fetching and synchronization are critical, React Query can be a valuable tool to manage remote data more efficiently.

Regardless of the state management approach chosen, it is crucial to ensure that state is managed in a way that maintains the performance and scalability of the application. This includes considering the implications of state updates on rendering performance and ensuring that the application remains responsive to user interactions. Properly managing state not only improves the user experience but also contributes to the maintainability and robustness of the application.

The integration of state management solutions in Next.js applications is a key aspect of building modern web applications that are both performant and maintainable. By understanding the various options available and implementing the appropriate tools and libraries, developers can effectively manage application state and build applications that meet their users' needs and expectations.

React Query, as a library designed for handling server state, can complement traditional state management solutions by abstracting away the complexities of data fetching and caching. It automates the management of server-side data, including caching, synchronization, and updates. This allows developers to focus more on the application's logic rather than on managing the data lifecycle.

Integrating React Query into a Next.js application involves setting up a `QueryClient` which acts as the core of the library's caching and data management system. The `QueryClient` is provided to the application through the `QueryClientProvider` component, which wraps around the application's component tree. This setup ensures that React Query's hooks are available throughout the application, enabling components to fetch and cache data seamlessly.

A key benefit of React Query is its ability to simplify data fetching with hooks like `useQuery` and `useMutation`. The `useQuery` hook is used to fetch data from an API and manage its loading, error, and success states automatically. It handles caching of data so that subsequent requests for the same data are served from the cache, reducing the number of network requests and improving performance. The `useMutation` hook, on the other hand, is used for creating, updating, or deleting data, and it provides utilities for handling optimistic updates, error handling, and retry mechanisms.

Combining React Query with Redux or MobX can also be beneficial in applications that require both client-side and server-side state management. While React Query efficiently handles server-side data fetching and caching, Redux or MobX can be employed to manage more complex client-side states such as user interactions, form state, or application-specific logic. This hybrid approach allows for a more modular state management strategy, leveraging the strengths of each library where they are most effective.

Another modern state management approach is the use of Zustand, a minimalistic state management library for React. Zustand focuses on simplicity and performance, offering a straightforward API for managing state with hooks. Zustand does not require complex configurations or boilerplate code, making it an appealing choice for applications that require a lightweight state management solution. Zustand's state management is based on hooks and can be easily integrated with Next.js without significant changes to the application architecture.

When choosing a state management solution for a Next.js application, it's crucial to consider the specific needs and scale of the project. For smaller applications or those that primarily handle local component state, the Context API or Zustand might be sufficient. For more complex scenarios involving extensive data interactions, Redux or MobX may offer more robust solutions. React Query excels in scenarios where server-side data management is a primary concern, providing automatic caching and synchronization.

In summary, handling state management effectively in Next.js applications involves selecting the right tools and libraries that match the project's requirements. Whether using the

Context API for simple state management, Redux or MobX for more comprehensive solutions, or React Query for server-side data fetching, integrating these tools appropriately can enhance the application's performance and maintainability. Understanding each tool's strengths and best use cases ensures that state management remains a manageable and efficient aspect of the development process, ultimately contributing to the overall success of the application.

CHAPTER 16: WORKING WITH FORMS AND VALIDATION

Forms are a cornerstone of interactive web applications, serving as a primary means for user input and data collection. In Next.js applications, building and managing forms efficiently involves several key considerations: handling user input, validating data, and managing form submission. Effective form management not only enhances user experience but also ensures data integrity and security. This chapter delves into the various techniques and libraries available for working with forms in Next.js, offering guidance on creating robust and user-friendly forms.

Handling user input in Next.js typically begins with understanding the controlled versus uncontrolled components paradigm. Controlled components rely on React state to manage form input values. Each input field's value is tied to a state variable, and updates to the input field trigger state updates, ensuring that the displayed value always reflects the state. This approach allows for a predictable and unified way to manage form state, making it easier to perform actions such as validation or conditional rendering based on user input.

Uncontrolled components, on the other hand, use React refs to access form values directly from the DOM. This approach is useful for simpler forms or scenarios where form values do not need to be tightly controlled. However, uncontrolled components can be less predictable and may complicate state management in more complex forms.

For form validation, various libraries and techniques can be employed to ensure that user inputs are both accurate and secure. One popular library is Formik, which simplifies the process of managing form state, handling validation, and performing form submission. Formik provides a set of hooks and components to streamline form handling and validation. It supports synchronous and asynchronous validation, allowing developers to define validation logic using schema-based libraries such as Yup. Yup provides a fluent API for defining complex validation schemas and handling validation errors, which can be easily integrated with Formik.

Another widely used library is React Hook Form. This library focuses on performance and ease of use, providing a lightweight solution for managing form state and validation. React Hook Form utilizes React hooks to manage form state and validation, reducing the need for boilerplate code and improving performance by minimizing re-renders. It supports schema validation with Yup and integrates well with various UI libraries and frameworks.

In addition to these libraries, custom validation solutions can be implemented directly using JavaScript or TypeScript. For example, custom validation functions can be used to enforce specific rules or constraints on form inputs. This approach allows for greater flexibility and control over validation logic, enabling developers to tailor validation to the specific needs of their application.

Form submission is another critical aspect of form

management. In Next.js applications, form submission can be handled in various ways, depending on the application's requirements. For simple forms, the default HTML form submission can be used, where the form data is sent to a specified endpoint using HTTP methods such as GET or POST. However, for more complex scenarios, such as those involving client-side validation or asynchronous data processing, JavaScript-based form submission methods can be employed. This involves using JavaScript to handle form data and submit it via AJAX requests, allowing for more interactive and dynamic user experiences.

Security is an essential consideration when working with forms. Proper validation and sanitization of user inputs are crucial to prevent security vulnerabilities such as cross-site scripting (XSS) and SQL injection. Input validation should be performed both on the client side and the server side to ensure data integrity and security. Client-side validation provides immediate feedback to users, while server-side validation acts as a final line of defense against malicious inputs.

Additionally, implementing secure handling of form data involves using HTTPS to encrypt data transmitted between the client and server. This helps protect sensitive information from being intercepted by malicious actors. Furthermore, employing techniques such as rate limiting and CAPTCHA can mitigate abuse and ensure that forms are not exploited for spam or other malicious activities.

In summary, working with forms in Next.js applications involves managing user input, implementing effective validation, and ensuring secure data handling. By leveraging libraries like Formik and React Hook Form, developers can streamline form management and validation processes. Custom validation solutions and secure handling practices further enhance the reliability and safety of forms. Understanding these techniques and tools will enable developers to build robust, user-friendly forms that meet the needs of their applications while maintaining high standards of security and performance.

Effective form management extends beyond the initial creation of input fields and validation. The entire form submission process is crucial for ensuring a smooth user experience and accurate data handling. In Next.js applications, this involves handling form submissions asynchronously, managing loading states, and providing user feedback.

To manage form submissions, it is common to use asynchronous functions, especially when interacting with external services or APIs. When a form is submitted, you can capture the data and send it to a backend server for processing. This is typically done using the `fetch` API or libraries like Axios. It is important to handle these submissions with care to ensure that users receive appropriate feedback, and any errors are managed effectively. For instance, you might display a loading spinner while the submission is in progress and show success or error messages based on the response.

Handling loading states and error messages is an integral part of user experience in form management. After a form submission, users should be informed about the success or failure of their action. Implementing loading indicators can help manage user expectations, while error handling can provide valuable feedback if something goes wrong. Ensuring that error messages are clear and actionable is key to improving the user experience.

In addition to validation and submission handling, accessibility is another crucial aspect of form management. Forms should be designed with accessibility in mind to ensure that all users, including those with disabilities, can interact with them effectively. This includes using semantic HTML elements, such as `<label>` tags associated with form inputs, and ensuring that forms are navigable using keyboard and screen reader technologies. Next.js, leveraging React's component-based architecture, allows developers to create accessible forms by following best practices and using ARIA (Accessible Rich Internet Applications) attributes where necessary.

When dealing with complex forms, such as those with dynamic fields or multi-step processes, careful planning is required. Dynamic forms, which change based on user input or other conditions, can be managed through conditional rendering and state management. Libraries like Formik and React Hook Form support dynamic field management, allowing developers to add or remove fields based on user interactions. Multi-step forms, where users progress through a series of steps, can be handled by managing form state across steps and validating each step independently before allowing users to proceed.

Security is another critical consideration when working with forms. Ensuring that user input is properly sanitized and validated on both the client and server sides is essential for preventing security vulnerabilities such as SQL injection or cross-site scripting (XSS) attacks. Input sanitization involves cleaning and validating user data before it is processed or stored, while validation ensures that the data conforms to expected formats and constraints. Utilizing libraries and frameworks that provide built-in security features can help mitigate these risks, but developers should always remain vigilant and follow best practices for web security.

For server-side validation and processing, it is crucial to ensure that data is consistently validated before being used or stored. While client-side validation enhances user experience by providing immediate feedback, server-side validation is necessary to guard against potentially malicious input. Combining both client-side and server-side validation helps to create a more secure and reliable application.

In conclusion, managing forms in Next.js involves several critical aspects: handling user input effectively, implementing robust validation and submission processes, addressing accessibility, and maintaining security. By leveraging libraries such as Formik and React Hook Form, and following best practices for form management, developers can build forms that are not only functional but also user-friendly and secure. The careful integration of these practices ensures that forms contribute positively to the overall user experience and reliability of the application.

When designing forms for web applications, it's essential to consider both client-side and server-side validation. Client-side validation helps provide immediate feedback to users, enhancing their experience by catching errors before the form is submitted. This can be achieved using JavaScript and various validation libraries, such as React Hook Form, which offer built-in validation rules and methods to ensure data integrity. However, client-side validation alone is not sufficient, as it can be bypassed by users with malicious intent. Therefore, server-side validation is equally important. It involves validating data on the server once it is submitted, ensuring that it meets the expected criteria and is free from potential security threats such as SQL injection or cross-site scripting (XSS) attacks. Combining both client-side and server-side validation helps safeguard the application and improve overall data quality.

In Next.js, integrating form validation libraries like Formik or React Hook Form simplifies the process of managing form states and validations. These libraries provide a structured approach to handling form inputs, validation errors, and submission processes. For example, Formik allows you to define validation schemas using Yup, a powerful schema builder that supports various validation rules and asynchronous validations. This integration streamlines the process of creating robust forms while ensuring that validation logic remains consistent and maintainable.

Moreover, user experience is significantly impacted by the design and functionality of forms. Ensuring that forms are intuitive and easy to navigate can greatly enhance user satisfaction and engagement. This involves designing forms with clear labels, helpful placeholder text, and appropriate input types for different data. For instance, using `<input type"email">` for email addresses or `<input type"number">` for numeric values can help guide users in providing the correct type of information. Additionally, implementing responsive design principles ensures that forms function well across various devices and screen sizes, making them accessible to a broader audience.

To further improve the user experience, consider adding features such as real-time validation feedback. This allows users to see errors or issues with their input as they type, rather than only after submitting the form. This can be implemented by leveraging event handlers that trigger validation checks on input changes. Real-time feedback helps users correct mistakes promptly, reducing frustration and increasing the likelihood of successful form submission.

Another aspect of form management is handling complex user interactions, such as dynamic form fields that change based on user input. Next.js, combined with React's component-based architecture, facilitates the creation of such dynamic forms. You can use state management to conditionally render form fields or sections based on user actions. For instance, if a form includes optional fields that appear only when a user selects a specific option, you can manage this behavior by updating the component state and re-rendering the form as needed.

In addition to these considerations, forms should be optimized for performance to ensure that they load quickly and respond efficiently to user interactions. Techniques such as debouncing input events and minimizing re-renders can help improve form performance. For example, using a debouncing function to limit the frequency of validation checks or input processing can reduce the load on the browser and enhance the overall responsiveness of the form.

Handling form submission securely is also paramount. It is essential to implement secure data transmission practices, such as using HTTPS to encrypt data sent between the client and server. Additionally, applying best practices for managing sensitive information, such as avoiding storing passwords in plain text and employing hashing algorithms, ensures that user data remains protected. When integrating with backend services, ensure that the form data is processed securely, with proper authentication and authorization mechanisms in place to prevent unauthorized access.

Lastly, testing forms is a critical step in ensuring their reliability and functionality. Automated tests can help validate that forms behave as expected under various conditions, including edge cases and error scenarios. Testing frameworks like Jest, combined with testing libraries such as Testing Library, allow you to write comprehensive tests for form components. These tests can simulate user interactions, verify form validation logic, and ensure that form submissions are handled correctly. Regular testing helps identify and resolve issues early in the development process, leading to more stable and reliable forms.

In conclusion, managing forms in Next.js involves a multifaceted approach that includes handling user input, implementing validation, ensuring accessibility, optimizing performance, and securing data. By leveraging tools and techniques for effective form management, you can create forms that not only meet functional requirements but also provide a positive and seamless user experience.

CHAPTER 17: CUSTOMIZING NEXT.JS WITH PLUGINS AND EXTENSIONS

Next.js is designed with flexibility in mind, allowing developers to enhance its core functionalities through a variety of plugins and extensions. This chapter delves into how you can leverage these tools to customize and extend Next.js applications, offering a streamlined development experience and improved performance. By integrating plugins and extensions, you can augment Next.js's built-in features, adding capabilities that align with specific project requirements or developer preferences.

Plugins and extensions in Next.js serve a multitude of purposes, from improving development efficiency to optimizing application performance. The process of integrating these tools generally involves installing the plugin or extension, configuring it to suit your application's needs, and then using it within your codebase. Understanding how to effectively implement these tools can significantly reduce development time and enhance the functionality of your Next.js projects.

One of the primary benefits of using plugins is the ability to automate and streamline repetitive tasks. For instance, the `next-optimized-images` plugin simplifies image handling by optimizing image loading and formats automatically. This plugin supports various image formats and offers performance enhancements by automatically compressing and resizing images. Integrating such a plugin involves installing it via npm or yarn, configuring it in your `next.config.js` file, and then using it to manage images throughout your application. By automating image optimization, developers can focus more on building features rather than managing assets manually.

Another valuable plugin is `next-auth`, which provides authentication and authorization functionalities. Authentication is a critical component for many applications, and `next-auth` simplifies the process of integrating various authentication providers, such as Google, Facebook, and GitHub. It offers a customizable and secure way to handle user sign-ins, sessions, and user management. To use `next-auth`, you need to install it, configure authentication providers in your application, and set up API routes to manage authentication flows. This plugin helps ensure that user authentication is handled efficiently and securely, reducing the need for custom authentication implementations.

For projects that require advanced state management, `redux` and its associated tools like `redux-thunk` or `redux-saga` can be beneficial. Redux provides a centralized store for managing state across an application, and integrating it with Next.js involves setting up the Redux store, connecting it to your components, and managing state through actions and reducers. Plugins like `next-redux-wrapper` facilitate the integration of Redux with Next.js by providing a higher-order component that integrates the Redux store into Next.js's server-side rendering process. This setup ensures that your application can efficiently manage state while taking full advantage of Next.js's SSR capabilities.

In addition to functional plugins, there are also tools designed to enhance development workflows. For example, `next-pwa` enables the creation of Progressive Web Apps (PWAs) with minimal configuration. PWAs offer offline capabilities and improved performance, making them an attractive option for modern web applications. Integrating `next-pwa` involves installing the plugin, configuring it in your `next.config.js`, and defining your service worker and caching strategies. This integration provides a straightforward path to converting your Next.js application into a PWA, enhancing user experience by delivering faster and more reliable performance.

Customizing Next.js with plugins also involves understanding how to extend its existing features. For instance, you might want to integrate analytics or monitoring tools into your application. Plugins such as `next-seo` provide an easy way to manage SEO-related configurations, including meta tags and structured data. By integrating `next-seo`, you can automatically generate meta tags for pages, configure Open Graph and Twitter Card metadata, and improve your application's search engine visibility with minimal effort. Configuring `next-seo` involves setting default SEO settings in your `next.config.js` and using its API to manage page-specific SEO settings.

Additionally, `next-sitemap` is a plugin that generates sitemaps automatically, aiding in SEO efforts by providing search engines with a structured map of your site's content. Integrating this plugin involves installing it, configuring the plugin options, and then generating the sitemap during your build process. This helps ensure that search engines can crawl and index your site effectively, contributing to better search rankings.

As with any tool or plugin, it is crucial to evaluate its compatibility and performance impact on your application. Plugins and extensions should be chosen based on their ability to integrate seamlessly with Next.js and their potential to enhance development efficiency without introducing unnecessary overhead. Testing and reviewing the documentation of each plugin can help ensure that it aligns with your project's needs and adheres to best practices.

In summary, customizing Next.js with plugins and extensions allows developers to significantly extend the framework's capabilities. By leveraging tools for image optimization, authentication, state management, and development workflows, you can enhance both the functionality and performance of your applications. Effective integration and configuration of these tools can streamline development processes and deliver a more robust and feature-rich user experience.

Expanding on the integration and customization of plugins, the ecosystem around Next.js provides numerous tools that can enhance development and application performance. One notable example is `next-seo`, a plugin designed to simplify the process of adding SEO metadata to your application. Proper SEO implementation is critical for ensuring that your application is indexed correctly by search engines and achieves optimal visibility. The `next-seo` plugin allows you to manage meta tags, structured data, and other SEO-related configurations directly within your Next.js project. By configuring `next-seo` in your application, you can ensure consistent and effective SEO practices without needing to manually insert meta tags into every page.

Similarly, the `next-i18next` plugin provides robust internationalization (i18n) support, making it easier to build applications that cater to multiple languages. Internationalization is essential for creating applications with a global user base. This plugin simplifies the process of translating content and managing language-specific resources by leveraging the i18next framework. Integrating `next-i18next` involves configuring your translation files, setting up the plugin in your Next.js configuration, and using it to manage translations in your components. This approach ensures that language switching and translation management are handled efficiently, improving the user experience for diverse audiences.

For applications requiring real-time data updates, integrating WebSocket support is crucial. The `next-websocket` plugin provides an easy way to set up WebSocket connections within a Next.js application. WebSockets enable real-time communication between the client and server, making them ideal for applications like chat systems, live notifications, or real-time data feeds. By incorporating `next-websocket`, you can establish WebSocket connections, handle events, and update your application's state in real-time, enhancing interactivity and responsiveness.

Another significant aspect of plugin customization involves performance optimization. The `next-pwa` plugin is designed to add Progressive Web App (PWA) capabilities to your Next.js project. PWAs offer a more app-like experience with offline capabilities, faster load times, and improved reliability. By integrating `next-pwa`, you can configure service workers and caching strategies to enhance the performance of your application. This plugin helps ensure that your application loads quickly and reliably, even in low-network conditions.

To manage and integrate these plugins effectively, understanding the configuration options and lifecycle events is essential. Most plugins offer configuration files or settings within the Next.js configuration file (`next.config.js`). This file acts as a central place for managing plugin configurations and integrating various tools into your application. For example, when using `next-pwa`, you would configure settings related to caching, offline support, and service worker registration within this configuration file. Similarly, other plugins like `next-auth` or `next-i18next` require specific setup steps that are outlined in their documentation. Familiarizing yourself with these configurations helps ensure that the plugins are used effectively and do not interfere with each other.

Furthermore, it is important to stay informed about updates and best practices related to the plugins and extensions you use. The Next.js ecosystem evolves rapidly, with new plugins and updates regularly introduced. Keeping abreast of these changes ensures that you are using the most current and effective tools available. Engaging with the Next.js community, reading documentation, and following release notes can help you stay updated on new features and improvements.

Customizing Next.js with plugins and extensions offers a powerful way to tailor your application to meet specific needs and enhance its functionality. By integrating tools like `next-optimized-images`, `next-auth`, and `next-i18next`, you can address a wide range of requirements, from image optimization and authentication to internationalization and real-time data updates. Each plugin provides unique capabilities that, when combined effectively, can lead to a more robust and feature-rich application.

As you explore and implement these plugins, consider the specific needs of your project and the potential impact on performance and maintainability. Plugins can significantly streamline development and add valuable features, but it is essential to balance their use with the overall architecture and goals of your application. By thoughtfully integrating and customizing these tools, you can build Next.js applications that are not only functional and efficient but also aligned with best practices and user expectations.

Effective integration and customization of Next.js plugins and extensions require a clear understanding of the Next.js configuration and plugin API. Most plugins are designed to be easily integrated into your Next.js application through the `next.config.js` file, which acts as the central configuration point. By modifying this configuration file, you can enable and customize plugins to suit the needs of your project.

For instance, the integration of `next-auth`, a popular authentication library, involves updating your `next.config.js` and adding specific authentication settings. `next-auth` simplifies user authentication by providing various authentication providers and session management tools. By configuring `next-auth`, you can manage user sign-ins, session handling, and access control seamlessly, enhancing the security and user experience of your application.

When working with plugins that affect build processes or runtime behavior, such as `next-bundle-analyzer`, it's essential to understand how these tools interact with your application's build pipeline. `next-bundle-analyzer` helps analyze and visualize the size of your application's bundles, which is invaluable for optimizing performance. By integrating this plugin, you can generate detailed reports on bundle sizes, identify large dependencies, and make informed decisions to reduce the overall size of your application, thus improving load times and performance.

Customization often extends beyond mere integration; it involves tailoring the behavior of plugins to fit specific project requirements. For example, when using `next-sitemap` for generating sitemaps, you might need to customize the configuration to include specific pages or exclude others based on your SEO strategy. `next-sitemap` provides options to control how sitemaps are generated, which can be adjusted through its configuration settings to ensure that the generated sitemaps align with your SEO objectives and best practices.

Moreover, managing dependencies and ensuring compatibility between various plugins is crucial for maintaining the stability of your application. Regularly updating plugins to their latest versions and checking their compatibility with your Next.js version helps prevent issues related to deprecated features or breaking changes. It is also beneficial to review the documentation and changelogs provided by plugin authors to stay informed about any new features or updates that could enhance your development process.

Testing is another important aspect of working with plugins and extensions. Ensuring that plugins do not introduce bugs or performance regressions involves incorporating them into your testing strategy. This includes writing test cases that validate the functionality provided by the plugins and performing integration tests to ensure that they work harmoniously with other parts of your application. For instance, if you integrate a plugin like `next-seo`, you should write tests to verify that the SEO metadata is correctly applied and rendered, thereby ensuring that it meets your SEO requirements.

In addition to testing, consider the impact of plugins on your application's security. When using third-party plugins, it is important to evaluate their security implications and ensure they do not introduce vulnerabilities. Reviewing the security practices of the plugin's maintainers, checking for recent updates, and following best practices for securing your application will help mitigate potential risks.

Overall, effectively leveraging Next.js plugins and extensions can significantly enhance your application's functionality, performance, and maintainability. By carefully integrating and customizing these tools, you can streamline development processes, optimize application performance, and deliver a superior user experience. As you continue to build and evolve your Next.js projects, staying informed about the latest plugins and best practices will ensure that your applications remain at the forefront of web development technology.

CHAPTER 18: IMPLEMENTING INTERNATIONALIZATION AND LOCALIZATION

Internationalization (i18n) and localization (l10n) are pivotal for developing web applications that serve users across various linguistic and cultural contexts. Implementing these features in Next.js applications involves careful planning and leveraging specific tools and strategies designed to handle diverse languages and regional settings. This chapter delves into the methodologies for integrating i18n and l10n into your Next.js application, focusing on the setup of translation files, locale management, and best practices for ensuring a seamless multilingual experience.

Internationalization is the process of designing an application so that it can be adapted to various languages and regions without requiring a redesign. It entails structuring the application in a way that supports the addition of new languages and regional settings as the need arises. In Next.js, internationalization can be approached by utilizing various libraries and built-in functionalities to manage language-specific content and locale-based formatting.

To start, one of the popular libraries for implementing i18n in Next.js applications is `next-i18next`. This library provides a straightforward way to handle translations and locales, integrating seamlessly with Next.js's features. Setting up `next-i18next` involves configuring the `next-i18next.config.js` file to define the supported languages, the default language, and the path to translation files. The configuration typically includes specifying the default locale and the available locales for the application, as well as setting up the directory structure for storing translation files.

The translation files themselves are central to the localization process. These files contain the key-value pairs that map text in the source language to its translation in the target languages. They are typically organized in JSON format, with each file representing a different language. For example, you might have `en.json` for English and `fr.json` for French. Each file would contain translations for the various strings used throughout the application. This organization allows for easy updates and expansions as new languages are added.

Managing different locales involves more than just providing translations. It also requires handling locale-specific formatting, such as date and time formats, number formats, and currency. Libraries like `date-fns` or `moment` can be integrated with `next-i18next` to handle locale-specific formatting. These libraries offer functionalities to format dates, numbers, and currencies according to the rules of the user's locale, enhancing the overall user experience.

Another important aspect of internationalization is routing. Next.js supports dynamic routing, which can be extended to handle localized routes. This means that you can create route paths that include locale identifiers, allowing users to navigate to pages in their preferred language. For example, you might have routes like `/en/about` for the English version of the about page and ` /fr/about` for the French version. Handling these routes typically involves setting up dynamic route parameters in Next.js and ensuring that your application can render the appropriate content based on the locale.

Locale switching is a user-facing feature that allows users to select their preferred language. Implementing a locale switcher involves creating a user interface component that allows users to choose from available languages. This component updates the application's state to reflect the selected locale and triggers the necessary updates to display content in the chosen language. It is also essential to handle the persistence of user preferences, which can be achieved using cookies or local storage to remember the user's language choice across sessions.

Testing your internationalized application is crucial to ensure that translations are accurate and that locale-specific features function correctly. Automated tests can be set up to verify that the correct translations are displayed and that locale-based formatting adheres to the expected rules. Manual testing should also be performed to catch any edge cases or issues related to different languages and regions that automated tests might miss.

In summary, implementing internationalization and localization in a Next.js application requires a combination of strategic planning, effective use of libraries, and careful management of translation files and locales. By setting up proper configurations, utilizing translation libraries, handling locale-specific formatting and routing, and ensuring a seamless user experience with locale switching, you can create an application that effectively serves a global audience. As you proceed, consider these elements and best practices to ensure that your application is both adaptable and user-friendly across different languages and regions.

To effectively implement internationalization and localization in a Next.js application, it is important to also consider the integration of language-switching mechanisms. Users should have a seamless experience when switching between different languages or regional settings. This involves providing an intuitive interface for users to select their preferred language and ensuring that the application dynamically updates to reflect these preferences.

One common approach to implementing a language-switching mechanism is to use a language selector component. This component typically presents a list of available languages and allows users to choose their preferred one. Upon selection, the application should update the language context or state and reload the relevant translations. The `next-i18next` library facilitates this by providing hooks and utilities for changing languages at runtime. The `useTranslation` hook, for instance, allows components to access the current language and change it based on user input.

The next challenge in internationalization is managing content that varies not only by language but also by region. Localization extends beyond mere translation to include adjustments for cultural norms, regional conventions, and specific formatting rules. For example, date formats differ between regions; the United States commonly uses the MM/DD/YYYY format, while many European countries use DD/MM/YYYY. Addressing these variations requires more than just translating text—it involves implementing locale-aware formatting throughout the application.

In Next.js, this can be achieved by combining the translation library with locale-specific formatting libraries. `react-intl` is another popular library that complements `next-i18next` by providing advanced formatting capabilities. It allows developers to format dates, numbers, and currencies based on locale settings, ensuring that all localized content adheres to the appropriate regional standards.

Another critical aspect of localization is the handling of right-to-left (RTL) languages such as Arabic and Hebrew. Implementing RTL support involves adjusting the layout and styling of your application to accommodate the directionality of the text. CSS frameworks or libraries that support RTL can be used in conjunction with Next.js to ensure that your application looks and behaves correctly for RTL languages. For instance, conditional stylesheets or dynamic CSS class adjustments can be employed to switch layouts and text directions based on the selected language.

Testing is also a key component in the localization process. It is essential to ensure that the application behaves as expected across different languages and locales. Automated tests can be set up to verify that translations are applied correctly and that locale-specific formatting is accurate. Manual testing is equally important, as it helps identify potential issues that automated tests might miss, such as text overflow in UI components or cultural insensitivity.

Additionally, considering SEO in the context of internationalization is crucial. Search engines need to index the localized versions of your application correctly. Implementing hreflang tags in your Next.js application can help search engines understand the relationship between different language versions of your pages. These tags indicate to search engines which language and regional version of a page should be served to users based on their preferences and location. Proper use of hreflang tags ensures that users are directed to the appropriate version of your content, improving the visibility and relevance of your application in search results.

Finally, handling fallback languages and default content is an important aspect of internationalization. In cases where translations are missing for specific text or components, the application should have a mechanism to fall back to a default language or provide a default message. This ensures that users always see meaningful content, even if certain translations are not yet available.

Implementing internationalization and localization in a Next.js application involves a comprehensive approach that includes setting up translation files, managing locale-specific formatting, supporting RTL languages, and ensuring SEO optimization. By integrating these strategies and tools effectively, you can create a globally accessible application that offers a seamless and user-friendly experience for users across different languages and regions.

When implementing internationalization and localization in a Next.js application, it is crucial to address the management of translation files and their integration with the application's routing system. Translation files, typically organized by language codes, contain key-value pairs where keys represent the text or messages in the application and values represent their translations. These files must be correctly structured and placed in an accessible directory for the application to utilize them effectively.

In a Next.js project using `next-i18next`, translation files are often stored in a `public/locales` directory. This structure allows for easy access and management of language-specific translations. For each language, a corresponding JSON file is created, containing all the translated strings needed for that language. For instance, a `en` folder might contain an `index.json` file with English translations, while a `fr` folder would contain a similar file with French translations.

Proper integration of these translation files into the application involves configuring the `next-i18next` library to recognize and load the files correctly. The `i18n` configuration object, often included in `next-i18next.config.js`, defines the paths to the translation files and specifies which languages are supported. This configuration ensures that the library can dynamically load and apply the appropriate translations based on the user's selected language.

Localization also entails handling dynamic content that may vary based on regional settings. For example, a date or time displayed in the application must be formatted according to the user's locale. Libraries such as `date-fns` or `moment` can be used in conjunction with `react-intl` to format dates and times according to locale-specific rules. This ensures that the content is not only translated but also presented in a way that is familiar and comprehensible to users in different regions.

Handling dynamic content also involves dealing with pluralization and gender-specific translations. Many languages have different rules for plural forms and gender agreements, which must be managed within the translation files. `react-intl` provides support for pluralization and gender-specific messages, allowing developers to define rules for different languages and ensure that the application can handle these variations correctly.

An additional consideration in internationalization is the application of fallback languages. If a translation is not available for a specific key in the selected language, the application should fall back to a default language, typically English. This fallback mechanism ensures that the user experience remains consistent even when certain translations are missing. Configuring fallback languages in `next-i18next` is straightforward and can be defined in the `i18n` configuration file.

The implementation of internationalization and localization should also be accompanied by thorough testing to ensure that the application behaves correctly across different languages and locales. Automated tests can be employed to verify that translation keys are present and that locale-specific content is displayed correctly. Additionally, manual testing with native speakers or testers familiar with the target languages can help identify any issues or inconsistencies in the translations or localized content.

Finally, it is essential to continuously update and maintain translation files as the application evolves. As new features are added or existing content is modified, the corresponding translations must be updated to reflect these changes. Establishing a process for managing and updating translations, including collaboration with translators or localization teams, is crucial for ensuring that the application remains accurate and relevant to its global audience.

In summary, implementing internationalization and localization in a Next.js application involves setting up translation files, managing dynamic content, handling locale-specific formatting, and ensuring a consistent user experience across different languages. By leveraging libraries such as `next-i18next` and `react-intl`, and by applying best practices for testing and maintenance, developers can create applications that are accessible and user-friendly for a global audience.

CHAPTER 19: MANAGING ASSETS AND STATIC FILES

Effective management of assets and static files plays a pivotal role in optimizing the performance and security of web applications. In the context of Next.js, which is renowned for its built-in static file handling capabilities, understanding how to manage and optimize these assets is crucial for delivering a seamless user experience. This chapter delves into best practices for handling static assets, including images, fonts, and other media files, and explores techniques to ensure these assets are served efficiently and securely.

In Next.js, static assets such as images, fonts, and other files are typically stored in the `public` directory of the project. Files placed in this directory are served directly at the root URL path, making them easily accessible throughout the application. For instance, an image saved in `public/images/logo.png` can be accessed at `/images/logo.png`. This straightforward approach simplifies asset management and allows for consistent referencing across different components and pages.

One of the fundamental practices in managing static assets is optimizing their size and format. Large files can significantly impact page load times, affecting overall application performance and user experience. Image optimization, for instance, involves compressing images without compromising quality, converting them to modern formats like WebP, and using responsive images to serve different sizes based on the user's device. Next.js offers built-in support for image optimization through the `next/image` component. This component automatically optimizes images for size and format, leveraging techniques like lazy loading and responsive resizing to enhance performance.

Beyond images, handling fonts is another crucial aspect of asset management. Web fonts can impact page load times, so it is essential to use them judiciously. Techniques such as font subsetting, which involves including only the characters used on the page, and utilizing font-display properties, which control how fonts are rendered while loading, can improve performance. The `@next/font` package in Next.js simplifies font management by providing a seamless way to load and optimize fonts, reducing the manual effort required for these tasks.

In addition to optimizing individual assets, it is important to manage the delivery of these assets effectively. Content Delivery Networks (CDNs) are a popular solution for serving static files efficiently. CDNs distribute content across multiple servers globally, ensuring that assets are delivered from a location closest to the user, thereby reducing latency and improving load times. Integrating a CDN with Next.js can be achieved by configuring the `next.config.js` file to include appropriate headers and by using the `assetPrefix` option to point to the CDN URL for serving static assets.

Security is another critical consideration when managing static files. Serving files securely involves ensuring that they are protected from unauthorized access and that any sensitive information is not exposed. Techniques such as setting appropriate HTTP headers, including Content Security Policy (CSP) headers to restrict the sources of assets, and using

HTTPS for secure file transfer are essential for maintaining the integrity and confidentiality of the files. Next.js applications can leverage various middleware and security modules to enforce these practices and safeguard assets against potential vulnerabilities.

Caching strategies also play a significant role in optimizing the performance of static assets. Proper caching ensures that assets are stored and served efficiently, reducing the need for repeated requests to the server. Next.js supports caching through various mechanisms, including HTTP cache headers and service workers. Configuring appropriate cache-control headers helps instruct browsers on how long to cache assets and when to request updated versions. Service workers, on the other hand, can intercept network requests and serve cached assets, enabling offline access and further improving performance.

Finally, it is essential to monitor and analyze the performance of static asset delivery continuously. Tools such as web performance analytics platforms and browser developer tools provide valuable insights into how assets are loaded and rendered. By analyzing metrics like load times, caching effectiveness, and network requests, developers can identify potential bottlenecks and make informed decisions on further optimizations.

In summary, managing assets and static files in a Next.js application requires a comprehensive approach that includes optimization, efficient delivery, security, and monitoring. By leveraging Next.js's built-in features, employing best practices for asset handling, and integrating with modern tools and techniques, developers can ensure that their applications perform optimally and provide a secure and smooth user experience.

Another critical aspect of managing assets in a Next.js application is implementing caching strategies to improve performance and reduce server load. Caching helps to minimize the time it takes to fetch assets by storing copies of these files closer to the end-user. The Next.js framework provides several mechanisms for caching assets effectively.

The use of HTTP caching headers is one approach to managing asset delivery. By setting appropriate cache headers, such as `Cache-Control` and `Expires`, you can instruct browsers and intermediary servers to cache assets for specified periods. This reduces the need for repeated downloads and accelerates page load times for returning users. In Next.js, custom server configurations or middleware can be employed to set these headers appropriately for static assets.

Another advanced technique for caching involves using service workers. Service workers are a type of web worker that can intercept network requests and serve cached responses. This is particularly useful for improving performance in Progressive Web Apps (PWAs) by allowing offline access to assets. Implementing service workers requires additional setup, including registering the service worker and managing the cache storage effectively. Tools like Workbox, which integrates well with Next.js, simplify the process of adding service workers and managing caching.

Efficient asset management also involves handling asset versioning. When you update an asset, such as an image or font, you need to ensure that users receive the latest version without facing caching issues. One common approach is to use hash-based versioning, where a unique hash is appended to the asset's filename. This ensures that browsers fetch the new version of the file whenever the content changes, as the filename will differ. Next.js supports this practice natively through its static file handling mechanism, where filenames are automatically hashed during the build process.

For secure asset handling, implementing proper access

controls is essential. While assets in the `public` directory are accessible to anyone, sensitive files should be protected to prevent unauthorized access. Techniques such as server-side rendering (SSR) or API routes in Next.js can be utilized to control access to these files. For instance, you can serve protected assets through API routes that verify user authentication before returning the file. This approach ensures that only authorized users can access certain resources, enhancing the security of your application.

Additionally, managing static files involves ensuring their integrity and authenticity. One effective method is to use Subresource Integrity (SRI) checks, which provide a way to verify that assets have not been tampered with. SRI involves including a cryptographic hash in the HTML link or script tag that references the asset. When the browser loads the asset, it checks the hash to confirm that the file has not been altered. This adds a layer of security by protecting against potential attacks that might inject malicious code into static files.

Handling large media files, such as videos, presents unique challenges in asset management. Streaming services and adaptive bitrate streaming are techniques used to handle large files effectively. Adaptive bitrate streaming adjusts the quality of the media based on the user's network conditions, ensuring smooth playback even on slower connections. For video assets in Next.js applications, you can integrate third-party services like Cloudflare Stream or AWS Media Services to handle video hosting, streaming, and optimization.

In summary, managing assets and static files in a Next.js application requires a comprehensive approach that includes optimizing file sizes, implementing efficient caching strategies, securing access, and ensuring integrity. By leveraging Next.js's built-in features, such as automatic image optimization and font handling, and integrating advanced techniques like CDN usage and service workers, you can significantly enhance the performance and security of your application. This holistic approach ensures that your web application delivers a fast, reliable, and secure user experience, catering to a diverse and global audience.

Ensuring the integrity and authenticity of assets is another vital aspect of managing static files. Subresource Integrity (SRI) is a powerful technique that helps protect your application from malicious modifications to third-party resources. By using SRI, you can include cryptographic hashes in your asset references, which the browser checks to verify that the file has not been altered since it was published. If the hash does not match, the browser will refuse to load the asset, thereby preventing potential security issues. Implementing SRI in Next.js involves adding integrity attributes to the `<link>` or `<script>` tags in your HTML, ensuring that all external resources adhere to expected integrity constraints.

Beyond these strategies, proper asset organization and maintenance are essential for long-term efficiency. As projects evolve, the number of assets can grow significantly, making it crucial to keep your asset directory well-organized. Using a structured folder hierarchy, such as separating images, fonts, and other media into distinct folders, can streamline asset management and make it easier to locate and update files as needed. Regularly auditing and cleaning up unused or obsolete assets can also help maintain an efficient asset pipeline, reducing unnecessary bloat and improving overall application performance.

When dealing with images specifically, leveraging modern formats and responsive techniques is key to optimizing load times and enhancing user experience. Formats such as WebP provide superior compression and quality characteristics compared to traditional formats like JPEG and PNG, making them an excellent choice for reducing image sizes without compromising visual fidelity. Next.js supports automatic image optimization through its `next/image` component, which handles various optimizations, including format conversion and lazy loading, out of the box. By using this component, you can ensure that images are served in the most efficient format and size for each user's device, contributing to faster page loads and better performance.

Additionally, implementing lazy loading for images is an effective strategy to improve initial page load times. Lazy loading delays the loading of images until they are about to enter the viewport, reducing the amount of data that needs to be fetched and rendered on initial page load. The `next/image` component includes built-in support for lazy loading, but it can also be applied to other assets using native browser features or JavaScript libraries designed for this purpose.

For fonts, adopting font optimization techniques can further enhance application performance. Web fonts can often be large in size, and their loading can impact the overall page render time. Strategies such as font subsetting, which involves including only the characters required for your application, can significantly reduce font file sizes. Font-display properties, like `font-display: swap`, can be used to control how fonts are rendered while they are loading, ensuring that text remains visible even if the custom font has not yet been downloaded. By carefully managing font loading and using appropriate CSS techniques, you can minimize their impact on performance and maintain a smooth user experience.

Security considerations also play a crucial role in asset management. Protecting sensitive assets and ensuring secure delivery are essential for safeguarding user data and maintaining the integrity of your application. Implementing HTTPS across all asset deliveries helps protect against man-in-the-middle attacks and ensures data is encrypted during transmission. Additionally, setting up Content Security Policy (CSP) headers can help prevent unauthorized access and mitigate risks associated with content injection attacks.

In summary, managing assets and static files effectively in a Next.js application involves a multifaceted approach that includes optimizing file delivery, implementing robust caching and security practices, and leveraging modern formats and technologies. By following best practices for asset management, you can enhance the performance, security, and user experience of your application, ensuring that it remains efficient and resilient in the face of evolving demands and challenges.

CHAPTER 20: DEPLOYING NEXT.JS APPLICATIONS

Deploying a Next.js application represents the culmination of development efforts and marks the transition from a local environment to the public internet. The deployment process involves several key steps, from choosing the right hosting solution to configuring the production environment and ensuring the application operates seamlessly once live.

To start, selecting an appropriate deployment platform is essential. Next.js applications can be deployed to a variety of environments, each offering distinct advantages depending on the project's needs. Traditional hosting platforms, such as shared hosting or virtual private servers (VPS), provide a foundational level of control and customization. However, they often require significant manual configuration and may not be as scalable as modern cloud solutions.

Cloud services have become a popular choice due to their scalability and ease of use. Providers like Vercel, the creators of Next.js, offer a platform specifically optimized for Next.js applications. Vercel simplifies deployment by integrating closely with the framework, automatically handling optimizations such as server-side rendering (SSR) and static site generation (SSG) out of the box. Deployment involves connecting a Git repository, configuring build settings, and letting Vercel manage the deployment process. This integration also facilitates continuous deployment, meaning that updates to your application are automatically deployed as changes are pushed to your repository.

Another cloud option is Netlify, which supports Next.js with features like serverless functions and edge caching. Netlify's deployment process is similar to Vercel's, involving repository integration and automated build and deploy pipelines. Both Vercel and Netlify offer user-friendly interfaces and extensive documentation to help streamline the deployment process, making them ideal choices for developers seeking simplicity and efficiency.

For applications requiring more control or specific configurations, cloud providers such as AWS, Google Cloud Platform, and Microsoft Azure offer flexible deployment options. AWS Amplify, for instance, provides a streamlined deployment process tailored for modern web applications, with support for serverless backend services, static site hosting, and continuous integration/continuous deployment (CI/CD) workflows. Google Cloud's App Engine and Azure App Service offer similar capabilities, allowing you to deploy Next.js applications with customizable environments and integrated services.

Serverless environments are another modern approach to deploying Next.js applications. Serverless platforms, such as AWS Lambda or Google Cloud Functions, enable you to run code in response to events without managing servers. This model is particularly well-suited for applications that need to scale dynamically based on user demand. Next.js can be configured to operate in a serverless environment by utilizing serverless functions to handle server-side rendering and API routes, allowing you to benefit from the scalability and cost-efficiency of serverless computing.

Regardless of the deployment platform chosen, preparing your application for production is crucial. This preparation involves several best practices to ensure that your application runs efficiently and securely once live. One of the first steps is to optimize the application for performance. This includes enabling production optimizations in Next.js, such as minifying JavaScript and CSS, optimizing images, and prefetching resources. These optimizations help reduce the initial load time and improve the overall user experience.

Another important aspect of preparation is environment configuration. Production environments often require different settings compared to development environments, such as API endpoints, database connections, and security settings. Next.js provides a built-in mechanism for managing environment variables through `.env` files, which can be used to define configuration settings for various stages of deployment. Ensuring that these environment variables are correctly configured is essential for maintaining the application's functionality in a production setting.

Security considerations also play a critical role in deployment. Implementing HTTPS is a fundamental step in securing communication between users and your application. Most deployment platforms offer built-in support for HTTPS, either through automated certificates or custom configurations. Additionally, you should review and apply security best practices, such as securing sensitive data, setting up appropriate access controls, and monitoring for vulnerabilities.

Finally, testing and monitoring post-deployment are crucial to maintaining application health and performance. Before going live, thoroughly test your application in a staging environment that mirrors the production setup as closely as possible. This testing should include functional testing, performance testing, and security assessments to identify and address any potential issues. Once deployed, implement monitoring and logging solutions to track application performance, detect errors, and ensure that your application remains reliable and responsive.

In summary, deploying a Next.js application involves selecting a suitable deployment platform, preparing the application for production, and implementing best practices for security and performance. By understanding and leveraging the available deployment options and preparing your application accordingly, you can ensure a successful transition from development to production, providing a robust and efficient experience for your users.

When preparing a Next.js application for deployment, several critical considerations must be addressed to ensure that the transition from development to production is smooth and successful. These considerations include optimizing the application for performance, ensuring security, and configuring the deployment environment to handle various aspects of application management effectively.

One of the first steps in preparing your application for deployment is to ensure that it is optimized for performance. Next.js offers several built-in features to enhance performance, including automatic code splitting, optimized bundling, and server-side rendering (SSR). Leveraging these features effectively can significantly reduce load times and improve user experience. During the build process, Next.js generates optimized static assets and JavaScript bundles. It is crucial to review and test these outputs to confirm that they meet performance expectations. Tools such as Lighthouse and WebPageTest can provide valuable insights into performance metrics and areas for improvement.

Minimizing the size of JavaScript bundles and optimizing images are additional strategies to enhance performance.

Next.js supports image optimization through the `next/ image` component, which automatically optimizes images for different devices and screen sizes. Configuring this component correctly can lead to significant reductions in image load times and overall page weight.

Security is another critical aspect of deploying a Next.js application. Implementing HTTPS is essential to secure data transmitted between the user and the server. Most modern deployment platforms, including Vercel and Netlify, provide built-in support for HTTPS, which should be enabled by default. Additionally, securing sensitive data, such as API keys and environment variables, is crucial. Environment variables should be managed through secure methods provided by the deployment platform, such as encrypted secrets or configuration settings that are not exposed to the client side.

When deploying to serverless environments or cloud platforms, it is also important to configure proper access controls and permissions. For instance, ensure that serverless functions or cloud services are only accessible to authorized users and that they adhere to the principle of least privilege. This principle involves granting only the minimum permissions necessary for the service or function to operate correctly, reducing the risk of unauthorized access or misuse.

Another key aspect of deployment is handling application configuration and environment variables. Next.js supports environment variables through `.env` files, which can be configured for different environments, such as development, staging, and production. Ensure that these environment variables are correctly set up in the deployment environment and that they are securely managed. For cloud platforms, environment variables can often be configured through the platform's management console or CLI tools.

Continuous integration and continuous deployment (CI/

CD) are also vital components of the modern deployment workflow. CI/CD pipelines automate the process of building, testing, and deploying applications, making it easier to maintain consistent quality and quickly roll out updates. Most cloud platforms and deployment services integrate with popular CI/CD tools like GitHub Actions, GitLab CI, and CircleCI. Setting up a CI/CD pipeline involves configuring build and test processes, automating deployment steps, and defining triggers for deploying changes to production.

Monitoring and logging are essential for maintaining the health and performance of your deployed application. Implementing robust logging mechanisms allows you to track and diagnose issues that arise in production. Tools such as Sentry, LogRocket, and Datadog provide comprehensive monitoring and logging solutions that integrate with Next.js applications. These tools can help you identify and address performance bottlenecks, errors, and other issues that may impact the user experience.

Finally, testing your application in the production environment is crucial before fully committing to deployment. Performing thorough testing, including end-to-end tests and user acceptance tests, ensures that the application functions as expected under real-world conditions. This testing phase helps identify potential issues that may not have been apparent during development and staging.

In summary, deploying a Next.js application involves careful consideration of performance optimization, security, environment configuration, and CI/CD practices. By leveraging the features provided by Next.js and employing best practices in deployment, you can ensure that your application performs efficiently, remains secure, and provides a positive user experience. As the deployment process is the final step in bringing your application to users, thorough preparation and attention to detail are essential for achieving a successful launch and maintaining a high-quality application in production.

Effective deployment of Next.js applications requires a comprehensive approach that encompasses configuration, monitoring, and troubleshooting to ensure that the application performs reliably in a production environment.

Configuration is a key step in the deployment process, involving the setup of various environment-specific settings and integrations. For instance, configuring a CDN (Content Delivery Network) can greatly enhance the performance of static assets by reducing latency and load times for users across different geographical regions. Many deployment platforms offer integrated CDN services that can be enabled with minimal configuration, which helps in serving static assets like images, fonts, and other files efficiently.

Additionally, setting up proper caching strategies is crucial. Next.js supports several caching mechanisms, including HTTP caching headers and cache invalidation strategies. By configuring these headers, you can control how long resources are cached on the client side and when they should be revalidated. Proper caching helps in reducing server load and improving application responsiveness.

Another aspect to consider is logging and monitoring. Implementing robust logging mechanisms allows you to capture and analyze errors and performance issues in real-time. Next.js applications can integrate with various monitoring and logging tools that provide insights into application health, error rates, and user behavior. Tools like Sentry or LogRocket can capture client-side errors and performance issues, while server-side monitoring can be managed using services like New Relic or Datadog. Setting up alerts for critical issues ensures that you can address problems promptly before they affect users.

Deploying a Next.js application often involves handling different environments, such as development, staging, and production. Each environment requires its configuration settings and deployment pipelines. Automated deployment processes, such as Continuous Integration and Continuous Deployment (CI/CD), can streamline the release process. CI/CD pipelines automate testing, building, and deploying applications, ensuring that code changes are consistently and reliably integrated and delivered. Popular CI/CD tools like GitHub Actions, GitLab CI, and CircleCI support various deployment strategies and can be configured to deploy your Next.js application to different environments seamlessly.

Testing in a staging environment that mirrors production is essential to identify and resolve issues before going live. This environment should replicate the production environment as closely as possible, including configurations, integrations, and data. Performing thorough testing in staging helps in catching issues that might not be evident in development and ensures that the deployment to production is smooth.

When deploying to different types of hosting environments, such as traditional servers, cloud platforms, or serverless environments, it's essential to understand the specific requirements and limitations of each. Traditional hosting platforms may involve manual server management and configuration, whereas cloud platforms and serverless environments often offer more managed services with built-in scalability and high availability. Understanding these differences helps in making informed decisions about deployment strategies and managing application resources effectively.

Finally, post-deployment practices are crucial for maintaining the application's health and performance. Regular updates and maintenance are necessary to address security vulnerabilities, implement new features, and optimize performance. Monitoring user feedback and application metrics helps in identifying areas for improvement and ensuring that the application continues to meet user needs effectively.

In summary, deploying a Next.js application involves a multifaceted approach that includes performance optimization, security measures, environment configuration, and monitoring. By adhering to best practices in these areas, you can ensure a successful deployment and maintain a high-quality user experience. Effective deployment not only brings your application to the public but also sets the stage for ongoing management and improvement, ultimately contributing to the long-term success of your web application.

CHAPTER 21: MONITORING AND LOGGING

In the landscape of modern web development, effective monitoring and logging are fundamental for ensuring the reliability, performance, and security of applications in production. As applications become more complex and serve a larger user base, the ability to track and diagnose issues swiftly can distinguish between seamless user experiences and critical service disruptions. This chapter delves into the principles and practices of monitoring and logging specifically tailored for Next.js applications, offering a comprehensive approach to maintaining and optimizing application performance.

Monitoring encompasses the continuous observation of application health and performance, providing real-time insights into various metrics such as response times, error rates, and resource usage. For Next.js applications, setting up robust monitoring involves selecting appropriate tools and configuring them to track both server-side and client-side metrics. Tools such as New Relic, Datadog, and Prometheus are popular choices for monitoring web applications. These platforms can be integrated with Next.js to gather data on application performance, server health, and infrastructure metrics.

One of the key aspects of monitoring is setting up performance metrics. Metrics such as page load times, API response times, and memory usage offer insights into the application's efficiency. For Next.js, this includes monitoring server-side rendering (SSR) performance, static site generation (SSG) times, and API routes. By analyzing these metrics, developers can identify bottlenecks, optimize code, and enhance user experience. For instance, if page load times are significantly high, it might indicate that certain components are rendering slowly or that server resources are strained. Tools that provide real-time performance insights can help in diagnosing these issues and taking corrective actions promptly.

In addition to performance monitoring, setting up alerts is crucial for proactive issue management. Alerts notify developers of potential problems before they impact users. Configuring alerts involves defining thresholds for various metrics and setting up notification channels. For example, if an API endpoint exceeds a predefined error rate, an alert can be triggered to notify the development team. Alerts can be integrated with communication tools such as Slack or email, ensuring that the team is promptly informed of critical issues.

Logging complements monitoring by providing detailed records of application events, errors, and user interactions. Effective logging is instrumental in diagnosing and troubleshooting issues. In Next.js applications, logging can be implemented on both the server-side and client-side. On the server-side, tools like Winston or Morgan can be used to log HTTP requests, errors, and other significant events. For client-side logging, integrating services like Sentry or LogRocket can capture JavaScript errors, user interactions, and performance metrics.

Configuring logging involves setting up log levels, defining what information to capture, and determining where logs should be stored. Log levels, such as DEBUG, INFO, WARN, and ERROR, allow for filtering and prioritizing log entries based on their importance. Debugging and error logs are particularly valuable for understanding the context of issues and tracing their origins. Ensuring that logs are detailed yet concise is important for effective troubleshooting without overwhelming developers with excessive data.

Furthermore, centralized logging solutions can aggregate logs from various sources, providing a unified view of application behavior. Tools like ELK Stack (Elasticsearch, Logstash, Kibana) or cloud-based solutions like AWS CloudWatch can be used to collect, search, and visualize logs from different environments. Centralized logging facilitates the analysis of patterns and trends, making it easier to identify recurring issues and improve application stability.

In practice, effective monitoring and logging strategies for Next.js applications involve a combination of tools and techniques tailored to the specific needs of the application. Setting up comprehensive monitoring requires integrating performance metrics, configuring alerts, and leveraging advanced tools for real-time insights. Complementing this with robust logging practices ensures that detailed records are available for diagnosing issues and understanding application behavior. Together, these practices enable developers to maintain a high level of application reliability, enhance user experience, and respond effectively to any operational challenges.

To establish a comprehensive logging strategy in a Next.js application, one must consider the nuances of both server-side and client-side logging. On the server-side, Next.js applications can utilize logging libraries such as Winston or Bunyan. These libraries provide structured logging, allowing developers to capture detailed logs including timestamps, log levels (e.g., info, warn, error), and custom metadata. Winston, for instance, supports multiple transports, enabling logs to be written to various destinations such as files, databases, or external services. This flexibility is crucial for maintaining a centralized log management system.

When implementing server-side logging, it's important to ensure that sensitive information is handled appropriately. Logs should not include sensitive user data or application secrets. Implementing log redaction or masking techniques helps mitigate risks associated with data breaches. Additionally, proper log rotation and retention policies should be established to manage the volume of logs and prevent storage issues.

Client-side logging in Next.js can be approached using browser-based logging libraries such as LogRocket or Sentry. These tools capture client-side errors and performance issues, providing valuable insights into user interactions and frontend performance. For example, LogRocket records user sessions, enabling developers to replay sessions and investigate issues in context. This capability is particularly useful for diagnosing complex UI problems that are difficult to reproduce in a development environment.

Integrating client-side logging involves embedding the logging library into the Next.js application and configuring it to capture relevant events and errors. Logs from the client-side can be sent to a centralized logging service, where they can be correlated with server-side logs to provide a comprehensive view of application health.

Combining monitoring and logging strategies ensures that developers have a holistic view of their application's performance and issues. For effective troubleshooting, logs should be searchable and correlated with monitoring data. This integration allows for more efficient diagnosis of issues by cross-referencing performance metrics with detailed error logs. For example, if a performance spike is detected, logs can be examined to identify specific errors or unusual events that coincide with the spike.

Another critical aspect of monitoring and logging is implementing error tracking. Error tracking tools like Sentry or Rollbar provide detailed reports on application errors, including stack traces, affected users, and frequency. These tools can be integrated into the Next.js application to capture both server-side and client-side errors. Proper error tracking setup involves configuring the tool to capture relevant exceptions and provide actionable insights into their causes. For instance, integrating Sentry with Next.js involves setting up the Sentry SDK and configuring it to capture errors from both the server-side and client-side environments.

Moreover, performance monitoring should include tracking user experience metrics such as Time to First Byte (TTFB) and Largest Contentful Paint (LCP). These metrics provide insights into how quickly users can interact with the application and can highlight performance issues that impact user satisfaction. Tools like Google Lighthouse or WebPageTest can be used to analyze these metrics and provide recommendations for performance improvements.

When setting up a monitoring and logging strategy, it is essential to establish a routine for reviewing and acting on the collected data. Regularly scheduled reviews of monitoring dashboards and log files help identify trends and recurring issues. This proactive approach enables developers to address potential problems before they escalate and ensures continuous improvement of application performance and reliability.

Finally, it's important to integrate monitoring and logging with the deployment pipeline. Continuous integration and deployment (CI/CD) pipelines can be configured to include monitoring and logging checks as part of the deployment process. This integration ensures that any changes made to the application are immediately monitored for issues and that logs are captured and analyzed for any anomalies. By incorporating these practices into the CI/CD pipeline, developers can achieve a more streamlined and automated approach to maintaining application health.

In summary, effective monitoring and logging are integral to maintaining the stability and performance of Next.js applications. By implementing robust monitoring tools, configuring detailed logging strategies, and integrating error tracking, developers can gain comprehensive insights into their application's behavior and performance. This approach not only facilitates swift issue resolution but also contributes to a more reliable and user-friendly application. As applications continue to evolve, the practices outlined in this chapter will serve as a foundation for ensuring that they remain robust and responsive in production environments.

Effective monitoring and logging also involve setting up proactive alerting mechanisms. Alerts are crucial for identifying issues before they impact users significantly. To establish a robust alerting system, you must integrate monitoring tools with notification services such as Slack, email, or SMS. Tools like Prometheus combined with Alertmanager can be configured to trigger alerts based on predefined thresholds or anomalies. For instance, you might set up alerts for high error rates or unusually long response times. This immediate feedback loop enables developers to address issues promptly, reducing downtime and enhancing user experience.

In addition to alerting, performance metrics play a vital role in understanding the application's health. Metrics such as response times, error rates, and resource usage provide insights into how well the application performs under various conditions. Next.js applications can be instrumented to emit performance metrics using tools like New Relic or Datadog. By integrating these tools, you can track key performance indicators and visualize them through dashboards. These dashboards provide a real-time overview of application health and can help identify performance bottlenecks or resource constraints.

Another important consideration is the integration of distributed tracing into your monitoring strategy. Distributed tracing tools like OpenTelemetry or Zipkin help track requests as they propagate through various services. This is especially beneficial in microservices architectures where a single request might involve multiple services. By tracing these requests, you can identify performance bottlenecks, service dependencies, and latency issues. Distributed tracing provides a comprehensive view of the application's operational flow, allowing for more effective debugging and performance optimization.

When it comes to diagnosing issues, combining logs with monitoring data can provide a more nuanced understanding of what went wrong. For example, if a specific endpoint experiences a surge in response times, correlating this with logs can reveal whether the slowdown is due to code issues, database performance, or external dependencies. Techniques like log aggregation and analysis enhance this process by consolidating logs from various sources into a single platform. Tools such as ELK Stack (Elasticsearch, Logstash, and Kibana) or Splunk facilitate log aggregation, indexing, and querying, making it easier to perform detailed analyses.

Lastly, implementing a logging and monitoring strategy involves continuous improvement. Regularly reviewing and updating logging configurations, alert thresholds, and monitoring dashboards ensures they remain relevant as the application evolves. Conducting post-mortem analyses after significant incidents helps refine these strategies and improve their effectiveness. By iteratively enhancing your monitoring and logging practices, you ensure that they adapt to the changing landscape of your application and its operational requirements.

In summary, effective monitoring and logging are critical for maintaining the stability and performance of Next.js applications. By leveraging server-side and client-side logging, integrating with error tracking and performance monitoring tools, and setting up proactive alerts, you can gain valuable insights into application health and address issues promptly. Combining these practices with distributed tracing and continuous improvement efforts ensures a comprehensive approach to application maintenance and troubleshooting.

CHAPTER 22: SECURING NEXT.JS APPLICATIONS

Security is a paramount concern in web development, particularly for applications that handle sensitive user data or operate within a high-risk environment. As web applications become increasingly sophisticated, so too do the techniques employed by malicious actors. In this chapter, we explore common security vulnerabilities and best practices for securing Next.js applications, focusing on securing API routes, handling user authentication and authorization, and protecting against common web security threats.

A fundamental aspect of securing a Next.js application involves safeguarding API routes. API routes in Next.js offer a convenient way to build backend functionality within the same application framework. However, this convenience can introduce security risks if not properly managed. One critical measure is to ensure that sensitive data is not exposed through these endpoints. Implementing proper authentication and authorization checks before processing API requests helps prevent unauthorized access. For instance, using JSON Web Tokens (JWT) or OAuth for authentication ensures that only authenticated users can access protected routes. Additionally, input validation and sanitization should be employed to mitigate risks such as SQL injection and cross-site scripting (XSS) attacks. Validating and sanitizing input data before it reaches the backend prevents malicious payloads from compromising application integrity.

Handling user authentication and authorization effectively is another crucial aspect of application security. Next.js supports various methods for managing user authentication, including integration with third-party authentication providers such as Auth0, Firebase Authentication, or implementing custom authentication mechanisms. Utilizing session-based authentication, where user sessions are managed securely on the server side, helps protect against common attacks such as session hijacking. Additionally, implementing secure password storage practices, such as hashing passwords with bcrypt, ensures that user credentials are not exposed even if a security breach occurs.

Authorization involves determining what actions authenticated users are allowed to perform. Implementing role-based access control (RBAC) or attribute-based access control (ABAC) models can help manage user permissions effectively. RBAC assigns permissions based on user roles, while ABAC evaluates user attributes to make authorization decisions. Both methods should be combined with principle of least privilege, ensuring users have only the necessary permissions required to perform their tasks.

Securing a Next.js application also involves defending against common web security threats. Cross-Site Request Forgery (CSRF) attacks exploit the trust between a user's browser and a web application, allowing unauthorized commands to be transmitted from a user that the web application trusts. Implementing anti-CSRF tokens, which are unique tokens associated with each user session, helps prevent such attacks by validating that requests originate from legitimate sources.

Cross-Site Scripting (XSS) attacks occur when malicious scripts are injected into web pages viewed by other users.

To protect against XSS, it is essential to escape user-generated content before rendering it in the application. Using libraries and frameworks that automatically handle escaping, such as React's built-in mechanisms, reduces the risk of XSS vulnerabilities. Additionally, employing Content Security Policy (CSP) headers helps control which resources can be loaded by the application, further mitigating XSS risks.

Another critical security concern is securing sensitive data in transit and at rest. Implementing HTTPS across your application ensures that data transmitted between the client and server is encrypted, protecting it from interception by unauthorized parties. For sensitive data stored on the server, such as user credentials or personal information, encrypting this data both at rest and during transmission is essential. Utilizing encryption algorithms like AES (Advanced Encryption Standard) for data at rest and TLS (Transport Layer Security) for data in transit helps maintain the confidentiality and integrity of user data.

Regular security updates and patching also play a vital role in maintaining application security. Keeping dependencies and libraries up-to-date ensures that known vulnerabilities are addressed promptly. Tools such as Snyk or Dependabot can help automate the process of monitoring and updating dependencies to avoid potential security risks.

In summary, securing a Next.js application involves a multi-faceted approach that addresses various aspects of security. From securing API routes and managing user authentication and authorization to defending against common web threats and ensuring data encryption, each layer of security contributes to the overall robustness of the application. Adopting best practices and staying informed about emerging security threats are crucial steps in safeguarding your Next.js application against potential vulnerabilities and attacks.

Effective protection against Cross-Site Request Forgery (CSRF) attacks requires implementing CSRF tokens. CSRF tokens are unique, random values generated by the server and included in forms and headers. When a request is made, the token is validated to ensure that it matches the one generated by the server. This approach prevents unauthorized requests from being executed on behalf of authenticated users. In Next.js applications, libraries such as `csurf` can be used to integrate CSRF protection into API routes seamlessly.

Another common threat is Cross-Site Scripting (XSS), which occurs when malicious scripts are injected into web pages viewed by other users. XSS attacks can compromise user data and application integrity. To defend against XSS, it is crucial to escape user-generated content and avoid directly inserting untrusted data into the HTML. Next.js provides built-in mechanisms for safely rendering content, such as using the `dangerouslySetInnerHTML` attribute with caution and employing libraries like `DOMPurify` to sanitize HTML.

Content Security Policy (CSP) is another important defense mechanism that helps prevent XSS and data injection attacks. CSP is a security feature that controls which resources the browser is allowed to load and execute. By setting appropriate CSP headers, developers can restrict the sources of scripts, styles, and other resources, mitigating the risk of malicious content being executed. Next.js applications can configure CSP headers through server-side middleware or custom server configurations.

For applications that handle sensitive information, securing data in transit and at rest is essential. Enforcing HTTPS ensures that data transmitted between the client and server is encrypted, protecting it from interception or tampering. Using HTTPS requires obtaining and installing SSL/TLS certificates. Modern web servers and cloud platforms often provide straightforward mechanisms for enabling HTTPS. Additionally, securing sensitive data stored in databases or other storage systems involves encrypting this data both in transit and at rest. Encryption algorithms like AES (Advanced Encryption Standard) can be used to secure stored data, while secure key management practices should be followed to protect encryption keys.

Implementing proper error handling and logging is also critical for security. While logging errors can be valuable for debugging and monitoring, it is important to ensure that logs do not expose sensitive information. Error messages should be generic and not reveal details about the underlying system or application architecture. This practice helps prevent attackers from gaining insights into potential vulnerabilities. In production environments, sensitive log data should be stored securely and access to logs should be restricted to authorized personnel only.

Regular security audits and vulnerability assessments are crucial for maintaining the security of a Next.js application. Conducting periodic reviews of code, dependencies, and configuration settings helps identify and address potential security issues before they can be exploited. Tools such as static code analyzers and dependency scanners can assist in detecting known vulnerabilities in code and third-party libraries. Additionally, staying informed about security best practices and updates from the Next.js community and security organizations helps ensure that your application remains protected against emerging threats.

In summary, securing a Next.js application involves a multi-faceted approach that addresses various aspects of security. By implementing robust measures for securing API routes, managing user authentication and authorization, defending against common web threats, and adhering to best practices for data protection, developers can significantly reduce the risk of security breaches. Continuous monitoring, regular updates, and a proactive approach to security are essential for maintaining a secure application environment. As threats evolve and new vulnerabilities are discovered, staying vigilant and adapting security practices accordingly is key to safeguarding your Next.js applications.

Securing API routes in Next.js is essential for protecting sensitive data and ensuring that only authorized users can access certain functionalities. To implement effective security measures, developers must consider several strategies. One key approach is to use authentication and authorization mechanisms that verify user identities and control access permissions. Authentication can be managed using various methods, including session-based authentication, token-based authentication (such as JWT), or integrating with third-party identity providers.

Next.js applications can leverage middleware or API route handlers to enforce authentication and authorization checks. For example, with JWT, an access token can be sent with API requests, and the server can verify this token to ensure it is valid and has the necessary permissions. Libraries like `jsonwebtoken` facilitate the creation and verification of JWTs, while tools like `next-auth` provide a comprehensive authentication solution that integrates with Next.js seamlessly.

Authorization, on the other hand, ensures that authenticated users have appropriate permissions to access specific resources or perform certain actions. Role-based access control (RBAC) is a common approach where users are assigned roles, and each role has specific permissions. Implementing RBAC involves defining roles and permissions, associating users with roles, and applying these rules in API route handlers to control access. This ensures that only users with the required roles can perform sensitive operations or access restricted areas of the application.

In addition to authentication and authorization, protecting

against common web security threats involves proactive measures and continuous monitoring. Regular security assessments, such as vulnerability scans and penetration testing, can help identify potential weaknesses in the application. These assessments should be part of a broader security strategy that includes regular updates to dependencies, patches for known vulnerabilities, and adherence to secure coding practices.

For comprehensive security, incorporating security headers into your application's responses is crucial. Security headers provide instructions to browsers on how to handle content and security-related aspects of web interactions. Important security headers include `Strict-Transport-Security` (HSTS), which enforces HTTPS connections, `X-Content-Type-Options` to prevent MIME-type sniffing, and `X-Frame-Options` to protect against clickjacking attacks. By configuring these headers, developers can enhance the security posture of their Next.js applications and mitigate various attack vectors.

Furthermore, securing application deployment environments is an integral part of maintaining overall security. This includes securing server infrastructure, applying proper network security measures, and configuring firewalls to restrict unauthorized access. In cloud environments, leveraging security features provided by cloud providers, such as Virtual Private Cloud (VPC) configurations, security groups, and managed security services, can significantly enhance the security of deployed applications.

Regularly reviewing and updating security policies, conducting security training for development teams, and staying informed about emerging security threats and best practices are essential components of a robust security strategy. As new vulnerabilities and attack techniques emerge, it is important to adapt security practices accordingly to protect applications from evolving threats.

In summary, securing Next.js applications requires a multifaceted approach that encompasses securing API routes, implementing robust authentication and authorization mechanisms, protecting against common web security threats, and ensuring secure deployment practices. By following these best practices and employing appropriate tools and techniques, developers can build resilient applications that safeguard user data and maintain the integrity of their systems. Continuous vigilance and proactive measures are essential for addressing security challenges and maintaining a secure application environment in today's ever-evolving digital landscape.

CHAPTER 23: PERFORMANCE TUNING AND OPTIMIZATION

In the realm of web development, ensuring that an application performs efficiently is crucial for delivering a positive user experience. Beyond the basic performance improvements, advanced techniques in performance tuning and optimization are essential for achieving high efficiency and responsiveness in Next.js applications. This chapter explores various strategies to optimize server response times, enhance client-side performance, and improve overall application efficiency.

A key area of focus for performance tuning is server response time. Reducing latency in server responses directly impacts the speed at which content reaches users. To achieve this, developers should start by optimizing server-side rendering (SSR) processes. Next.js applications rely on SSR to generate pages on the server before sending them to the client, which can be resource-intensive. Techniques such as implementing caching strategies are vital. Caching can be done at multiple levels: server-side caching of rendered pages, in-memory caching for frequently accessed data, and CDN (Content Delivery Network) caching to distribute content geographically closer to users.

Additionally, employing server-side optimizations, such as database query optimizations and efficient data fetching, can further enhance performance. For instance, using techniques like indexing, query optimization, and reducing unnecessary database calls can significantly decrease the time required to fetch and process data. Moreover, implementing incremental static regeneration (ISR) allows pages to be updated incrementally, rather than regenerating the entire site, which can dramatically improve server performance and reduce deployment times.

On the client side, optimizing performance involves reducing the amount of JavaScript and CSS that needs to be processed by the browser. Next.js provides several tools and techniques for this purpose. Code splitting is one effective method, where only the necessary code for a particular route is loaded, rather than the entire application's codebase. This minimizes the initial load time and enhances responsiveness. Dynamic imports and React's `lazy` and `Suspense` components can be utilized to load components only when they are needed.

Another aspect of client-side performance optimization is managing and optimizing assets such as images and fonts. Large images can be a major contributor to slow page loads. Next.js offers built-in support for the `next/image` component, which provides automatic image optimization, including resizing, lazy loading, and format conversion to WebP. This component ensures that images are delivered in an optimized format and size, improving both load times and user experience. Similarly, optimizing fonts by using only the necessary font weights and styles, and employing font loading strategies like `font-display: swap`, can reduce render-blocking and improve page speed.

Client-side performance can also benefit from efficient state management. Overuse of global state or frequent state updates can lead to unnecessary re-renders and degraded performance. Using memoization techniques and React's `useMemo` and `useCallback` hooks helps avoid unnecessary computations and re-renders, thereby improving performance. Additionally, optimizing how components handle state changes and ensuring that state updates are batched can help maintain a smooth and responsive user interface.

In terms of overall application efficiency, monitoring and analyzing performance metrics play a crucial role. Tools like Google Lighthouse and WebPageTest can provide valuable insights into performance bottlenecks and areas for improvement. By regularly auditing the application's performance, developers can identify issues such as slow loading times, inefficient resource usage, and opportunities for further optimization.

Integrating performance monitoring tools into the development workflow allows for continuous performance assessment. Tools like New Relic, Datadog, and Sentry offer real-time monitoring and detailed performance analytics, helping developers track and address performance issues as they arise. These tools can monitor server response times, identify slow database queries, and detect client-side performance issues, providing actionable insights for ongoing optimization efforts.

To sum up, advanced performance tuning and optimization in Next.js applications involve a multifaceted approach. By focusing on optimizing server response times through caching and efficient data fetching, enhancing client-side performance through code splitting and asset optimization, and continuously monitoring application efficiency, developers can achieve a high-performing, responsive, and efficient web application. Implementing these strategies not only improves user experience but also contributes to the overall success and scalability of the application.

A significant factor in improving client-side performance is optimizing JavaScript execution. The JavaScript bundle size can greatly affect load times and overall application speed. Next.js facilitates this by enabling features such as automatic static optimization and code splitting. Automatic static optimization ensures that pages that do not require server-side rendering are served as static files, reducing the need for server processing. Code splitting, on the other hand, breaks down the application into smaller chunks that are loaded only when needed, rather than loading the entire JavaScript bundle at once.

To complement these techniques, it is crucial to analyze and improve the performance of React components. Utilizing React's built-in performance profiling tools, such as the React DevTools profiler, can help identify performance bottlenecks. Techniques such as memoization, which involves using `React.memo` or the `useMemo` hook, can prevent unnecessary re-rendering of components, thereby improving rendering performance. Additionally, employing efficient state management practices and minimizing the number of state updates can help reduce the computational overhead during rendering.

Another important aspect of performance optimization is ensuring efficient data fetching and management. When working with APIs or external data sources, minimizing the number of network requests and optimizing the data retrieval process can lead to substantial performance improvements. Implementing techniques such as batching requests, caching responses, and pre-fetching data can reduce the time spent waiting for data to load. Next.js provides tools like `getStaticProps` and `getServerSideProps` for data fetching, which can be leveraged to fetch data at build time or request time, respectively, optimizing the performance based on the application's needs.

Client-side performance also benefits from optimizing web fonts and ensuring they do not adversely affect page load times. Using modern font formats such as WOFF2, which provide better compression and faster loading, can improve performance. Additionally, techniques such as font-display CSS property configuration, which controls how fonts are displayed while they are loading, can enhance user experience by reducing the visibility of unstyled text during font loading.

Beyond these optimizations, it is essential to address overall application efficiency through practices such as performance monitoring and continuous assessment. Tools like Lighthouse, which provides audits for performance, accessibility, and best practices, can be integrated into the development workflow to continuously assess and improve application performance. Regular performance audits and monitoring can help identify areas for improvement and ensure that optimization efforts are effective.

Incorporating performance best practices into the development lifecycle ensures that Next.js applications are not only responsive and efficient but also scalable. Performance tuning is an ongoing process that requires regular evaluation and adjustment as new features are added and user expectations evolve. By adopting a proactive approach to performance optimization and leveraging the tools and techniques provided by Next.js and modern web development practices, developers can create applications that deliver exceptional user experiences and operate efficiently at scale.

When addressing server performance, it is crucial to consider both server configuration and the handling of dynamic content. Efficient server response times can be achieved by leveraging server-side caching mechanisms. Caching strategies such as HTTP caching and server-side caching using solutions like Redis can store frequently accessed data, reducing the time needed to generate responses. Next.js integrates with various caching solutions, allowing for configuration that suits specific application needs, whether through edge caching, CDNs, or API caching.

Additionally, optimizing server performance involves fine-tuning server settings and scaling strategies. For applications deployed on cloud platforms, utilizing auto-scaling features ensures that resources are dynamically adjusted based on traffic. This approach helps handle varying loads without compromising performance. Serverless environments, a key feature of Next.js, can also optimize server operations by handling server management automatically, which can lead to better scalability and reduced latency.

To further enhance performance, the use of CDN (Content Delivery Network) services can be invaluable. CDNs distribute content across multiple geographic locations, reducing the distance between users and the content they are requesting. This results in faster load times and reduced latency. Next.js applications can be configured to take advantage of CDNs for static assets and media files, ensuring that content is delivered swiftly and efficiently to users worldwide.

Application efficiency can also be improved through the optimization of build processes. Efficient build configurations and practices, such as using incremental builds, can significantly reduce the time required for deploying changes. Next.js supports incremental static regeneration, which allows static pages to be updated incrementally without needing a full rebuild, thereby enhancing build efficiency and deployment times.

Another advanced technique for performance tuning involves monitoring and analyzing the performance of third-party integrations. Many modern applications rely on external services for functionalities such as payment processing, analytics, or content delivery. Ensuring that these integrations do not become performance bottlenecks is critical. By monitoring the response times and impact of third-party services, developers can identify and address potential issues that may affect overall application performance.

Furthermore, applying best practices for image optimization is essential. Images often represent a significant portion of a web application's payload and can substantially impact load times. Next.js provides built-in support for image optimization through its `next/image` component, which automatically optimizes images on-demand, serving them in modern formats such as WebP when appropriate. This component also includes features for responsive images and lazy loading, which enhance the loading experience and overall performance.

In conclusion, optimizing Next.js applications involves a multifaceted approach that addresses both server and client-side performance. By leveraging advanced techniques such as server-side caching, auto-scaling, CDN integration, incremental builds, and third-party performance monitoring, developers can enhance the efficiency and responsiveness of their applications. Additionally, practices such as image optimization and continuous performance assessment play a critical role in maintaining high performance standards. Through these strategies, applications can deliver a seamless and fast user experience, ensuring that they meet the demands of modern web performance expectations.

CHAPTER 24: INTEGRATING WITH EXTERNAL APIS

Integrating with external APIs is a fundamental aspect of modern web development, enhancing the functionality and reach of applications by leveraging third-party services. In the context of Next.js, integrating external APIs involves several key considerations, including making API requests, managing authentication, and implementing error handling strategies to ensure robust and reliable interactions.

To begin with, making API requests in Next.js can be approached in multiple ways, depending on the application's architecture and requirements. Next.js provides several methods to handle API interactions, including server-side and client-side fetching. For server-side data fetching, Next.js offers functions such as `getServerSideProps` and `getStaticProps`. These functions enable developers to fetch data from external APIs during the server-side rendering process, providing data that is available when the page is initially loaded. This approach is beneficial for SEO and initial load performance, as the data is already included in the server-rendered HTML.

In contrast, client-side data fetching can be achieved using JavaScript libraries such as Axios or the native `fetch` API. Client-side fetching is useful for dynamic interactions where the data needs to be updated without a full page reload. By making API calls directly from React components, developers can update the UI based on the latest data from external sources, enhancing the interactivity and responsiveness of the application.

When interacting with external APIs, managing authentication is a critical aspect of ensuring secure and authorized access. Many APIs require authentication, typically through mechanisms such as API keys, OAuth tokens, or JWT (JSON Web Tokens). For secure storage and handling of sensitive credentials, environment variables are commonly used in Next.js applications. By placing API keys and tokens in environment variables, developers can keep sensitive information out of the codebase and configuration files, reducing the risk of exposure.

Implementing authentication strategies often involves creating API routes within the Next.js application that handle token management and authentication logic. For example, a custom API route can be set up to handle the exchange of credentials for tokens or to validate existing tokens before making further API requests. This setup ensures that the client-side code does not directly handle sensitive authentication details, adding an additional layer of security.

Error handling is another crucial aspect of integrating with external APIs. Effective error handling ensures that the application can gracefully handle unexpected situations and provide informative feedback to users. Common types of errors include network issues, server errors, and API rate limits. Implementing robust error handling involves checking the status codes of API responses and managing different error scenarios accordingly. For example, if an API request fails due to a network issue, the application should retry the request or display a user-friendly message indicating that there was a problem with connectivity.

To handle errors systematically, developers can use error boundaries in React to catch JavaScript errors in component trees and log them appropriately. Additionally, managing API response errors within client-side components involves implementing conditional logic to display error messages or alternative content when the API call fails.

Rate limiting and quota management are additional considerations when integrating with external APIs. Many APIs impose rate limits to prevent abuse and ensure fair usage. When designing the integration, it is essential to be aware of these limits and handle scenarios where the application exceeds the allowed number of requests. Implementing strategies such as request throttling, caching responses, and optimizing API calls can help mitigate the impact of rate limits and improve the application's efficiency.

Caching strategies also play a significant role in optimizing interactions with external APIs. By caching API responses, applications can reduce the number of requests sent to the external service, decreasing latency and improving performance. In Next.js, server-side caching can be implemented using various techniques, such as in-memory caching with libraries like Node-cache or external caching solutions like Redis.

Finally, integrating with external APIs often requires adhering to the API provider's terms of service and usage guidelines. Ensuring compliance with these guidelines helps maintain a positive relationship with API providers and avoids potential legal or operational issues.

In summary, integrating with external APIs in Next.js involves managing API requests effectively, handling authentication securely, and implementing robust error handling strategies. By leveraging Next.js's capabilities and best practices, developers can create applications that interact seamlessly with external services, providing enhanced functionality and a better user experience.

When integrating with external APIs, a key component to consider is error handling, which ensures that your application can deal with failures in a graceful and user-friendly manner. Effective error handling involves not only managing API request failures but also providing meaningful feedback and recovery options for users.

To start with, it is essential to handle various types of errors that may occur during API interactions. These include network errors, which occur when the application cannot reach the API server due to connectivity issues, and HTTP errors, which are returned by the server and indicate that something went wrong with the request. Common HTTP errors include 404 (Not Found), 500 (Internal Server Error), and 401 (Unauthorized), among others.

In the case of network errors, implementing retry mechanisms can be beneficial. For example, you might configure your application to retry the request a certain number of times before showing an error message to the user. This can be achieved using libraries like Axios, which provide built-in support for request retries, or by implementing custom retry logic using JavaScript.

Handling HTTP errors typically involves inspecting the response status code and providing appropriate feedback based on the type of error. For instance, a 404 error might trigger a message informing the user that the requested resource could not be found, while a 500 error could prompt a message indicating a server issue and suggesting the user try again later. Ensuring that error messages are user-friendly and actionable can significantly enhance the user experience.

Another crucial aspect of integrating with external APIs is managing data and state changes in response to API interactions. As data is fetched from external sources, it is vital to handle it efficiently and update the application's state accordingly. In Next.js, client-side data fetching often involves using React's state management features or third-party state management libraries. For instance, React hooks like `useState` and `useEffect` can be used to manage and update state based on API responses. Similarly, libraries such as Redux or Zustand can provide more advanced state management solutions for larger applications.

When it comes to server-side data fetching, Next.js offers utilities like `getServerSideProps` and `getStaticProps` to ensure that data is available before rendering the page. `getServerSideProps` runs on every request, making it suitable for dynamic data that needs to be fetched at runtime. On the other hand, `getStaticProps` is used for static generation and is called at build time, making it ideal for data that does not change frequently.

For both client-side and server-side data fetching, caching can play a significant role in optimizing performance. Implementing caching strategies reduces the number of API requests and speeds up data retrieval. Client-side caching can be managed using in-memory stores or libraries like React Query, which provide built-in caching mechanisms. For server-side caching, solutions such as Redis or in-memory caches can be employed to store frequently accessed data and reduce latency.

Moreover, integrating external APIs often involves dealing with rate limits imposed by API providers. Rate limits restrict the number of API requests that can be made within a given time frame. To manage rate limits effectively, you can implement strategies such as request throttling, which involves limiting the rate at which requests are made, and handling rate limit errors by either queuing requests or implementing exponential backoff strategies.

Another important consideration is the security of data exchanged between your application and external APIs. Ensuring that data is transmitted securely involves using HTTPS for all API requests to encrypt data in transit. Additionally, for APIs that require authentication, securely managing and storing authentication tokens is critical. This can be achieved by using secure storage mechanisms such as HTTP-only cookies or secure client-side storage options.

In addition to these practices, thorough testing of API integrations is essential to identify potential issues and ensure reliability. Testing involves verifying that API requests return the expected results, handling various error scenarios, and ensuring that the application behaves correctly under different conditions. Tools like Postman can be used for manual API testing, while automated testing frameworks such as Jest and Cypress can be employed for integration and end-to-end tests.

By implementing robust error handling, managing data and state effectively, addressing rate limits, and ensuring data security, developers can create reliable and user-friendly applications that make effective use of external APIs. Properly handling these aspects ensures that the application remains performant, secure, and capable of providing a seamless user experience even when interacting with third-party services.

Incorporating external APIs into your Next.js application also involves dealing with authentication and authorization, which are critical for accessing secure resources and maintaining application security. Many APIs require authentication, usually via tokens or API keys, to ensure that only authorized users or applications can access their endpoints.

To manage API authentication effectively, it's important to understand the different methods used for securing API requests. One common approach is using API keys, which are simple tokens included in the request headers or query parameters. When using API keys, ensure they are stored securely, such as in environment variables or configuration files, and never exposed directly in your codebase. For Next.js applications, you can manage environment variables through `.env.local` files, which provide a secure way to handle sensitive information.

Another common method for authentication is OAuth, which provides a more secure and flexible approach for user authentication. OAuth involves exchanging tokens between the application and the API provider. The OAuth process typically includes redirecting users to the authentication provider, receiving an authorization code, and exchanging it for an access token. In a Next.js application, you can use libraries like `next-auth` to simplify OAuth integration and manage session states securely.

When integrating with APIs that require authentication, handling tokens and managing session states are crucial. For client-side requests, store tokens securely in cookies or local storage, and ensure they are transmitted over HTTPS to prevent interception. On the server side, validate tokens and handle token refresh logic as needed to maintain session security. This approach helps in protecting your application from unauthorized access and ensures secure communication between your application and external services.

Additionally, consider the performance implications of external API integration. APIs can introduce latency due to network communication and server processing times. To mitigate these effects, employ strategies such as caching API responses. Caching can significantly improve response times by storing frequently accessed data temporarily, reducing the need to make repetitive requests to the API. Next.js supports various caching mechanisms, including HTTP caching and server-side caching using libraries like `swr` or `react-query`.

Moreover, implement rate limiting and throttling to manage the frequency of API requests and prevent overwhelming external services. Rate limiting can be handled on both the client and server sides, ensuring that your application adheres to the API provider's usage policies and minimizes the risk of hitting rate limits. On the server side, you might use middleware to enforce rate limits, while client-side strategies can include request debouncing or batching to optimize the number of requests made.

Error handling, as discussed earlier, also extends to API interactions. Implement robust logging and monitoring to track API request performance and identify any issues. Tools like LogRocket or Sentry can help you capture and analyze errors, providing valuable insights into the cause of failures and allowing you to address issues proactively. Monitoring API usage and response times helps in optimizing performance and ensuring that your application remains reliable and responsive.

In summary, integrating with external APIs in Next.js involves a comprehensive approach that includes handling authentication, managing session states, optimizing performance, and ensuring robust error handling. By understanding the various authentication methods, securing sensitive information, implementing caching strategies, and monitoring API interactions, you can build a resilient and efficient application that leverages external services effectively. This approach not only enhances the functionality of your application but also contributes to a seamless and secure user experience.

CHAPTER 25: IMPLEMENTING REAL-TIME FEATURES

Real-time features have become integral to modern web applications, offering enhanced interactivity and user engagement. These features include functionalities such as live chat, notifications, and live updates, which rely on maintaining an open, continuous connection between the client and server. Implementing such functionalities in Next.js applications involves leveraging various technologies that facilitate real-time communication, including WebSockets and Server-Sent Events (SSE).

At the core of real-time communication in web applications is the need for efficient, bidirectional data transfer. Traditional HTTP requests are stateless and cannot maintain an ongoing connection, which poses a challenge for real-time features. This is where WebSockets and Server-Sent Events come into play, providing the mechanisms necessary to establish and maintain real-time connections.

WebSockets offer a robust solution for real-time communication by enabling a full-duplex communication channel over a single, long-lived connection. This protocol establishes a persistent connection between the client and server, allowing data to flow freely in both directions. In Next.js applications, integrating WebSockets involves using libraries and tools such as `socket.io`, which simplifies the implementation process. The `socket.io` library provides a straightforward API for managing WebSocket connections and handling events, making it an ideal choice for developers looking to add real-time features.

To begin integrating WebSockets into a Next.js application, first install the `socket.io` client and server packages. On the server side, set up a WebSocket server using `socket.io` by creating a new server instance and attaching it to the existing HTTP server. This configuration allows you to broadcast and listen for events across connected clients. On the client side, establish a connection to the WebSocket server using the `socket.io-client` library. This setup enables you to send and receive real-time updates, such as chat messages or notifications.

Another technology for implementing real-time updates is Server-Sent Events (SSE). Unlike WebSockets, SSE is a unidirectional protocol that allows the server to push updates to the client over an HTTP connection. SSE is particularly useful for scenarios where the client only needs to receive updates, such as live notifications or real-time feeds. The implementation of SSE in Next.js involves setting up an endpoint on the server that streams events to clients and handling these events on the client side using the `EventSource` API.

To use SSE in a Next.js application, create an API route that responds with a `Content-Type` of `text/event-stream`. This API route will continuously send events to connected clients. On the client side, instantiate an `EventSource` object with the URL of the SSE endpoint. This object listens for incoming messages from the server and processes them as they arrive. SSE is less complex than WebSockets and does not require a separate library, making it a lightweight option for certain real-time features.

When implementing real-time features, consider the performance implications and potential scalability challenges. Maintaining multiple open connections can strain server resources and impact application performance. To address these issues, use techniques such as load balancing and message queuing. Load balancing distributes incoming connections across multiple servers, while message queuing systems, such as Redis Pub/Sub, manage and deliver messages efficiently.

Security is also a critical aspect of real-time communication. Ensure that all real-time data transmissions are secure by using HTTPS and implementing proper authentication and authorization mechanisms. For WebSockets, you can use token-based authentication to validate clients before establishing a connection. For SSE, consider using secure tokens or sessions to ensure that only authorized users receive updates.

Finally, monitor and test the real-time features of your application to ensure they perform as expected under various conditions. Use performance monitoring tools and logs to track connection stability, message delivery, and server resource usage. Regular testing helps identify and resolve issues related to real-time communication, ensuring a smooth user experience.

In summary, implementing real-time features in Next.js applications involves choosing the appropriate technology— WebSockets for bidirectional communication and SSE for server-to-client updates. By leveraging these technologies, you can enhance user engagement with live chat, notifications, and other interactive elements. Careful consideration of performance, scalability, and security will ensure that your real-time features provide a seamless and reliable experience for users.

When implementing Server-Sent Events (SSE) in a Next.js application, you start by setting up a dedicated endpoint on your server to handle the streaming of events. Unlike WebSockets, SSE operates over standard HTTP connections and is inherently simpler to implement for scenarios where only server-to-client communication is required.

To set up SSE, create a new API route in your Next.js application that will serve as the SSE endpoint. This endpoint should configure the response headers to indicate that the content is being streamed as an event stream, setting `Content-Type` to `text/event-stream` and `Cache-Control` to `no-cache`. The endpoint will use a continuous response stream to send events to the client. Each event is formatted as a series of lines, with a single event separated from the next by a pair of newlines. The server sends these events whenever there is new data to push, allowing clients to receive real-time updates.

On the client side, you utilize the `EventSource` API to connect to the SSE endpoint. This API is built into modern browsers and provides a straightforward way to listen for incoming messages. You instantiate an `EventSource` object with the URL of your SSE endpoint and attach event listeners to handle incoming messages. The `EventSource` API also supports reconnections if the connection is lost, making it a reliable choice for real-time data updates.

Both WebSockets and SSE offer unique benefits depending on the specific requirements of your application. WebSockets provide a full-duplex communication channel suitable for scenarios requiring bidirectional data flow, such as live chat applications where users need to send and receive messages in real-time. In contrast, SSE is optimized for scenarios where only server-to-client communication is needed, such as updating live notifications or news feeds.

Integrating real-time features into Next.js applications also involves considerations for scalability and performance. For instance, when using WebSockets, managing multiple concurrent connections can become challenging, particularly under high traffic. Implementing a load balancer and scaling your WebSocket server horizontally can help manage these connections more efficiently. Additionally, using a message broker or pub/sub system like Redis or Kafka can help distribute messages across multiple instances of your application, ensuring that all connected clients receive updates consistently.

For applications using SSE, managing server resources is typically less intensive compared to WebSockets, as SSE connections are simpler and less resource-intensive. However, you still need to consider the potential impact on server load, especially if your application has a large number of clients connected simultaneously. Techniques such as connection pooling and efficient message broadcasting can help mitigate performance issues.

Incorporating real-time features also necessitates robust error handling and user experience considerations. For both WebSockets and SSE, handling reconnections and managing connection states is crucial to providing a seamless user experience. Implementing logic to detect and handle disconnections, retries, and errors ensures that users receive updates reliably and that your application remains resilient in the face of network issues.

Security is another important aspect when integrating real-time features. With WebSockets, ensuring that connections are secure (using `wss://` for WebSocket connections) and validating incoming data to prevent injection attacks is essential. For SSE, while the protocol is less susceptible to certain types of attacks, ensuring that your server is protected against potential abuse, such as excessive connection requests, is still important.

Lastly, the choice between WebSockets and SSE should be guided by the specific use cases and requirements of your application. WebSockets offer greater flexibility for two-way communication and are suitable for applications with complex interactions. SSE, on the other hand, provides a simpler and more efficient solution for one-way updates. Evaluating these needs will help you select the most appropriate technology and ensure that your real-time features are implemented effectively.

By leveraging these technologies, you can significantly enhance the interactivity and responsiveness of your Next.js applications, providing users with real-time updates and a more engaging experience.

When implementing real-time features, security and error handling are paramount to ensure a smooth and secure user experience. With WebSockets, establishing secure connections is crucial to protect data integrity and prevent unauthorized access. To secure WebSocket connections, use the `wss` (WebSocket Secure) protocol rather than the plain `ws` protocol. This involves configuring your server with SSL/TLS certificates, which encrypt the data transmitted between the server and client, safeguarding it from eavesdropping and tampering.

In addition to using `wss`, consider implementing authentication mechanisms for WebSocket connections. This can be done by requiring clients to provide a token or some form of credential when initiating the connection. On the server side, you should verify these credentials before allowing the connection to proceed. This ensures that only authorized users can access the real-time features of your application.

For SSE, while the protocol is less complex than WebSockets, security considerations remain important. Ensure that your SSE endpoints are also served over HTTPS to protect the data transmitted from being intercepted. Similarly, implement authentication checks to restrict access to your SSE endpoints. You can achieve this by including authentication tokens or session identifiers in the initial connection request and verifying them on the server before streaming events.

Error handling is another critical aspect of implementing real-time features. WebSocket connections can be interrupted due to network issues, server errors, or other unforeseen problems. Both on the client and server sides, it's important to handle these errors gracefully. On the client side, implement logic to detect connection drops and attempt to reconnect automatically. This might involve setting up retry mechanisms with exponential backoff to avoid overwhelming the server with frequent reconnection attempts. On the server side, monitor WebSocket connections for errors and implement fallback mechanisms to ensure the reliability of your real-time features.

For SSE, error handling is somewhat more straightforward. The `EventSource` API provides built-in support for automatic reconnections. However, you should still handle scenarios where events are lost or the connection is temporarily disrupted. Implement mechanisms to ensure that critical events are re-sent if a connection is re-established. This may involve storing recent events on the server and re-sending them to the client upon reconnection.

Performance optimization is another key area to consider when implementing real-time features. For both WebSockets and SSE, efficient handling of messages and minimizing latency are crucial for a responsive user experience. Optimize the server-side logic to handle incoming messages and broadcast updates efficiently. This might involve using message queues or caching mechanisms to manage the flow of data and reduce the processing time for each message.

On the client side, ensure that your real-time updates are processed in a manner that doesn't adversely affect the user experience. For example, avoid performing heavy computations directly in response to real-time events, as this can lead to performance bottlenecks. Instead, offload such tasks to web workers or use asynchronous processing techniques to keep the main thread responsive.

To further enhance performance, consider using techniques such as batching updates or aggregating data on the server before sending it to the client. This reduces the frequency of messages sent and ensures that clients receive updates in a consolidated form, which can help to minimize the impact on network and rendering performance.

In summary, integrating real-time features into Next.js applications using WebSockets or SSE involves a combination of secure implementation practices, robust error handling, and performance optimization techniques. By carefully considering these aspects, you can build real-time functionalities that enhance user engagement while ensuring reliability, security, and efficiency.

CHAPTER 26: ADVANCED ROUTING TECHNIQUES

Routing in Next.js extends far beyond the basics, offering a robust set of tools and patterns for managing complex navigation and rendering scenarios. While earlier chapters may have covered fundamental routing concepts, this chapter explores more advanced techniques that cater to intricate applications requiring sophisticated navigation structures. Understanding and implementing these techniques can significantly enhance the functionality and user experience of your Next.js applications.

Nested routes represent a crucial advancement in routing. In traditional web applications, nested routes allow for a hierarchical structure of pages and components, where each level of nesting can have its own route. Next.js, by default, supports file-based routing where the file structure in the `pages` directory directly translates to routes. To implement nested routes in Next.js, you can leverage dynamic routing alongside nested file structures. For instance, if you need a route structure where `/dashboard/settings` is nested under `/dashboard`, you can create a directory structure within the `pages` folder like `/dashboard/index.js` and `/dashboard/settings/index.js`. This organization enables you to manage complex route hierarchies efficiently, with each component corresponding to a specific route segment.

Dynamic route matching is another advanced routing technique in Next.js that enhances the flexibility of your routes. Dynamic routing allows you to create routes with variable segments, making it possible to match different URLs using parameters. In Next.js, dynamic routes are defined by adding square brackets to the file names within the `pages` directory. For example, a file named `[id].js` within the `pages/posts` directory will match routes like `/posts/1` and `/posts/42`, with the `id` parameter dynamically available for use in the component. This approach facilitates the creation of pages that display data based on URL parameters, such as blog posts or user profiles.

When working with dynamic routes, it is essential to understand how to handle the route parameters effectively. In your component, you can use the `useRouter` hook from Next.js to access these parameters. This hook provides an object containing the route parameters, which can be used to fetch and display content dynamically. For instance, in a blog application, you might use the `id` parameter from the route to fetch and display the specific blog post associated with that ID.

Custom route handlers offer another layer of flexibility in Next.js routing. By default, Next.js routes are handled according to the file structure within the `pages` directory. However, there are scenarios where you might need to implement custom logic for handling routes. This can be achieved by using Next.js middleware or custom server configurations. Middleware allows you to intercept and modify requests before they reach your pages, providing an opportunity to implement custom routing logic. For example, you could use middleware to handle authentication checks, redirect users based on specific criteria, or modify request headers.

In Next.js, middleware can be implemented in the `middleware.js` file located at the root of your project. This file allows you to define custom logic that executes on every request, enabling you to manipulate the request and response objects as needed. Additionally, you can use custom servers with Next.js to gain even more control over routing. Custom servers, such as those built with Express.js or another Node.js framework, allow you to define custom routes and handlers outside of the default file-based routing system. This approach is particularly useful for integrating Next.js with other backend services or APIs, handling complex routing requirements, and managing server-side logic.

As you delve into these advanced routing techniques, it is crucial to balance complexity with maintainability. While advanced routing capabilities provide powerful tools for handling intricate scenarios, they can also introduce additional complexity to your application. To manage this complexity effectively, consider the following practices:

1. Modularize Route Logic: Break down complex routes into smaller, manageable components. This modular approach helps maintain clarity and facilitates easier debugging and testing.

2. Document Route Structures: Clearly document your route structures and custom routing logic to ensure that team members can understand and navigate the routing system effectively.

3. Optimize Performance: Keep performance considerations in mind when implementing advanced routing techniques. For example, be mindful of how dynamic routes impact server performance and optimize data fetching strategies accordingly.

4. Test Thoroughly: Ensure thorough testing of all routing

scenarios, including edge cases and potential error conditions. This helps identify issues early and ensures a smooth user experience across different routes.

By mastering these advanced routing techniques, you can create Next.js applications that offer a sophisticated and seamless navigation experience. Whether implementing nested routes, handling dynamic parameters, or integrating custom route handlers, these techniques provide the tools necessary to build complex and high-performing applications.

The implementation of custom route handlers is an advanced technique that extends the built-in routing capabilities of Next.js. These handlers offer a way to manage complex routing scenarios that go beyond the default file-based routing system. Custom handlers can be particularly useful when dealing with routing requirements that involve specific business logic, authentication rules, or URL rewriting.

To begin with custom route handling in Next.js, you can utilize the concept of API routes. API routes allow you to define server-side logic directly within the Next.js application, making it possible to handle requests and responses without needing a separate backend server. For instance, you might use API routes to handle complex routing rules or to process requests based on custom criteria before sending responses to the client. By creating files in the `pages/api` directory, you can define endpoints that respond to HTTP requests, enabling you to manage various backend functionalities directly within your Next.js application.

In addition to API routes, Next.js also supports custom server configurations using Node.js. By creating a custom server, you gain greater control over the request and response lifecycle, which can be useful for implementing advanced routing logic. For example, you might need to rewrite URLs based on specific patterns or redirect requests under certain conditions. To achieve this, you can create a custom server using Express.js or another Node.js framework and configure your routes accordingly. This approach allows you to integrate custom routing behaviors with your Next.js application, providing a high degree of flexibility in managing your routing requirements.

Moreover, custom route handlers can also be used to manage middleware functions that are executed before reaching the actual route handler. Middleware functions can perform tasks such as authentication checks, request logging, or URL validation, and they can be applied to specific routes or globally across the application. By leveraging middleware, you can enhance the security and functionality of your routing logic, ensuring that requests are processed according to your application's needs.

When dealing with advanced routing scenarios, it is important to consider the impact of your routing decisions on application performance. Complex routing logic can introduce additional overhead, so it is essential to optimize your routing configurations to maintain efficient performance. This includes minimizing the number of route handlers, avoiding unnecessary redirects or rewrites, and ensuring that your middleware functions are as efficient as possible.

Another consideration is the management of route state and transitions. In more complex applications, you may need to handle state changes that occur as users navigate between different routes. Next.js provides several tools for managing route state, including the `useRouter` hook, which allows you to programmatically navigate between routes and access the current route information. By combining this hook with state management solutions like React's Context API or external libraries such as Redux, you can maintain and synchronize route state effectively across your application.

Additionally, handling route transitions smoothly is crucial for maintaining a positive user experience. As users navigate between routes, it is important to manage transitions in a way that minimizes delays and visual disruptions. Techniques such as prefetching route data or implementing loading indicators can help improve the perceived performance of your application. Next.js supports automatic static optimization and prefetching, which can be leveraged to enhance route transition performance by loading data and components ahead of time.

In summary, advanced routing techniques in Next.js provide a range of options for managing complex navigation and rendering scenarios. By understanding and implementing nested routes, dynamic route matching, and custom route handlers, you can build sophisticated applications that meet diverse routing requirements. Additionally, optimizing routing performance and managing route state are essential considerations for ensuring a seamless user experience. With these advanced techniques, you can harness the full potential of Next.js routing to create robust and efficient web applications.

In addition to the considerations mentioned, managing state and transitions in complex routing scenarios is crucial for maintaining a smooth user experience. When navigating between routes, especially in applications with deeply nested routes or those that rely on dynamic parameters, it is essential to manage and persist state effectively. Next.js's routing system supports this by allowing you to pass state through the query parameters or leverage client-side state management libraries like Redux or Context API to handle state transitions seamlessly.

Dynamic routing is a significant aspect of advanced routing in Next.js. This technique enables you to create routes that are based on variable parts of the URL. Dynamic routes are defined using file names enclosed in brackets, such as `[id].js` for a route where `id` is a variable. This flexibility allows for the creation of routes that can handle a range of URL structures without needing to define each possible path explicitly. For instance, an e-commerce site might use dynamic routing to generate product pages based on unique product IDs.

However, while dynamic routing offers substantial flexibility, it also requires careful handling to ensure that the application performs efficiently. One key aspect to manage is the data fetching associated with dynamic routes. Next.js provides several methods for fetching data, including `getStaticProps` for static generation and `getServerSideProps` for server-side rendering. Each method has its use cases and performance implications. When working with dynamic routes, it is important to choose the appropriate data-fetching strategy based on the nature of the data and how frequently it changes.

Nested routes further enhance the routing capabilities by allowing for hierarchical URL structures. This is particularly useful in applications with a complex layout, such as dashboards or admin panels. To implement nested routes in Next.js, you can structure your `pages` directory to mirror the desired route hierarchy. For example, placing a file in `pages/dashboard/settings.js` would correspond to the `/dashboard/settings` route. This approach simplifies the management of related routes and helps maintain a logical and organized routing structure.

Managing complex routing scenarios also involves handling URL parameters and query strings effectively. In Next.js, URL parameters are accessed through the `useRouter` hook from the `next/router` package. This hook provides access to the current route's parameters and query strings, allowing you to extract and use these values within your components. Proper handling of these parameters is crucial for ensuring that the application behaves as expected and that navigation between different states is handled correctly.

Customizing routing behaviors can also include implementing advanced features like route guards and conditional redirects. Route guards can restrict access to certain routes based on user authentication or permissions. For instance, you might implement a guard that checks whether a user is logged in before allowing access to a particular page. Conditional redirects allow you to redirect users based on specific conditions, such as redirecting to a login page if they attempt to access a restricted route. These features enhance the security and usability of your application, ensuring that users are guided appropriately based on their context and permissions.

Error handling is another critical aspect of advanced routing. In complex routing scenarios, it is important to provide meaningful feedback to users in the event of errors or invalid routes. Next.js offers built-in error pages, but you can also create custom error handling pages to provide a more tailored experience. Handling errors gracefully and providing users with clear information about what went wrong helps maintain a positive user experience even when issues arise.

In summary, advanced routing techniques in Next.js offer powerful tools for managing complex navigation scenarios. By understanding and implementing dynamic routing, nested routes, and custom route handlers, you can create sophisticated routing structures that enhance the functionality and user experience of your application. Effective state management, data fetching strategies, and error handling are crucial for ensuring that these advanced routing techniques are applied successfully. As you work with Next.js's routing capabilities, remember to balance flexibility with performance and maintainability to build robust and user-friendly applications.

CHAPTER 27: BUILDING PROGRESSIVE WEB APPS (PWAS)

Progressive Web Apps (PWAs) represent a significant evolution in web application development, providing users with a native app-like experience while leveraging the capabilities of the web. They combine the best features of web and mobile applications, including offline functionality, performance improvements, and an enhanced user experience. In this chapter, we will delve into the process of transforming a Next.js application into a PWA, covering key aspects such as setting up service workers, implementing caching strategies, and ensuring robust offline support.

To begin with, understanding the fundamental components of a PWA is crucial. A PWA is designed to work seamlessly across different platforms, providing a reliable and engaging user experience. This is achieved through three primary technologies: service workers, a web app manifest, and responsive design. Each plays a pivotal role in enhancing the performance and functionality of your web application.

Service workers are scripts that run in the background, separate from the web page, enabling features such as offline support and push notifications. They act as a network proxy, intercepting network requests and serving cached responses when the user is offline or on a slow network. To integrate a service worker into a Next.js application, you can use libraries like `next-pwa`, which simplifies the process of setting up and configuring service workers. This library provides an easy way to add PWA capabilities to your application with minimal configuration.

Once you have integrated a service worker, configuring caching strategies is essential for optimizing performance and ensuring that your application remains functional offline. Caching strategies dictate how and when resources are stored and retrieved. Common strategies include cache-first, network-first, and stale-while-revalidate. Each strategy serves a different purpose and can be tailored to meet the specific needs of your application. For instance, a cache-first strategy might be used for static assets such as images and stylesheets, ensuring that these resources are always available even when the network is unreliable. In contrast, a network-first strategy might be employed for dynamic content, allowing the application to fetch the latest data while falling back on cached content if the network is unavailable.

Another critical aspect of building a PWA is creating a web app manifest. The web app manifest is a JSON file that provides metadata about your application, such as its name, icons, and theme colors. This file is used to configure how your PWA appears when installed on a user's device. For example, it allows you to specify the application's icon, which will be displayed on the home screen or app launcher, and define the theme color, which affects the appearance of the browser's address bar. By including a manifest file in your Next.js application, you ensure that users have a consistent and branded experience when interacting with your PWA.

Responsive design is another key component of PWAs, ensuring that your application provides a seamless experience across various devices and screen sizes. Next.js facilitates responsive design through its built-in support for CSS modules and styled-components. By leveraging these tools, you can create flexible layouts that adapt to different screen sizes, enhancing the usability of your application on mobile devices and tablets.

Additionally, incorporating features such as push notifications can further enhance the user experience by keeping users informed and engaged with your application. Push notifications allow you to send timely updates and alerts to users, even when they are not actively using the app. To implement push notifications in a Next.js PWA, you will need to integrate with a push notification service, such as Firebase Cloud Messaging (FCM), and configure the service worker to handle incoming notifications. This involves setting up the necessary permissions, managing notification payloads, and implementing appropriate handlers within the service worker script.

Testing and debugging are crucial steps in the development process of a PWA. Given the complexity of PWAs and their reliance on service workers and caching, it is important to thoroughly test the application to ensure that it functions as expected in various scenarios. Tools such as Lighthouse, available in Chrome DevTools, can be used to audit your PWA and provide actionable insights on performance, accessibility, and best practices. Lighthouse assesses the application's adherence to PWA standards and offers recommendations for improvements.

Furthermore, monitoring the performance and reliability of your PWA in production is essential for maintaining a high-quality user experience. Implementing monitoring and analytics tools can help track user interactions, identify potential issues, and gather valuable feedback for ongoing improvements. By analyzing data such as user engagement, network requests, and error rates, you can make informed decisions on how to optimize your PWA and address any challenges that arise.

In summary, transforming a Next.js application into a Progressive Web App involves several key steps, including setting up service workers, configuring caching strategies, creating a web app manifest, and ensuring responsive design. By leveraging these technologies and best practices, you can enhance the performance, reliability, and user experience of your application, providing users with a seamless and engaging experience that rivals native apps.

Creating a web app manifest involves defining essential properties that allow users to add your web application to their home screens, configure the application's appearance, and provide a seamless launch experience. The manifest file typically includes parameters such as the application's name, short name, start URL, display mode, background color, theme color, and a set of icons in various sizes. These details ensure that when users install your PWA on their devices, it provides a cohesive and branded look and feel, similar to native apps.

Integrating the manifest into your Next.js application requires placing the `manifest.json` file in the `public` directory and linking it in your HTML head. This can be achieved by modifying the `_document.js` file within your Next.js project. Here, you will include a link tag that points to the manifest file, enabling browsers to recognize and utilize it. This step is crucial for the web app manifest to function correctly, as it allows browsers to fetch the file and apply its configurations.

In addition to the manifest and service workers, another aspect of PWAs is ensuring that your application provides an optimal experience across various devices and network conditions. This involves implementing responsive design practices to ensure that your application looks and performs well on different screen sizes and orientations. Using CSS media queries, flexible grid layouts, and scalable vector graphics (SVGs) can help maintain a consistent and adaptive user interface.

Performance optimization is a fundamental component of PWAs, and it involves more than just setting up caching. Techniques such as lazy loading, code splitting, and preloading are essential for enhancing the speed and responsiveness of your application. Lazy loading defers the loading of non-essential resources until they are needed, which reduces the initial load time and improves overall performance. Code splitting breaks down your application's JavaScript into smaller chunks, allowing users to download only the necessary parts of your application when they are needed. Preloading key resources can also ensure that critical assets are available immediately when required, further improving the user experience.

Ensuring that your PWA performs well in various network conditions is another important consideration. Implementing strategies such as background synchronization and network resilience can help maintain a seamless user experience even when connectivity is intermittent. Background synchronization allows your application to defer updates and send data when a stable connection is available, reducing the impact of network fluctuations on user interactions. Network resilience techniques, such as using service workers to handle fetch requests and provide fallback responses, can help mitigate the effects of unreliable networks and enhance the reliability of your application.

User engagement features, such as push notifications, are another significant benefit of PWAs. Push notifications allow you to communicate with users even when they are not actively using your application, providing timely updates, alerts, and promotional messages. Integrating push notifications involves configuring a push notification service, such as Firebase Cloud Messaging (FCM), and handling subscription and notification logic within your service worker. Ensuring that notifications are relevant and non-intrusive is key to maintaining user engagement without causing annoyance.

Finally, testing and debugging are critical to ensuring that your PWA functions correctly across different environments and devices. Tools such as Lighthouse, a built-in auditing tool in Chrome DevTools, can help you evaluate your application's PWA performance, accessibility, best practices, and SEO. Running audits with Lighthouse provides actionable insights into areas that need improvement, helping you refine your PWA to meet industry standards and user expectations.

In summary, transforming a Next.js application into a Progressive Web App involves a comprehensive approach that includes setting up service workers, configuring caching strategies, creating a web app manifest, and ensuring optimal performance and user engagement. By implementing these techniques, you can enhance the user experience, provide reliable and performant functionality, and deliver a native app-like experience through the web. As PWAs continue to evolve, staying informed about best practices and emerging technologies will be crucial for maintaining a competitive edge and delivering exceptional web applications.

Optimizing a Progressive Web App (PWA) also involves ensuring that the app's interactions are seamless and responsive, even in offline or low-network conditions. One advanced technique is the implementation of background sync, which allows the app to defer tasks, such as sending data to a server, until a stable network connection is available. This ensures that user actions are not lost if they occur during a period of poor connectivity. The Background Sync API, which is supported by many modern browsers, provides this functionality by allowing you to register tasks that the service worker can perform when connectivity is restored.

Another key aspect of building effective PWAs is ensuring that they handle navigation and routing efficiently. In a PWA, routing can be managed through the service worker, which intercepts network requests and serves cached responses when appropriate. This approach not only enhances the app's offline capabilities but also ensures that it can load quickly and reliably under varying network conditions. Implementing service worker-based routing requires careful consideration of cache strategies, such as cache-first, network-first, and stale-while-revalidate approaches, each of which has its use cases and implications for performance and user experience.

Moreover, integrating push notifications into your PWA can significantly enhance user engagement by providing timely updates and interactions. Push notifications allow your app to communicate with users even when the application is not actively open. To implement push notifications, you need to configure your service worker to handle push events and manage notification display. Additionally, you must set up a push service, which can be handled using various third-party services or custom solutions that interact with the Push API and Notification API.

Testing and debugging PWAs is crucial to ensure that they perform well across different scenarios and devices. Tools like Lighthouse, which is integrated into Chrome DevTools, provide valuable insights into your app's performance, accessibility, and PWA compliance. Lighthouse can audit various aspects of your PWA, including its responsiveness, offline capabilities, and adherence to best practices, offering recommendations for improvements. Regular testing on real devices and under different network conditions is also essential to identify and address potential issues that automated tools may not catch.

In conclusion, building a Progressive Web App with Next.js involves a series of steps to transform a standard web application into one that provides a robust, app-like experience. By setting up service workers, implementing effective caching strategies, integrating offline support, and ensuring proper routing and notifications, you can create a PWA that delivers high performance, reliability, and user engagement. The process also involves continuous testing and optimization to adapt to evolving standards and user expectations, ensuring that your application remains cutting-edge and competitive in a rapidly advancing digital landscape.

CHAPTER 28: INTEGRATING WITH HEADLESS CMS

The integration of a headless Content Management System (CMS) with Next.js represents a powerful approach to managing and delivering content in modern web applications. Unlike traditional CMS platforms, which couple content management with presentation, headless CMSs operate independently of the front-end, providing content through APIs. This separation allows developers to use Next.js for its rich, React-based features while leveraging the headless CMS for flexible and scalable content management.

To begin integrating a headless CMS with Next.js, the first step involves selecting a suitable headless CMS platform. Popular choices include Contentful, Strapi, and Sanity, each offering robust API interfaces and various features suited to different project needs. Once a CMS is chosen, the next step is to set up the CMS and configure it to serve the content required by your Next.js application.

The setup process generally involves creating content types and defining their fields within the CMS. Content types could range from blog posts and product listings to custom entities relevant to your application. For example, if you are building a blog, you might create content types for articles, authors, and categories. Each content type is configured with fields such as titles, body text, images, and metadata. This configuration ensures that your content is structured in a way that facilitates efficient querying and retrieval.

With the content model in place, the integration with Next.js can proceed by establishing a connection between the CMS and your application. This typically involves using the CMS's API to fetch content. Most headless CMSs provide RESTful or GraphQL APIs for this purpose. In Next.js, you can utilize these APIs to retrieve data at build time using `getStaticProps` or dynamically on the server with `getServerSideProps`, depending on your content needs and update frequency.

For example, when using Contentful with Next.js, you would start by installing the Contentful SDK and configuring it with your space ID and access token. This setup allows Next.js to communicate with Contentful's API. You can then create asynchronous functions to fetch the necessary content from Contentful, ensuring that your application can dynamically retrieve and render this content. The data fetched from the CMS can be passed to your React components as props, where it can be used to render pages with up-to-date content.

Managing content workflows involves ensuring that content updates in the CMS are reflected in the Next.js application in a timely and efficient manner. This may include setting up webhooks provided by the CMS to trigger rebuilds or invalidations of the application's cache when content changes. Webhooks notify your Next.js application of content updates, allowing you to regenerate static pages and serve the latest content without manual intervention. Implementing this mechanism ensures that users always see the most recent content, enhancing the overall user experience.

Another consideration in integrating a headless CMS with Next.js is managing authentication and access control. Depending on the CMS and the level of content protection required, you may need to implement authentication mechanisms to control access to certain parts of the content. For instance, some CMS platforms allow for role-based access control (RBAC), enabling you to manage who can create, edit, or publish content. This functionality helps maintain the integrity and security of your content management processes.

Testing and debugging the integration between Next.js and a headless CMS is essential to ensure that content is retrieved and displayed correctly. This involves verifying that the API requests are functioning as expected, handling any errors gracefully, and ensuring that the content is rendered correctly in your application. Utilizing tools like Postman for API testing and browser developer tools for debugging can assist in identifying and resolving issues related to content retrieval and display.

In summary, integrating a headless CMS with Next.js involves selecting an appropriate CMS, configuring it to manage your content, and setting up the necessary API connections to fetch and display content within your application. By leveraging the flexibility of a headless CMS and the capabilities of Next.js, you can create a dynamic and efficient content management system that meets the needs of modern web applications.

Managing content workflows within a headless CMS integration involves orchestrating how content is created, updated, and published. The primary advantage of using a headless CMS is its ability to decouple content management from the presentation layer, providing a flexible environment for content creators while allowing developers to handle content delivery as needed. Effective content workflow management ensures that content updates are accurately reflected in your Next.js application and that content creation processes are streamlined.

A key aspect of managing content workflows is implementing version control and approval processes. Many headless CMS platforms offer features that allow content creators to draft and review content before publishing. This workflow helps maintain content quality and consistency. For instance, in Contentful, you can use content publishing workflows to manage drafts, reviews, and final approvals. Similarly, in Strapi, you can set up custom roles and permissions to control who can create, edit, or publish content. This level of control is crucial for ensuring that only validated content appears on your site, reducing the risk of errors or inconsistencies.

Once content is published, it needs to be reflected in the Next.js application. This process involves querying the CMS API to fetch the latest content updates. For applications requiring real-time updates, implementing webhook notifications can be beneficial. Many headless CMS platforms support webhooks, which trigger an endpoint in your Next.js application whenever content changes. By setting up a webhook, you can automate the process of invalidating cached content and triggering a re-render or rebuild of affected pages. This ensures that your application always displays the most current content without manual intervention.

Another important consideration is handling content caching. For performance optimization, it's essential to cache the content retrieved from the CMS to reduce the load on the API and improve page load times. In Next.js, this can be achieved using static site generation (SSG) or incremental static regeneration (ISR). By using SSG with `getStaticProps`, you can generate static pages at build time, which are then served from a CDN, providing fast load times and reducing server load. For content that updates frequently but does not require real-time updates, ISR allows you to update static pages incrementally, ensuring that users receive fresh content without the need for a full rebuild.

For dynamic content that changes more frequently, such as user-generated content or real-time updates, server-side rendering (SSR) can be employed. With SSR, Next.js fetches content from the CMS on each request, ensuring that users see the latest content. This approach, while more resource-intensive than static generation, is suitable for scenarios where content freshness is critical.

Additionally, managing relationships between content types is another aspect of integrating with a headless CMS. Many headless CMS platforms allow you to establish relationships between different content types, such as linking blog posts to authors or categories. When fetching related content, ensure that your queries and data handling accommodate these relationships. For instance, if you have a blog post that references an author, you will need to fetch both the blog post and the author's details to render them correctly in your Next.js application.

Incorporating search functionality is also crucial for improving the user experience. Many headless CMS platforms offer search capabilities or integration with external search services. For example, integrating with services like Algolia or Elasticsearch can enhance search performance and provide users with an efficient way to find content within your application. Implementing a search feature involves configuring the CMS to index content and integrating the search functionality into your Next.js application, allowing users to query and retrieve relevant content seamlessly.

Finally, testing and debugging the integration are essential to ensure a smooth user experience. Regularly test your content retrieval processes, content updates, and rendering logic to identify and resolve issues promptly. Tools like Postman can help in testing API endpoints, while browser developer tools can assist in debugging issues related to data fetching and rendering in your Next.js application.

In summary, integrating a headless CMS with Next.js involves setting up content models, retrieving and displaying content through APIs, and managing content workflows efficiently. By leveraging features such as version control, webhooks, caching strategies, and search capabilities, you can create a robust content management system that enhances the user experience while maintaining flexibility and scalability. As headless CMS platforms continue to evolve, staying updated with best practices and emerging technologies will further enhance your ability to manage and deliver content effectively in modern web applications.

When integrating a headless CMS with Next.js, developers often encounter challenges related to content formatting and presentation. Each CMS has its own way of structuring content, which can vary significantly from the default data models in Next.js. Therefore, transforming this content into a format that suits your application's requirements is essential. This involves mapping the data received from the CMS to the components used in your Next.js application, ensuring that the content is not only accurate but also visually appealing and functional.

To handle this transformation effectively, create a set of utility functions or data transformation layers. These functions should parse and format the raw data from the CMS, making it compatible with your React components. For instance, if you are using a CMS like Sanity, you might need to handle rich text fields and embedded media. Sanity provides its own rich text editor, which stores content in a structured format. To render this content in Next.js, you may need to use the Sanity client library to fetch the data and then process it into HTML or React components using a rich text renderer such as `@portabletext/react`.

Managing media assets is another crucial aspect of integrating a headless CMS. Many CMS platforms support various media types, such as images, videos, and documents, which need to be handled appropriately. Typically, media files are stored in cloud-based storage and referenced through URLs in the CMS. To integrate these assets into your Next.js application, ensure that your application can handle external URLs, manage image optimization, and provide fallback mechanisms in case assets are unavailable. Next.js's built-in Image component can be particularly useful for handling responsive images and optimizing performance by automatically adjusting image sizes and formats.

Handling different content types within your application often involves setting up conditional rendering logic. This ensures that each type of content is displayed in the most appropriate manner. For instance, blog posts may be displayed with a different layout compared to product pages or user profiles. By leveraging Next.js's dynamic routing capabilities, you can create a flexible routing structure that caters to various content types, using parameters and query strings to fetch and display the relevant content.

Testing and debugging are essential in the process of integrating a headless CMS with Next.js. It's important to ensure that content is correctly fetched, displayed, and updated across different scenarios. Implementing automated tests using tools such as Jest and React Testing Library can help identify and resolve issues early. Additionally, thorough manual testing is necessary to verify the end-to-end functionality of content delivery and presentation.

Finally, consider the implications of content localization and internationalization. Many applications need to support multiple languages or regional variations of content. Headless CMS platforms often offer localization features, allowing you to manage different language versions of content. When integrating with Next.js, you will need to handle language-specific routes and content variations. This involves configuring your application to serve the correct content based on the user's language preferences and implementing mechanisms to switch between different locales seamlessly.

The process of integrating a headless CMS with Next.js involves several intricate steps, from initial setup and data retrieval to content transformation and presentation. By following best practices in data handling, caching, and testing, you can create a robust and dynamic application that leverages the flexibility of a headless CMS while providing a high-quality user experience.

CHAPTER 29: IMPLEMENTING SEARCH FUNCTIONALITY

In the landscape of modern web applications, search functionality serves as a cornerstone for enhancing user experience by enabling users to quickly locate information. Implementing effective search features in Next.js applications involves choosing the right approach based on the application's needs and scale. This chapter provides a comprehensive guide on integrating search capabilities, examining client-side and server-side solutions, as well as leveraging third-party search services.

To begin with, implementing client-side search is a straightforward approach for applications with relatively small datasets or when immediate feedback is necessary. This method involves executing search queries directly in the user's browser, usually by filtering data that has already been loaded. The simplicity of client-side search lies in its implementation: it requires minimal server-side interaction, making it ideal for static data or small collections. Common techniques for client-side search include using JavaScript libraries such as Fuse.js or implementing custom search algorithms. These libraries often provide features like fuzzy searching and ranking, which enhance the search experience by offering relevant results even when user input is imprecise.

For larger datasets or more dynamic content, server-side search becomes essential. This approach involves delegating the search operations to the server, where the data is stored and queried. Server-side search can handle larger volumes of data efficiently by performing complex queries and aggregations. Implementing server-side search in a Next.js application typically involves setting up an API endpoint that processes search requests. This endpoint interacts with a database or search index to retrieve relevant results, which are then sent back to the client. Technologies like Elasticsearch or Algolia are commonly used to power server-side search functionalities. Elasticsearch, for example, is a distributed search engine capable of full-text search and real-time analytics, while Algolia offers a hosted search solution with a focus on speed and relevance.

Integrating search functionality often requires considering how to handle and display search results. For instance, implementing pagination or infinite scrolling can help manage large result sets, improving performance and user experience. Pagination involves dividing search results into pages and allowing users to navigate between them, whereas infinite scrolling automatically loads more results as the user scrolls down the page. Both methods aim to balance user interaction with performance considerations, and the choice between them depends on the specific needs of the application.

Beyond traditional search approaches, modern applications frequently integrate third-party search services to leverage advanced features and scalability. These services, such as Algolia and Swiftype, offer out-of-the-box solutions for indexing and querying large datasets with minimal configuration. They often provide a range of features including typo tolerance, relevance tuning, and analytics.

Integrating a third-party search service involves setting up API connections between the service and your Next.js application. The integration process typically includes configuring the service with your data schema, sending search queries from the client or server, and processing the search results to present them in the application. These services can significantly reduce development time and effort while delivering powerful search capabilities.

Security and performance are critical aspects of implementing search functionality, regardless of the approach chosen. When dealing with server-side search, it's important to ensure that search queries are sanitized to prevent injection attacks and that user data is protected. Performance optimization involves strategies such as caching frequent queries or results to reduce load times and server load. On the client-side, optimizing search performance can include techniques such as debouncing search input to limit the number of queries sent to the server and using efficient data structures for search operations.

In summary, implementing search functionality in a Next.js application requires a thoughtful approach to meet the needs of users and handle data efficiently. Whether opting for client-side search for simplicity, server-side search for handling larger datasets, or third-party services for advanced features, it is crucial to integrate search features that are both effective and scalable. As you advance through the implementation process, consider the trade-offs and benefits of each approach, and align your choice with the specific requirements of your application to deliver a robust and user-friendly search experience.

Implementing search functionality often involves integrating third-party search services to leverage advanced features and scalability that might be challenging to develop in-house. Services such as Algolia, ElasticSearch, and Typesense offer powerful search capabilities with various features including full-text search, faceting, and real-time indexing.

Algolia is renowned for its speed and ease of integration. It provides a hosted search API that allows developers to add search functionality without managing infrastructure. To integrate Algolia with a Next.js application, you would start by creating an Algolia account and indexing your data into Algolia's service. The next step involves setting up the Algolia client in your Next.js application. This typically includes installing the Algolia client library and configuring it with your API keys. Once configured, you can query Algolia's indices from your Next.js server-side code or directly from client-side code, depending on the architecture of your application. Algolia also provides an extensive library of UI components to help streamline the development of search interfaces.

Elasticsearch, another robust solution, is a distributed search engine that offers advanced search capabilities and real-time analytics. Unlike Algolia, Elasticsearch requires managing a search cluster, which can add complexity but provides greater flexibility and control. To use Elasticsearch with Next.js, you need to set up an Elasticsearch cluster, either on-premises or through a managed service like Elastic Cloud. After setting up the cluster, you would integrate it with your Next.js application by using the Elasticsearch client library to perform searches and retrieve results. Elasticsearch's powerful querying capabilities allow for complex searches, including full-text searches, aggregations, and filtering, making it suitable for applications with extensive search requirements.

Typesense is another third-party search service that provides a balance between simplicity and performance. It offers a straightforward setup process and an intuitive API for integrating search capabilities. Similar to Algolia and Elasticsearch, integrating Typesense involves creating an account, indexing your data, and then using the Typesense client library in your Next.js application. Typesense's API is designed to be easy to use, with features such as typo tolerance and relevance tuning, which help to improve the search experience for users.

When integrating any third-party search service, it is important to consider the impact on performance and user experience. Search services often provide advanced caching and indexing features to ensure fast response times, but the effectiveness of these features can depend on the volume of data and the complexity of the queries. It is also crucial to manage API usage efficiently to avoid exceeding rate limits or incurring unexpected costs. Implementing search involves not only fetching and displaying results but also managing user interactions, such as query suggestions and result ranking, to enhance the search experience.

In addition to integrating with external search services, you may need to handle search-related challenges such as internationalization and localization. If your application supports multiple languages or regions, you will need to ensure that your search functionality accommodates different character sets and languages. Some search services offer built-in support for multilingual search, which can simplify the process. For client-side and server-side searches, you may need to implement additional logic to handle different languages and ensure that search results are relevant and accurate for users across various locales.

Another critical aspect of implementing search functionality is security and privacy. When handling user queries and search results, it is essential to ensure that sensitive data is protected and that your search implementation adheres to best practices for data privacy. This includes securing API keys, implementing authentication and authorization mechanisms for sensitive data, and ensuring that search logs and user data are handled in compliance with relevant regulations.

To summarize, implementing search functionality in Next.js applications involves choosing the right approach based on the application's scale and needs. Client-side search is suitable for small datasets and provides immediate feedback, while server-side search and third-party services offer solutions for larger, more complex search requirements. By integrating third-party search services such as Algolia, Elasticsearch, or Typesense, you can enhance your application's search capabilities and provide a better user experience. Addressing challenges such as internationalization, localization, and security will further ensure that your search functionality is robust and effective.

When implementing search functionality, careful attention must be paid to the user interface and experience to ensure that the search feature is both intuitive and effective. This involves not only integrating the search service but also designing an interface that supports user interaction and provides meaningful results.

For client-side search, the search component typically needs to handle user input and display results dynamically. This often involves using JavaScript to filter data on the client side. A common approach is to use libraries such as Fuse.js, which provide fuzzy searching capabilities. Fuse.js allows for client-side searching through a dataset by providing functionalities for exact and fuzzy matching, which is especially useful when dealing with large datasets that do not require server-side querying.

The client-side search implementation involves setting up a search input field and binding it to a function that performs the search operation. As users type, the search function processes the input, queries the dataset, and updates the displayed results in real-time. This method is best suited for smaller datasets where the entire dataset can be loaded into the client's memory without performance issues. For larger datasets, client-side search might become impractical due to memory and performance constraints.

In contrast, server-side search is ideal for handling larger datasets or complex queries. With server-side search, the search query is sent to the server, which processes it and returns the results. This method is typically implemented using a combination of API routes in Next.js and a search service like Elasticsearch or Algolia. The server-side search process involves receiving search requests from the client, querying the search service, and then returning the results to the client. This approach not only offloads the search processing from the client but also allows for more complex and efficient querying, leveraging the capabilities of the search service.

An important aspect of server-side search is managing the query performance and ensuring scalability. This involves optimizing the search queries to reduce latency and efficiently handle large volumes of data. Techniques such as query optimization, indexing, and caching are essential to achieving high performance in server-side search. Additionally, implementing pagination or infinite scrolling can enhance the user experience by managing the volume of results displayed at once and reducing the load on both the server and the client.

Integrating with third-party search services often involves additional considerations, such as managing API keys and handling rate limits imposed by the service providers. Most search services provide documentation and SDKs to facilitate integration and offer best practices for optimizing the search experience. Ensuring robust error handling is crucial when working with third-party services, as network issues, service outages, or API changes can affect the search functionality. Implementing error handling mechanisms such as retries, fallbacks, and user notifications can help manage these challenges and maintain a smooth user experience.

Additionally, search functionality should be complemented with features such as search suggestions, autocomplete, and filters to improve usability. Search suggestions and autocomplete provide users with real-time suggestions as they type, helping them refine their queries and find relevant results more quickly. Filters enable users to narrow down search results based on specific criteria, such as categories, tags, or date ranges, enhancing the relevance and precision of the search results.

To summarize, implementing search functionality in Next.js applications involves several key considerations, including choosing the right approach—whether client-side, server-side, or a combination of both—integrating with third-party search services, and designing a user-friendly interface. By addressing these aspects, developers can create effective and scalable search features that enhance user engagement and provide a seamless experience.

CHAPTER 30:
BUILDING AND USING
CUSTOM HOOKS

In modern React development, custom hooks have emerged as a powerful tool for managing and reusing logic across components. By allowing developers to encapsulate stateful logic and side effects into reusable functions, custom hooks offer a clean and modular approach to code organization and functionality. This chapter delves into the creation and utilization of custom hooks within Next.js applications, emphasizing their role in enhancing code reusability and maintainability.

The fundamental concept behind custom hooks is to abstract logic that is shared between components into standalone functions. These hooks, prefixed with "use" as per React's convention, enable developers to extract complex logic from components, making the code more readable and manageable. For instance, consider a scenario where multiple components require similar functionality, such as managing form input states or fetching data from an API. Instead of duplicating the same logic in each component, you can encapsulate it in a custom hook and use it wherever needed.

Creating a custom hook involves defining a function that uses built-in React hooks, such as `useState` or `useEffect`, to manage state or handle side effects. The custom hook can then be imported and utilized in any component requiring that specific functionality. For example, a custom hook for managing form input might look like this:

```javascript
import { useState } from 'react';

function useForm(initialValues) {
 const [values, setValues] useState(initialValues);

 const handleChange (event) > {
 const { name, value } event.target;
 setValues((prevValues) > ({
  ...prevValues,
  [name]: value,
 }));
 };

 return {
 values,
 handleChange,
 };
}
export default useForm;
```

In this example, the `useForm` hook manages form state and updates it based on user input. By encapsulating this logic into a hook, you can reuse it across different components without repeating the same code. To use this hook in a component, you simply import it and call it within the component's function:

```javascript
import useForm from './useForm';

function MyForm() {
 const { values, handleChange } useForm({ name: ", email: " });

 return (
```

```
<form>
 <input
  type"text"
  name"name"
  value{values.name}
  onChange{handleChange}
 />
 <input
  type"email"
  name"email"
  value{values.email}
  onChange{handleChange}
 />
</form>
);
}
```

Custom hooks can also manage more complex scenarios involving side effects, such as data fetching or subscriptions. For instance, a custom hook for data fetching might use `useEffect` to initiate an API call and `useState` to store the fetched data. Consider the following example of a hook that fetches data from an API:

```javascript
import { useState, useEffect } from 'react';

function useFetch(url) {
 const [data, setData] useState(null);
 const [loading, setLoading] useState(true);
 const [error, setError] useState(null);

 useEffect(() > {
  async function fetchData() {
   try {
    const response await fetch(url);
```

```javascript
  if (!response.ok) {
    throw new Error('Network response was not ok');
  }
  const result  await response.json();
  setData(result);
  } catch (error) {
  setError(error);
  } finally {
  setLoading(false);
  }
 }

  fetchData();
 }, [url]);

 return { data, loading, error };
}

export default useFetch;
```

In this `useFetch` hook, `useEffect` is used to perform the data fetching operation when the component mounts or when the URL changes. The hook returns the fetched data, a loading state, and any potential errors, which can be utilized in any component:

```javascript
import useFetch from './useFetch';

function DataDisplayComponent() {
    const { data, loading, error }    useFetch('https://api.example.com/data');

  if (loading) return <div>Loading...</div>;
 if (error) return <div>Error: {error.message}</div>;

 return (
  <div>
```

```
  {data.map(item > (
   <div key{item.id}>{item.name}</div>
  ))}
  </div>
 );
}
` ` `
```

Through these examples, it is evident that custom hooks play a crucial role in streamlining code by encapsulating reusable logic and managing state and side effects in a clean and modular fashion. Their flexibility and composability enable developers to handle complex scenarios with ease, contributing to a more maintainable and scalable codebase. As you advance in your Next.js development journey, leveraging custom hooks will significantly enhance your ability to write efficient and organized React code.

To further illustrate the use of custom hooks in Next.js applications, let's delve into scenarios where they can provide substantial benefits, particularly in managing side effects and data fetching. Custom hooks are especially valuable in these contexts because they allow you to abstract away complex logic and maintain a clean separation of concerns within your components.

Consider a situation where multiple components in your Next.js application need to fetch and display data from an external API. Without custom hooks, you might end up duplicating the data fetching logic across different components, leading to redundancy and increased potential for bugs. Instead, you can create a custom hook to handle the data fetching and state management, which can then be reused wherever needed.

Here is an example of a custom hook for fetching data from an API:

```javascript
import { useState, useEffect } from 'react';

function useFetch(url) {
 const [data, setData] useState(null);
 const [loading, setLoading] useState(true);
 const [error, setError] useState(null);

  useEffect(() > {
   const fetchData  async () > {
    try {
     const response  await fetch(url);
     if (!response.ok) {
      throw new Error('Network response was not ok');
     }
     const result  await response.json();
     setData(result);
    } catch (error) {
     setError(error);
    } finally {
     setLoading(false);
    }
   };

    fetchData();
  }, [url]);

  return { data, loading, error };
}

export default useFetch;
```

In this `useFetch` hook, the `useEffect` hook is used to perform the data fetching asynchronously when the component mounts or when the `url` dependency changes. The hook manages three pieces of state: `data` to store the fetched data, `loading` to indicate whether the request is in progress, and `error` to capture any errors that occur during the fetch operation. By using this hook, components can handle data fetching with minimal boilerplate code.

To use the `useFetch` hook in a component, you would do the following:

```javascript
import useFetch from './useFetch';

function DataDisplay() {
    const { data, loading, error }    useFetch('https://
api.example.com/data');

  if (loading) return <p>Loading...</p>;
  if (error) return <p>Error: {error.message}</p>;

  return (
   <div>
    <h1>Data</h1>
    <pre>{JSON.stringify(data, null, 2)}</pre>
   </div>
  );
}

export default DataDisplay;
```

In this component, the `useFetch` hook abstracts away the data fetching logic and provides a simple API to access the results. The component handles different states (loading, error, and data) based on the values returned by the hook. This approach keeps the component logic concise and focused on rendering the UI.

Beyond handling data fetching, custom hooks can also be used to encapsulate more complex state management logic. For example, a custom hook might be used to manage the state of a multi-step form. By breaking down the form logic into a custom hook, you can avoid cluttering the component with intricate state management code.

Here's an example of a custom hook managing a multi-step form:

```javascript
import { useState } from 'react';

function useMultiStepForm(initialValues, steps) {
 const [values, setValues] useState(initialValues);
 const [currentStep, setCurrentStep] useState(0);

 const handleChange (event) > {
 const { name, value } event.target;
 setValues((prevValues) > ({
   ...prevValues,
   [name]: value,
 }));
 };

 const nextStep () > {
     setCurrentStep((prevStep) > Math.min(prevStep + 1,
steps.length - 1));
 };

 const prevStep () > {
 setCurrentStep((prevStep) > Math.max(prevStep - 1, 0));
 };

 return {
 values,
 currentStep,
 handleChange,
 nextStep,
 prevStep,
 step: steps[currentStep],
 };
}
```

```
export default useMultiStepForm;
` ` `
```

In this `useMultiStepForm` hook, `useState` is used to manage the form values and the current step of the form. The `handleChange` function updates form values based on user input, while `nextStep` and `prevStep` functions navigate between steps. This hook encapsulates all logic related to form state and navigation, making it reusable across different multi-step forms.

To implement a multi-step form using this hook, you might have:

```javascript
import useMultiStepForm from './useMultiStepForm';

function MultiStepForm() {
 const steps ['Step 1 Content', 'Step 2 Content', 'Step 3 Content'];
   const { values, currentStep, handleChange, nextStep,
prevStep, step } useMultiStepForm(
  { name: '', email: '' },
  steps
 );

 return (
 <div>
  <h1>{step}</h1>
  {currentStep 0 && (
   <input
    type"text"
    name"name"
    value{values.name}
    onChange{handleChange}
    placeholder"Name"
   />
  )}
```

```
{currentStep 1 && (
 <input
  type"email"
  name"email"
  value{values.email}
  onChange{handleChange}
  placeholder"Email"
 />
)}
               <button    type"button"    onClick{prevStep}
disabled{currentStep 0}>
  Previous
 </button>
               <button    type"button"    onClick{nextStep}
disabled{currentStep steps.length - 1}>
  Next
 </button>
 </div>
);
}

export default MultiStepForm;
``` `
```

In this component, the `useMultiStepForm` hook is employed to manage form values and step transitions. This approach ensures that the form logic is separated from the presentation, making the component cleaner and more manageable.

By leveraging custom hooks in Next.js applications, developers can encapsulate complex logic, enhance code reusability, and maintain a clean separation of concerns. Custom hooks enable you to write modular and maintainable code, improving the overall quality of your applications.

Custom hooks are not only useful for handling side effects such as data fetching but also for managing complex state interactions and encapsulating reusable logic.
```

For instance, suppose you need to implement a form with complex validation rules across various components. Managing form state, validation, and error handling can quickly become unwieldy if each component handles these concerns independently. A custom hook can simplify this by centralizing the form logic and state management.

Here's an example of a custom hook designed to handle form state and validation:

```javascript
import { useState } from 'react';

function useForm(initialValues, validate) {
 const [values, setValues] useState(initialValues);
 const [errors, setErrors] useState({});
 const [touched, setTouched] useState({});

 const handleChange (e) > {
 const { name, value } e.target;
 setValues((prevValues) > ({
   ...prevValues,
   [name]: value,
 }));
 setTouched((prevTouched) > ({
   ...prevTouched,
   [name]: true,
 }));
 };

 const handleBlur (e) > {
 const { name } e.target;
 setTouched((prevTouched) > ({
   ...prevTouched,
   [name]: true,
 }));
 };
```

```javascript
  const validateForm () > {
  const validationErrors validate(values);
  setErrors(validationErrors);
  return Object.keys(validationErrors).length 0;
  };

  const handleSubmit (e, onSubmit) > {
  e.preventDefault();
  if (validateForm()) {
   onSubmit(values);
  }
  };

  return {
  values,
  errors,
  touched,
  handleChange,
  handleBlur,
  handleSubmit,
  };
}

export default useForm;
  ` ` `
```

In this `useForm` hook, `initialValues` represents the starting state of the form, while `validate` is a function that performs validation and returns error messages. The hook manages form values, validation errors, and touch state to keep track of which fields have been interacted with. It provides functions to handle input changes, form submission, and validation, encapsulating all form-related logic into a reusable hook.

To utilize this custom hook in a component, you might write:

` ` `javascript

```
import React from 'react';
import useForm from './useForm';

const validate (values) > {
 const errors  {};
 if (!values.email) {
  errors.email 'Email is required';
 } else if (!/\S+@\S+\.\S+/.test(values.email)) {
  errors.email 'Email address is invalid';
 }
 // Additional validation rules can be added here
 return errors;
};

function MyForm() {
 const {
  values,
  errors,
  touched,
  handleChange,
  handleBlur,
  handleSubmit,
 } useForm({ email: '' }, validate);

  const submitForm (values) > {
  console.log('Form Submitted:', values);
  // Handle form submission
 };

 return (
  <form onSubmit{(e) > handleSubmit(e, submitForm)}>
   <div>
    <label htmlFor"email">Email</label>
    <input
     type"text"
     id"email"
     name"email"
```

```
    value{values.email}
    onChange{handleChange}
    onBlur{handleBlur}
   />
   {touched.email && errors.email && <span>{errors.email}</
span>}
    </div>
    <button type"submit">Submit</button>
   </form>
  );
}

export default MyForm;
```

In this `MyForm` component, `useForm` provides the necessary state and handlers for form input and validation. The `validate` function defines the rules for validating the form fields, and the `handleSubmit` method handles the form submission process, ensuring validation is completed before proceeding.

Custom hooks also facilitate the management of complex stateful logic that spans multiple components. For instance, if your application includes a notification system where notifications can be triggered from different parts of the app, a custom hook can centralize the notification management logic, making it accessible throughout your application.

Here is an example of a custom hook for managing notifications:

```javascript
import { useState } from 'react';

function useNotifications() {
 const [notifications, setNotifications] useState([]);

 const addNotification (notification) > {
```

```
  setNotifications((prevNotifications) > [
    ...prevNotifications,
    notification,
  ]);
};

  const removeNotification (id) > {
  setNotifications((prevNotifications) >
    prevNotifications.filter((notification) > notification.id ! id)
  );
};

  return {
  notifications,
  addNotification,
  removeNotification,
  };
}

export default useNotifications;
` ` `
```

In this `useNotifications` hook, `addNotification` adds new notifications to the state, while `removeNotification` filters out notifications by their unique `id`. This hook encapsulates the logic for managing notifications, making it easy to integrate into any component that needs to display or trigger notifications.

By leveraging custom hooks, you can streamline your Next.js applications, improving code readability, maintainability, and reusability. Custom hooks are instrumental in managing state, handling side effects, and encapsulating complex logic in a modular and clean manner, thus enhancing the overall architecture of your React-based applications.

CHAPTER 31: WORKING WITH GRAPHQL

GraphQL, an innovative alternative to traditional REST APIs, provides a more dynamic approach to querying and manipulating data. Unlike REST, which exposes multiple endpoints for different resources, GraphQL offers a single endpoint that responds to complex queries with precisely the data requested. This chapter delves into the integration of GraphQL with Next.js, focusing on the setup of a GraphQL server, constructing and executing queries, and managing responses effectively.

The integration of GraphQL into a Next.js application begins with setting up a GraphQL server. There are several ways to establish this server, but one of the most common approaches involves using Apollo Server or similar libraries. Apollo Server is a community-driven, open-source GraphQL server that can be seamlessly integrated with Next.js to provide a robust solution for handling GraphQL queries.

To start, you need to install the necessary dependencies. For Apollo Server, this includes `apollo-server-micro` and `graphql`. These packages can be installed using npm or yarn:

```bash
npm install apollo-server-micro graphql
```

After installing these packages, you can set up your GraphQL server. Create a file, for instance, `pages/api/graphql.js`, and configure Apollo Server:

```javascript
import { ApolloServer, gql } from 'apollo-server-micro';
import typeDefs from '../../graphql/typeDefs';
import resolvers from '../../graphql/resolvers';

const server new ApolloServer({ typeDefs, resolvers });

export const config {
 api: {
  bodyParser: false,
 },
};

export default server.createHandler({ path: '/api/graphql' });
```

In this setup, `typeDefs` and `resolvers` are imported from separate files where you define your GraphQL schema and the corresponding resolver functions. The `typeDefs` file describes the shape of your data and the operations available. For instance, you might define a simple schema for querying user information:

```javascript
import { gql } from 'apollo-server-micro';

const typeDefs gql`
 type User {
  id: ID!
  name: String!
  email: String!
 }

 type Query {
  users: [User!]!
```

```
}
`;

export default typeDefs;
```

The `resolvers` file contains the logic for fetching data. It maps the operations defined in `typeDefs` to actual data retrieval:

```javascript
const resolvers {
 Query: {
  users: () > {
   // Fetch users from a data source, e.g., a database
   return [
    { id: '1', name: 'Alice', email: 'alice@example.com' },
    { id: '2', name: 'Bob', email: 'bob@example.com' },
   ];
  },
 },
};

export default resolvers;
```

With the GraphQL server set up, the next step involves querying data from your Next.js application. This is typically achieved using a client-side library like Apollo Client, which simplifies the process of sending queries and handling responses. To install Apollo Client and its dependencies, use:

```bash
npm install @apollo/client graphql
```

After installation, configure Apollo Client to connect with your GraphQL server. Create an instance of Apollo Client and wrap your application with an `ApolloProvider` in `_app.js`:

```javascript
import { ApolloProvider, InMemoryCache } from '@apollo/
client';

const client new ApolloClient({
 uri: '/api/graphql',
 cache: new InMemoryCache(),
});

function MyApp({ Component, pageProps }) {
 return (
  <ApolloProvider client{client}>
   <Component {...pageProps} />
  </ApolloProvider>
 );
}

export default MyApp;
```

Now, you can start making queries from your components. For example, to fetch the list of users, you would use the `useQuery` hook provided by Apollo Client:

```javascript
import { useQuery, gql } from '@apollo/client';

const GET_USERS gql`
 query GetUsers {
  users {
   id
   name
   email
  }
 }
`;

function Users() {
```

```
const { loading, error, data }  useQuery(GET_USERS);

 if (loading) return <p>Loading...</p>;
 if (error) return <p>Error :(</p>;

 return (
  <ul>
   {data.users.map(({ id, name, email }) > (
    <li key{id}>
     {name} - {email}
    </li>
   ))}
  </ul>
 );
}

export default Users;
` ` `
```

This `Users` component demonstrates how to fetch and display data from the GraphQL server. The `useQuery` hook manages the query lifecycle, including loading states and errors, making it easier to work with data in a declarative manner.

Integrating GraphQL into a Next.js application enhances its ability to handle complex data requirements with efficiency. By centralizing the data retrieval logic in a single endpoint and utilizing tools like Apollo Client, you can streamline your data management processes and create a more responsive, flexible application.

Once you have set up your GraphQL server, the next step is to focus on querying data. GraphQL allows clients to specify exactly what data they need, which can result in more efficient queries compared to REST, where each endpoint returns a fixed set of data. To execute queries from your Next.js application, you can use Apollo Client, which integrates well with React and Next.js.

First, install Apollo Client and its dependencies:

```bash
npm install @apollo/client graphql
```

In your Next.js project, configure Apollo Client to connect to your GraphQL server. This involves creating an Apollo Client instance and wrapping your application with the ApolloProvider to provide the client instance throughout your component tree. Typically, you would configure Apollo Client in a file like `lib/apolloClient.js`:

```javascript
import { ApolloClient, InMemoryCache } from '@apollo/client';

const client  new ApolloClient({
 uri: '/api/graphql',
 cache: new InMemoryCache(),
});

export default client;
```

Next, wrap your application with ApolloProvider in `_app.js` to ensure that Apollo Client is available in all components:

```javascript
import { ApolloProvider } from '@apollo/client';
import client from '../lib/apolloClient';

function MyApp({ Component, pageProps }) {
 return (
  <ApolloProvider client{client}>
   <Component {...pageProps} />
  </ApolloProvider>
 );
}
```

```javascript
export default MyApp;
```

With Apollo Client set up, you can now start querying data within your Next.js pages or components. You use the `useQuery` hook from Apollo Client to fetch data. Here is an example of how you might query for user data and display it in a Next.js page:

```javascript
import { gql, useQuery } from '@apollo/client';

const GET_USERS gql`
 query GetUsers {
  users {
   id
   name
   email
  }
 }
`;

export default function UsersPage() {
 const { loading, error, data } useQuery(GET_USERS);

 if (loading) return <p>Loading...</p>;
 if (error) return <p>Error: {error.message}</p>;

 return (
  <ul>
   {data.users.map(user > (
    <li key{user.id}>
     {user.name} - {user.email}
    </li>
   ))}
  </ul>
 );
}
```

```
```

This example demonstrates a basic query that fetches a list of users from the GraphQL server. The `useQuery` hook manages the loading and error states and provides the queried data once it is available.

In addition to querying, GraphQL also supports mutations for creating, updating, and deleting data. You can use the `useMutation` hook from Apollo Client to perform these operations. Here's an example of how to use a mutation to add a new user:

```javascript
import { gql, useMutation } from '@apollo/client';

const ADD_USER gql`
 mutation AddUser($name: String!, $email: String!) {
  addUser(name: $name, email: $email) {
   id
   name
   email
  }
 }
`;
export default function AddUserForm() {
 let name, email;
     const [addUser, { data, loading, error }] useMutation(ADD_USER);

  const handleSubmit (e) > {
  e.preventDefault();
     addUser({ variables: { name: name.value, email: email.value } });
  name.value ";
  email.value ";
 };
```

```
  if (loading) return <p>Loading...</p>;
  if (error) return <p>Error: {error.message}</p>;

  return (
   <form onSubmit{handleSubmit}>
    <input ref{node > name  node} placeholder"Name" />
    <input ref{node > email  node} placeholder"Email" />
    <button type"submit">Add User</button>
    {data && <p>User added: {data.addUser.name}</p>}
   </form>
  );
}
` ` `
```

This example shows how to define a mutation and integrate it into a component. The `useMutation` hook handles the mutation request, and the component updates based on the mutation's result.

Effective management of GraphQL responses is crucial for optimizing performance and user experience. By using Apollo Client, you gain built-in tools for caching and state management. Apollo Client's cache ensures that your application avoids unnecessary network requests by reusing previously fetched data. For example, after performing a mutation that adds a user, the cache automatically updates to reflect this change, preventing the need for additional queries.

In summary, integrating GraphQL with Next.js enhances the flexibility and efficiency of data management within your application. By setting up a GraphQL server, configuring Apollo Client, and leveraging GraphQL queries and mutations, you can build a powerful and responsive application. The ability to specify precisely the data needed and handle complex queries and mutations with ease makes GraphQL a valuable addition to modern web development practices.

In addition to querying data, managing responses and mutations in a GraphQL setup involves careful consideration of how to handle state and data updates efficiently. This is particularly important in dynamic applications where user interactions may require changes to the data stored on the server.

When dealing with mutations, which are GraphQL operations that modify data, the approach is somewhat similar to querying but involves sending data to the server to create, update, or delete resources. In Apollo Client, you use the `useMutation` hook to handle these operations. For example, if you need to create a new user, you would define a mutation and use it within your component to execute the operation.

Here's a simplified example of how you might handle user creation in a Next.js application:

```javascript
import { gql, useMutation } from '@apollo/client';
import { useState } from 'react';

const CREATE_USER gql`
  mutation CreateUser($name: String!, $email: String!) {
   createUser(name: $name, email: $email) {
    id
    name
    email
   }
  }
`;

export default function CreateUserForm() {
  const [name, setName] useState("");
  const [email, setEmail] useState("");
      const [createUser, { data, loading, error }]
useMutation(CREATE_USER);
```

```
const handleSubmit async (e) > {
e.preventDefault();
try {
 await createUser({ variables: { name, email } });
 // Optionally reset form fields or handle post-mutation logic
} catch (e) {
 // Handle error
 console.error('Error creating user:', e);
}
};

return (
 <form onSubmit{handleSubmit}>
  <input
   type"text"
   value{name}
   onChange{(e) > setName(e.target.value)}
   placeholder"Name"
   required
  />
  <input
   type"email"
   value{email}
   onChange{(e) > setEmail(e.target.value)}
   placeholder"Email"
   required
  />
  <button type"submit" disabled{loading}>
   {loading ? 'Creating...' : 'Create User'}
  </button>
  {error && <p>Error: {error.message}</p>}
  {data && <p>User created: {data.createUser.name}</p>}
 </form>
);
}
```

` ` `

Handling GraphQL responses and mutations effectively requires a good understanding of caching and state management, especially in client-side applications. Apollo Client provides a sophisticated caching mechanism that can help with managing data locally, reducing the need for repeated network requests and improving performance.

To handle real-time updates, GraphQL subscriptions can be used. Subscriptions enable your application to receive updates from the server in real time, which is ideal for features like live chat or notifications. To implement subscriptions in a Next.js app, you need to set up a WebSocket link along with your Apollo Client configuration.

Here's an example of how you might configure a WebSocket link for GraphQL subscriptions:

```javascript
import { ApolloClient, InMemoryCache, ApolloProvider, split }
from '@apollo/client';
import { WebSocketLink } from '@apollo/client/link/ws';
import { HttpLink } from '@apollo/client/link/http';
import { getMainDefinition } from '@apollo/client/utilities';

const httpLink new HttpLink({
 uri: '/api/graphql',
});

const wsLink new WebSocketLink({
 uri: `ws://localhost:4000/graphql`,
 options: {
  reconnect: true,
 },
});

const splitLink split(
 ({ query }) > {
```

```javascript
    const definition  getMainDefinition(query);
    return (
      definition.kind 'OperationDefinition' &&
      definition.operation 'subscription'
    );
  },
  wsLink,
  httpLink
);

const client  new ApolloClient({
  link: splitLink,
  cache: new InMemoryCache(),
});

function MyApp({ Component, pageProps }) {
  return (
    <ApolloProvider client{client}>
      <Component {...pageProps} />
    </ApolloProvider>
  );
}

export default MyApp;
```

In your components, you can use the `useSubscription` hook from Apollo Client to listen to real-time updates:

```javascript
import { gql, useSubscription } from '@apollo/client';

const MESSAGE_SUBSCRIPTION  gql`
  subscription OnMessageAdded {
    messageAdded {
      id
      content
      author
```

```
    }
  }
`;

function Messages() {
        const    {    data,    loading,    error    }
useSubscription(MESSAGE_SUBSCRIPTION);

  if (loading) return <p>Loading messages...</p>;
  if (error) return <p>Error: {error.message}</p>;

  return (
   <ul>
    {data.messageAdded.map((message) > (
     <li key{message.id}>
      <strong>{message.author}:</strong> {message.content}
     </li>
    ))}
   </ul>
  );
}
```
` ` `

By integrating GraphQL with your Next.js application in this manner, you gain access to a powerful toolset for managing data, optimizing performance, and enhancing user experience with real-time capabilities. This approach allows for a more flexible and efficient way of handling data compared to traditional REST APIs, ultimately leading to more dynamic and responsive web applications.

CHAPTER 32: ENHANCING USER EXPERIENCE WITH ANIMATIONS

Animations have become a crucial aspect of modern web design, offering not only aesthetic appeal but also functional benefits that enhance user experience. They can make applications feel more interactive and responsive, guiding users through their tasks with a seamless flow. In the context of Next.js applications, integrating animations involves a blend of CSS animations, JavaScript libraries, and React-specific tools to create engaging and smooth transitions.

To start, CSS animations provide a straightforward method for incorporating movement and transitions into your application. CSS animations are defined using `@keyframes` rules, which describe the sequence of the animation, and the `animation` property, which controls the timing and application of these keyframes. For instance, you might use CSS to create a fade-in effect for elements as they appear on the screen. This approach is efficient for simple animations and transitions because it leverages the browser's optimized rendering engine, ensuring smooth performance with minimal overhead.

Here is a basic example of a fade-in animation using CSS:

```css
@keyframes fadeIn {
 from {
  opacity: 0;
 }
 to {
  opacity: 1;
 }
}

.fade-in {
 animation: fadeIn 2s ease-in-out;
}
```

Applying the `fade-in` class to an HTML element will trigger the animation, making it gradually appear over a duration of 2 seconds. CSS animations are particularly beneficial for static elements or simple interactive components that do not require complex logic.

For more complex interactions or animations tied to component state changes, JavaScript libraries offer greater flexibility. Libraries such as Framer Motion and React Spring are popular choices in the React ecosystem. These libraries provide hooks and components that simplify the process of animating React components, allowing for more intricate animations that respond to user input or state changes.

Framer Motion, for example, is a powerful library designed for React that enables declarative animations with simple syntax. It provides components like `motion.div` and hooks like `useAnimation` to control animations programmatically. Here's an example of how you might use Framer Motion to animate a component's entrance:

```javascript
```

```
import { motion } from 'framer-motion';

const AnimatedComponent () > {
 return (
  <motion.div
   initial{{ opacity: 0 }}
   animate{{ opacity: 1 }}
   transition{{ duration: 1 }}
  >
   Hello, world!
  </motion.div>
 );
};
` ` `
```

In this example, the `motion.div` component starts with an opacity of 0 and animates to full opacity over 1 second. The `initial`, `animate`, and `transition` props control the starting state, ending state, and timing of the animation, respectively. This approach is particularly useful for animating components based on their lifecycle or user interactions.

React Spring is another robust library that allows for the creation of complex animations and transitions by leveraging spring physics. It offers hooks like `useSpring` and `useTrail` that provide detailed control over animation behavior. For example, to animate a component with a bouncing effect, you might use `useSpring` as follows:

```javascript
import { useSpring, animated } from 'react-spring';

const BouncingComponent () > {
 const props useSpring({
  from: { transform: 'translateY(-100px)' },
  to: { transform: 'translateY(0px)' },
  config: { tension: 200, friction: 15 },
```

```
});

  return <animated.div style{props}>Bounce!</animated.div>;
};
` ` `
```

Here, `useSpring` generates animation styles based on a spring configuration, creating a bouncing effect as the component moves from `-100px` to `0px` on the Y-axis.

Integrating animations into Next.js applications also requires attention to performance and accessibility. Excessive or poorly optimized animations can lead to sluggishness, particularly on lower-end devices or in resource-intensive scenarios. Thus, it is essential to ensure that animations are smooth and do not hinder the overall performance of the application.

For accessibility, it is important to consider users who may experience motion sensitivity. Providing options to reduce or disable animations can greatly enhance inclusivity. You can achieve this by respecting the `prefers-reduced-motion` media query in CSS:

```css
@media (prefers-reduced-motion: reduce) {
 .fade-in {
   animation: none;
 }
}
```

This CSS rule disables animations for users who have indicated a preference for reduced motion, aligning your application with accessibility best practices.

In conclusion, animations are a powerful tool for enhancing user experience in Next.js applications. By utilizing CSS animations for simple effects, and JavaScript libraries like Framer Motion or React Spring for more complex interactions, developers can create engaging and responsive applications. However, balancing aesthetics with performance and accessibility considerations is key to ensuring that animations contribute positively to the overall user experience.

When advancing from basic CSS animations to more dynamic effects, JavaScript libraries become indispensable. These libraries offer sophisticated control and flexibility, allowing animations to respond to complex user interactions and application state changes. React Spring and Framer Motion are two notable libraries that integrate seamlessly with React applications, including those built with Next.js.

React Spring, a popular choice for handling animations in React, is based on spring physics, making it well-suited for creating natural, fluid animations. Unlike CSS animations, which use keyframes and are often rigid in their timing, React Spring's approach allows for animations that are more responsive to user interactions and application state. For instance, if you want to animate an element based on user drag or scroll events, React Spring provides a straightforward way to interpolate values and animate properties in response to these changes.

Consider a scenario where you need to animate a card that expands and contracts based on user input. Using React Spring, you can define a spring animation that adjusts the card's size in response to a click event:

```javascript
import { useSpring, animated } from 'react-spring';

const ExpandableCard () > {
 const [isOpen, setIsOpen] React.useState(false);
 const props useSpring({
  to: { width: isOpen ? '300px' : '150px' },
  from: { width: '150px' },
 });
```

```
  return (
   <animated.div
    style{props}
    onClick{() > setIsOpen(!isOpen)}
    className"card"
   >
    Click to expand
   </animated.div>
  );
 };
 ` ` `
```

In this example, `useSpring` is used to interpolate the width of the card between two states. The `animated.div` component automatically applies the animation properties defined in the `props` object, creating a smooth transition effect when the card is clicked.

Framer Motion, on the other hand, offers a more declarative approach to animations. It provides high-level components and hooks that abstract away much of the complexity involved in setting up animations. With Framer Motion, you can create animations using a straightforward syntax and define transitions directly within your JSX. For example, if you wanted to animate a component's opacity and scale when it mounts, you could use the `motion.div` component with its `initial`, `animate`, and `exit` props:

```javascript
import { motion } from 'framer-motion';

const AnimatedComponent () > (
 <motion.div
  initial{{ opacity: 0, scale: 0.5 }}
  animate{{ opacity: 1, scale: 1 }}
  exit{{ opacity: 0, scale: 0.5 }}
  transition{{ duration: 0.5 }}
```

```
  >
  Fade in and scale up
  </motion.div>
);
` ` `
```

Here, the `motion.div` element transitions from an initial opacity of 0 and scale of 0.5 to a final opacity of 1 and scale of 1. The `transition` prop defines the duration and timing of the animation, providing a smooth and visually appealing effect when the component mounts and unmounts.

Incorporating animations can enhance user engagement by providing visual feedback that aligns with user actions and application states. However, it is crucial to use animations judiciously. Overuse or poorly designed animations can lead to a cluttered interface and may detract from the user experience. Ensuring that animations are smooth, performant, and serve a clear purpose in guiding or informing the user is essential.

Performance optimization is another key consideration when implementing animations. Animations that are not optimized can lead to sluggish performance, especially on devices with lower processing power. Using CSS animations where possible can leverage hardware acceleration and reduce the strain on the JavaScript thread. Additionally, monitoring and profiling animations to identify potential performance bottlenecks is advisable. Tools like the React DevTools and browser performance profilers can help in diagnosing issues and improving the efficiency of your animations.

In conclusion, animations are a powerful tool for enhancing user experience in Next.js applications. By leveraging CSS animations for straightforward transitions and JavaScript libraries like React Spring and Framer Motion for more complex and interactive effects, developers can create engaging and visually appealing interfaces. Balancing the use of animations with performance considerations and user-centric design principles ensures that they contribute positively to the overall application experience.

Framer Motion's syntax allows you to easily define animations for React components. For instance, to animate an element's opacity and scale upon its appearance, you might use the `motion.div` component with predefined animation properties:

```javascript
import { motion } from 'framer-motion';

const FadeInCard () > (
 <motion.div
  initial{{ opacity: 0, scale: 0.8 }}
  animate{{ opacity: 1, scale: 1 }}
  transition{{ duration: 0.5 }}
  className"card"
 >
  This card fades in and scales up
 </motion.div>
);
```

In this example, `initial` sets the starting state of the component, `animate` defines the target state, and `transition` specifies the duration and type of animation. This approach simplifies the implementation of animations and provides a clear and concise way to achieve complex visual effects.

In addition to JavaScript libraries, combining animations with user interactions requires careful consideration of performance. Animations can impact the responsiveness of your application if not managed properly. To ensure smooth performance, use `requestAnimationFrame` for animations that are tied to frame updates, and offload heavy computations to Web Workers when possible. Additionally, minimizing reflows and repaints by reducing DOM manipulations and using GPU-accelerated CSS properties can help maintain a responsive user experience.

Another important aspect of implementing animations in a Next.js application is the server-side rendering (SSR) of animated components. Since Next.js performs server-side rendering to improve performance and SEO, animations must be handled in a way that does not disrupt this process. Typically, you can manage this by using conditional logic to ensure that animations only run on the client side. For example, you might check if the code is running in the browser before applying animations:

```javascript
import { useEffect, useState } from 'react';

const ClientOnly ({ children }) > {
 const [isClient, setIsClient] useState(false);

 useEffect(() > {
 setIsClient(true);
 }, []);

 if (!isClient) {
 return null;
 }

 return children;
};

const AnimatedComponent () > (
 <ClientOnly>
  <motion.div
   initial{{ opacity: 0 }}
   animate{{ opacity: 1 }}
   transition{{ duration: 0.5 }}
   className"animated"
```

```
    >
    This component animates only on the client side
    </motion.div>
  </ClientOnly>
);
` ` `
```

In this setup, the `ClientOnly` component ensures that the child component only renders in the client environment, thereby avoiding potential issues with SSR.

Lastly, testing animations and their impact on the user experience is crucial. Automated testing frameworks such as Jest, in conjunction with testing libraries like React Testing Library, can help you validate that animations are triggered correctly and perform as expected. However, testing animations can be more challenging than testing static components. It often involves asserting that animations occur within the expected timeframes and checking visual correctness. For this purpose, you may use tools like Cypress, which provide end-to-end testing capabilities and can simulate user interactions to ensure that animations behave as intended in real-world scenarios.

In summary, enhancing user experience through animations in Next.js applications involves a multifaceted approach. Leveraging CSS animations for simpler effects and JavaScript libraries such as React Spring and Framer Motion for more complex interactions allows you to create engaging and dynamic interfaces. Ensuring performance optimization and compatibility with server-side rendering, along with implementing thorough testing practices, will help deliver a seamless and high-quality user experience. As the field of web development continues to evolve, keeping abreast of new tools and techniques for animation will be vital in maintaining an engaging and interactive user interface.

CHAPTER 33: OPTIMIZING IMAGES AND MEDIA

Efficient handling of images and media is fundamental for enhancing the performance and user experience of modern web applications. In Next.js, this optimization is crucial due to its impact on load times, responsiveness, and overall user satisfaction. This chapter delves into various techniques for optimizing images and media, including the use of responsive images, lazy loading, and image optimization libraries.

To start with, responsive images are a pivotal aspect of performance optimization. In Next.js, the built-in `next/image` component facilitates this by automatically providing different image sizes based on the viewport size. This approach ensures that users receive an appropriately sized image for their device, reducing unnecessary data transfer and speeding up page load times. By using the `next/image` component, you can specify the layout, width, and height of images, and the component will handle the rest. For example:

```javascript
import Image from 'next/image';

const ResponsiveImage () > (
 <Image
  src"/path/to/image.jpg"
  alt"Description"
```

```
  layout"responsive"
  width{700}
  height{475}
 />
);
` ` `
```

This component automatically generates multiple image sizes and serves the most suitable one based on the user's device. It also optimizes images in terms of format and quality, delivering a balance between visual fidelity and performance.

In addition to responsive images, lazy loading is another critical optimization technique. Lazy loading defers the loading of images until they are needed, which helps reduce the initial load time and improves the perceived performance of your application. With Next.js, lazy loading is built into the `next/image` component, which means images are loaded only when they enter the viewport. For further control over lazy loading, the `loading` attribute can be set to `"lazy"`:

```javascript
<Image
 src"/path/to/image.jpg"
 alt"Description"
 layout"intrinsic"
 width{500}
 height{300}
 loading"lazy"
/>
` ` `
```

This attribute instructs the browser to defer loading of the image until it is close to being visible on the screen. For media files other than images, such as videos, similar principles apply. Using the HTML `loading` attribute with the `video` element can also enable lazy loading:

```html
<video controls width"600" loading"lazy">
 <source src"/path/to/video.mp4" type"video/mp4" />
 Your browser does not support the video tag.
</video>
```

However, images and videos are not the only media types to consider. For other types of media such as audio files or large datasets, effective handling is equally important. Audio files should be compressed and delivered in formats that provide a good balance between quality and file size. Utilizing streaming protocols for large datasets can also enhance performance by reducing the initial load time.

Another crucial technique for optimizing media is the use of image optimization libraries. Next.js integrates seamlessly with image optimization services like ImageKit, Cloudinary, and Imgix. These services offer advanced features such as automatic format conversion (e.g., WebP), compression, and resizing. For instance, by integrating Cloudinary, you can automatically transform images to a more efficient format and reduce their size while maintaining quality. This can be achieved by configuring the `next.config.js` file to use an image loader that interfaces with Cloudinary:

```javascript
module.exports {
 images: {
  loader: 'cloudinary',
   path: 'https://res.cloudinary.com/your-cloud-name/image/
upload/',
 },
};
```

By configuring the image loader, all images served by

the `next/image` component will benefit from Cloudinary's optimization features. This setup provides a significant performance boost and ensures that images are delivered in the most efficient format and size.

In addition to image optimization services, local image optimization is also essential. Tools like ImageMagick and Squoosh can be used to manually optimize images before deploying them to your Next.js application. These tools allow you to compress images, adjust quality settings, and convert them to more efficient formats. Employing these techniques ensures that images are optimized before they even reach the user, further enhancing performance.

Lastly, it is important to monitor and measure the impact of your image and media optimizations. Tools such as Google Lighthouse and WebPageTest provide valuable insights into how well your media optimization strategies are performing. These tools evaluate various performance metrics, including load times and rendering speed, and offer recommendations for further improvements.

In summary, optimizing images and media in Next.js involves a multifaceted approach that includes using responsive images, implementing lazy loading, leveraging image optimization libraries, and applying local optimization techniques. By employing these strategies, you can ensure that your Next.js applications load quickly, perform efficiently, and deliver a superior user experience.

Beyond responsive images and lazy loading, leveraging image optimization libraries can significantly enhance the performance of a Next.js application. Image optimization involves compressing images to reduce their file sizes while maintaining acceptable quality, which can lead to faster load times and improved user experiences. Several libraries and tools can assist with this process, and integrating them into a Next.js project can be done seamlessly.

One of the most popular tools for image optimization is `sharp`, a high-performance Node.js image processing library. It provides a range of features, including resizing, cropping, and format conversion, which are essential for optimizing images. In a Next.js application, you can use `sharp` in conjunction with a custom server or within a build process to handle image optimization tasks. For instance, integrating `sharp` with an image processing pipeline can look like this:

```javascript
const sharp require('sharp');

sharp('input.jpg')
 .resize(800, 600)
 .toFile('output.jpg', (err, info) > {
  if (err) throw err;
  console.log(info);
 });
```

This example demonstrates how to resize an image using `sharp`, but the library also supports advanced features like converting images to different formats (e.g., WebP), adjusting quality, and performing various transformations. By incorporating such tools into your build process, you can ensure that your images are optimized before they are served to users.

Another approach is to use cloud-based image optimization services. These services offer automatic optimization and delivery of images through a Content Delivery Network (CDN). Services such as Imgix, Cloudinary, and Imgproxy integrate with Next.js by providing APIs or plugins that automatically handle image processing and optimization. For example, with Cloudinary, you can upload images to their service and then use their URLs in your Next.js application. Cloudinary also offers dynamic image transformations via URL parameters, which allows you to adjust image size, quality, and format on-the-fly:

```javascript
const imageUrl  'https://res.cloudinary.com/demo/image/upload/w_800,h_600,c_fill/sample.jpg';
```

This URL transformation automatically resizes the image to 800x600 pixels and applies a fill crop, all while benefiting from Cloudinary's CDN for fast delivery.

In addition to optimizing images, handling other media types, such as videos and audio files, requires similar considerations. For videos, it's important to use modern formats and codecs, such as MP4 with H.264 or WebM with VP8, which provide good compression and compatibility across browsers. Additionally, leveraging adaptive streaming technologies like HLS (HTTP Live Streaming) or DASH (Dynamic Adaptive Streaming over HTTP) can enhance video delivery by adjusting quality based on the user's network conditions.

Integrating video optimization can involve using video processing libraries or cloud services similar to those used for images. For instance, tools like FFmpeg can be employed to compress and transcode videos as part of your build process:

```bash
ffmpeg -i input.mp4 -vcodec libx264 -crf 23 output.mp4
```

This command uses FFmpeg to convert a video to the H.264 codec with a constant rate factor (CRF) of 23, balancing quality and file size.

For audio files, optimization focuses on compression and bitrate management. Using formats like MP3 or AAC, which offer good compression ratios while preserving audio quality, is beneficial. Tools and libraries like `ffmpeg` can also be used for audio processing tasks, ensuring that audio files are delivered efficiently.

As you integrate these optimization techniques into your Next.js application, it's also essential to consider the impact on user experience. Ensuring that media files load quickly and efficiently will contribute to a smoother, more engaging application. Regularly testing your application's performance using tools such as Google Lighthouse or WebPageTest can help identify areas for improvement and validate the effectiveness of your optimization strategies.

By combining responsive images, lazy loading, image and media optimization libraries, and cloud-based services, you can achieve a high level of performance and user satisfaction in your Next.js application. These techniques not only enhance load times and reduce bandwidth usage but also contribute to a more polished and professional user experience.

In addition to optimizing images, handling other media types, such as videos and audio files, also plays a critical role in improving the performance of a Next.js application. Effective management of these media assets ensures that they do not become a bottleneck, affecting load times and overall user experience.

For videos, implementing techniques such as adaptive streaming and efficient encoding can significantly impact performance. Adaptive streaming allows the video to be delivered in multiple quality levels, automatically adjusting based on the user's network conditions and device capabilities. Formats like HLS (HTTP Live Streaming) and DASH (Dynamic Adaptive Streaming over HTTP) are commonly used for this purpose. Using a video hosting platform that supports adaptive streaming, such as Vimeo or YouTube, can simplify the process. These platforms often provide built-in optimization and efficient delivery via CDNs.

Incorporating video players that support lazy loading can further enhance performance. Lazy loading ensures that videos are only loaded when they come into the viewport, reducing initial page load times. Libraries and components such as `react-lazy-load` or `react-intersection-observer` can be utilized to implement this feature effectively in a Next.js application. For instance, using `react-lazy-load`, you can delay the loading of a video until the user scrolls near it:

```javascript
import LazyLoad from 'react-lazy-load';

const VideoComponent () > (
 <LazyLoad>
  <video controls width"100%">
   <source src"video.mp4" type"video/mp4" />
   Your browser does not support the video tag.
  </video>
 </LazyLoad>
);
```

Similarly, audio files should be optimized to balance quality and file size. Compressing audio files and using efficient formats such as MP3 or AAC can help reduce their impact on performance. Audio files should also be lazy-loaded or streamed as needed to avoid unnecessary delays in loading.

Implementing a comprehensive strategy for optimizing images and media extends to proper caching strategies. Leveraging browser caching for static assets ensures that once an asset is downloaded, it does not need to be fetched again on subsequent visits. Next.js automatically handles caching for static assets stored in the `public` directory, but you can further control caching policies for dynamic content using HTTP headers. For instance, configuring `Cache-Control` headers allows you to specify how long browsers should cache your assets:

```javascript
import express from 'express';

const app express();

app.use(express.static('public', {
  maxAge: '1d' // Cache static assets for one day
}));
```

Beyond caching, utilizing a Content Delivery Network (CDN) can significantly enhance media delivery performance. CDNs distribute media files across various edge servers around the globe, reducing latency by serving files from locations closer to the user. Many cloud providers, including AWS CloudFront and Google Cloud CDN, offer easy integration with Next.js applications. By configuring your Next.js application to use a CDN, you can ensure that your media files are delivered swiftly and efficiently.

When integrating these optimization techniques, it is essential to test and measure their impact on performance. Tools such as Lighthouse and WebPageTest provide insights into how your media assets affect load times and overall performance. Regularly monitoring these metrics allows you to adjust your strategies as needed, ensuring that your application remains fast and responsive.

In conclusion, optimizing images and media in Next.js applications involves a multifaceted approach. By combining responsive images, lazy loading, image optimization libraries, adaptive streaming for videos, and effective caching and CDN strategies, you can significantly enhance the performance and user experience of your application. Implementing these techniques requires a thoughtful approach and ongoing monitoring, but the benefits in terms of faster load times and improved user satisfaction are well worth the effort.

CHAPTER 34: IMPLEMENTING CUSTOM ERROR PAGES

In the realm of web development, the handling of errors and the presentation of error messages play a crucial role in maintaining a positive user experience. When users encounter issues such as broken links, server errors, or other disruptions, the response provided by an application can significantly impact their perception and overall satisfaction. Custom error pages in Next.js are instrumental in enhancing this experience by offering clear, informative, and branded messages that guide users through their troubles rather than leaving them confused or frustrated.

Next.js provides a robust framework for managing errors through its built-in error handling mechanism. By default, Next.js displays a generic error page for various types of errors, including 404 (Not Found) and 500 (Internal Server Error). However, to deliver a more tailored and engaging experience, you can customize these error pages to align with the specific needs and branding of your application.

To create custom error pages in Next.js, you begin by defining error page components. Next.js allows you to create custom error pages by placing specific files in the `pages` directory of your project. For instance, a file named `404.js` will be used to handle 404 errors, while `500.js` will manage 500 errors. These files should export React components that define how the error page should be rendered.

A basic example of a custom 404 error page might look like this:

```javascript
// pages/404.js
import React from 'react';

const Custom404 () > {
 return (
  <div>
   <h1>Page Not Found</h1>
   <p>Sorry, the page you are looking for does not exist.</p>
   <a href"/">Go back to the homepage</a>
  </div>
 );
};

export default Custom404;
```

In this example, the `Custom404` component provides a friendly message and a link back to the homepage, enhancing the user experience by offering a clear path forward. You can style this page according to your application's design guidelines to maintain consistency in branding and visual appeal.

Similarly, for server errors, you can create a `500.js` file to handle internal server issues. A typical `500` error page might include a message indicating a problem on the server side and encourage users to try again later or contact support. An example might be:

```javascript
```

```
// pages/500.js
import React from 'react';

const Custom500 () > {
 return (
  <div>
   <h1>Internal Server Error</h1>
     <p>Something went wrong on our end. Please try again
later.</p>
    <a href"/">Return to the homepage</a>
   </div>
 );
};

export default Custom500;
` ` `
```

In this scenario, the `Custom500` component offers a straightforward message about the error and provides a way for users to navigate back to the homepage, helping to mitigate the impact of unexpected server issues.

For a more advanced setup, you may also handle additional HTTP status codes by creating custom pages for other types of errors. For example, you might want to handle errors like 403 (Forbidden) or 401 (Unauthorized) in a manner that is consistent with the rest of your application's error handling strategy. This approach involves creating corresponding files such as `403.js` or `401.js` and implementing similar components to manage those scenarios.

Beyond the basic implementation, custom error pages can be enhanced with more sophisticated features. For instance, you might integrate analytics to track the occurrence of specific errors and gather insights on how users interact with error pages. This data can be invaluable for improving the overall application and addressing recurring issues.

Additionally, incorporating links to support resources, such as a help center or contact form, can further assist users who encounter problems. Providing context-specific guidance, such as a troubleshooting section for common issues, can also enhance the user experience by offering more immediate help.

Overall, the goal of implementing custom error pages in Next.js is to provide users with a clear, helpful, and consistent experience even when things go wrong. By thoughtfully designing and customizing these pages, you not only maintain the professionalism of your application but also help users navigate challenges with greater ease and confidence.

In addition to customizing basic error pages, handling dynamic errors and integrating error boundaries can further enhance the resilience and user experience of your Next.js application. Dynamic errors, such as those arising from specific user actions or external integrations, often require more sophisticated handling beyond static error pages.

For instance, if your application interacts with external APIs or services, you may encounter various types of errors that are specific to those interactions, such as timeouts or invalid responses. In these cases, it is beneficial to create error boundaries to catch and handle these errors gracefully. Error boundaries are React components that catch JavaScript errors anywhere in their child component tree, log those errors, and display a fallback UI instead of crashing the whole component tree.

To implement an error boundary in a Next.js application, you can create a component that uses the `componentDidCatch` lifecycle method to catch errors and log them. Here's a simplified example of an error boundary component:

```javascript
// components/ErrorBoundary.js
```

```javascript
import React from 'react';

class ErrorBoundary extends React.Component {
 constructor(props) {
  super(props);
  this.state { hasError: false };
 }

 static getDerivedStateFromError() {
  return { hasError: true };
 }

 componentDidCatch(error, errorInfo) {
  // Log error to an error reporting service
    console.error("Error caught by Error Boundary:", error,
errorInfo);
 }

 render() {
  if (this.state.hasError) {
   return (
    <div>
     <h1>Something went wrong.</h1>
     <p>We are sorry, but an unexpected error occurred. Please
try again later.</p>
    </div>
   );
  }

   return this.props.children;
 }
}

export default ErrorBoundary;
```

You can wrap your application or specific components with this `ErrorBoundary` to ensure that any errors within its children are caught and managed. This approach prevents the entire application from crashing and allows you to provide a fallback UI, improving the overall robustness of your application.

Another important aspect of error handling in Next.js involves managing client-side errors. While custom error pages address server-side issues effectively, client-side errors such as form validation errors or JavaScript runtime exceptions require a different approach. Implementing client-side validation and providing clear, actionable feedback to users can greatly enhance the user experience.

For instance, if your application includes a form that users submit, you should validate the form data before sending it to the server. Client-side validation helps catch errors early and provides immediate feedback, which can prevent common issues and improve the form submission process. Here is an example of how you might handle form validation:

```javascript
// components/MyForm.js
import React, { useState } from 'react';

const MyForm () > {
 const [formData, setFormData] useState({ name: '', email: '' });
 const [errors, setErrors] useState({ name: '', email: '' });

  const validateForm () > {
  let valid true;
  let errors { name: '', email: '' };

   if (!formData.name) {
   errors.name 'Name is required';
   valid false;
   }
   if (!formData.email || !/\S+@\S+\.\S+/.test(formData.email))
 {
    errors.email 'Valid email is required';
```

```
    valid false;
  }
   setErrors(errors);
  return valid;
};
  const handleSubmit (event) > {
  event.preventDefault();
  if (validateForm()) {
   // Submit form data
   console.log('Form submitted:', formData);
  }
};

  return (
   <form onSubmit{handleSubmit}>
    <div>
     <label>Name:</label>
     <input
      type"text"
      value{formData.name}
           onChange{(e) > setFormData({ ...formData, name:
e.target.value })}
     />
     {errors.name && <p>{errors.name}</p>}
    </div>
    <div>
     <label>Email:</label>
     <input
      type"email"
      value{formData.email}
           onChange{(e) > setFormData({ ...formData, email:
e.target.value })}
     />
     {errors.email && <p>{errors.email}</p>}
    </div>
```

```
  <button type"submit">Submit</button>
 </form>
);
};

export default MyForm;
```
` ` `

In this example, the form component performs client-side validation and displays error messages directly on the page. This method ensures that users receive immediate feedback on their input, reducing the likelihood of submission errors and enhancing the overall form experience.

Customizing error pages and handling errors effectively in Next.js involves a combination of strategies, including defining static error pages, implementing error boundaries for dynamic errors, and providing client-side validation. By applying these techniques, you can significantly improve the user experience, making your application more resilient and user-friendly in the face of unexpected issues.

In refining the user experience with custom error pages, it's essential to consider both the design and functionality aspects to ensure that they are both informative and user-friendly. Effective error pages should not only communicate that something went wrong but also guide users on what steps to take next, thereby minimizing frustration and improving the overall experience.

When designing custom error pages, it's beneficial to incorporate several key elements. First, clear and concise messaging is crucial. The user should immediately understand that an error has occurred without being overwhelmed by technical jargon. For example, a 404 error page, which indicates that a page could not be found, might include a friendly message like, "Oops! The page you're looking for doesn't exist." Accompanying this message with a search bar or a link to the homepage can help users navigate to relevant content or return to a familiar location within the site.

Additionally, providing context-specific error pages can further enhance user experience. For instance, a 500 Internal Server Error page might include a message such as, "Sorry, something went wrong on our end. We're working to fix it." This page can also include options to contact support or report the issue, which helps users feel that their concerns are being addressed.

A best practice for implementing custom error pages in Next.js involves leveraging the built-in error handling capabilities while customizing the experience according to the needs of your application. Next.js provides a straightforward mechanism for defining custom error pages. By creating a `pages/_error.js` file, you can handle HTTP status codes and render error pages accordingly. For example:

```javascript
// pages/_error.js
import React from 'react';
import { NextPageContext } from 'next';

const ErrorPage ({ statusCode }) > {
 return (
  <div>
   {statusCode 404 ? (
    <div>
     <h1>Page Not Found</h1>
     <p>Sorry, the page you are looking for does not exist.</p>
     <a href"/">Go back to the homepage</a>
    </div>
   ) : (
    <div>
     <h1>Something Went Wrong</h1>
        <p>We are experiencing some issues. Please try again
```

```
later.</p>
    </div>
  )}
  </div>
 );
};

ErrorPage.getInitialProps async (ctx: NextPageContext) > {
 const statusCode ctx.res ? ctx.res.statusCode : 404;
 return { statusCode };
};

export default ErrorPage;
` ` `
```

This approach provides a robust mechanism to handle different error scenarios and render appropriate content based on the error type.

Furthermore, integrating analytics and monitoring tools can help you track the occurrence of errors and gather insights on their impact. Tools like Sentry, LogRocket, or New Relic can be integrated to capture error logs and user interactions leading up to an error. This data can be invaluable for diagnosing issues, understanding user behavior, and improving the overall reliability of your application.

Incorporating feedback mechanisms on error pages can also be useful. Allowing users to report issues directly from the error page provides immediate insights into problems they encounter. Implementing a simple form where users can describe the issue and submit feedback can enhance user engagement and help you identify areas for improvement.

Finally, testing and iterating on your custom error pages is crucial. Regularly reviewing how these pages perform under different conditions and user scenarios ensures that they meet the intended goals of improving user experience and providing effective guidance during error situations. User feedback, analytics data, and periodic reviews can help refine the design and functionality of your error handling strategy.

In summary, custom error pages in Next.js play a critical role in maintaining a positive user experience during unexpected issues. By providing clear messaging, offering navigation options, integrating with monitoring tools, and allowing user feedback, you can ensure that your application remains user-friendly even when things go wrong. Through careful design and continuous improvement, custom error pages can transform potentially frustrating experiences into opportunities for guiding users effectively and maintaining their trust.

CHAPTER 35:
HANDLING FILE
UPLOADS

Handling file uploads is a fundamental aspect of modern web applications, enabling users to interact with the system by submitting documents, images, or other files. In Next.js, managing file uploads involves several steps: setting up user interfaces for file selection, processing the uploaded files on the server, and managing file storage and retrieval. This chapter delves into each of these components to provide a comprehensive guide on implementing file upload functionality in a Next.js application.

The first step in handling file uploads is creating a user interface that allows users to select files. This typically involves a file input element within a form. In Next.js, you can create a file upload form using React components. The form should include an `<input>` element with the `type"file"` attribute, which prompts the user to choose files from their local system. For example:

```javascript
import React, { useState } from 'react';

const FileUploadForm () > {
  const [file, setFile] useState(null);

  const handleFileChange (event) > {
```

```
  setFile(event.target.files[0]);
};

 const handleSubmit  async (event) > {
 event.preventDefault();
 const formData  new FormData();
 formData.append('file', file);

  try {
  const response  await fetch('/api/upload', {
   method: 'POST',
   body: formData,
  });
  if (response.ok) {
   console.log('File uploaded successfully.');
  } else {
   console.error('File upload failed.');
  }
 } catch (error) {
  console.error('An error occurred:', error);
 }
};

 return (
  <form onSubmit{handleSubmit}>
   <input type"file" onChange{handleFileChange} />
   <button type"submit">Upload</button>
  </form>
 );
};

export default FileUploadForm;
` ` `
```

In this example, `FileUploadForm` provides a simple interface for file selection and submission. The `handleFileChange` function updates the component's state with the selected file, while `handleSubmit` handles the form submission, sending the file to the server via a `POST` request.

Once the file is submitted, the server-side handling of file uploads comes into play. Next.js allows you to define API routes within the `pages/api` directory. For processing file uploads, you would typically use a library such as `formidable` or `multer` to handle multipart form data. Here, I'll illustrate using `formidable`:

First, install `formidable`:

```bash
npm install formidable
```

Next, create an API route to handle the file upload. For example, in `pages/api/upload.js`:

```javascript
import formidable from 'formidable';
import fs from 'fs';
import path from 'path';

export const config {
 api: {
  bodyParser: false,
 },
};

const uploadDir path.join(process.cwd(), 'public/uploads');

const handler async (req, res) > {
 const form new formidable.IncomingForm();
 form.uploadDir uploadDir;
 form.keepExtensions true;

 form.parse(req, (err, fields, files) > {
  if (err) {
   return res.status(500).json({ error: 'Failed to upload file' });
```

```
}
```

    const file files.file[0];
            const   newFilePath   path.join(uploadDir,
file.originalFilename);
    fs.renameSync(file.filepath, newFilePath);

    res.status(200).json({ message: 'File uploaded successfully',
filePath: newFilePath });
  });
};

export default handler;
` ` `

In this API route, `formidable` is used to parse incoming form data, handle file uploads, and save files to a specified directory. By setting `bodyParser: false` in the `config` object, Next.js knows to defer the body parsing to `formidable`. The uploaded file is then moved from a temporary location to the desired upload directory.

Managing file storage and retrieval requires consideration of where to store the uploaded files and how to access them. For simplicity, the example stores files in the `public/uploads` directory, which makes them accessible via URLs. In a production environment, you might opt for cloud storage solutions like AWS S3, Google Cloud Storage, or Azure Blob Storage for better scalability and reliability.

To retrieve and serve the uploaded files, you can create an API route to list or fetch files. This involves reading the directory contents and sending the list of files to the client. For instance, a simple implementation to list files might look like:

` ` `javascript
import fs from 'fs';
import path from 'path';
```
```

```
const uploadDir path.join(process.cwd(), 'public/uploads');

const handler async (req, res) > {
 fs.readdir(uploadDir, (err, files) > {
  if (err) {
   return res.status(500).json({ error: 'Failed to list files' });
  }

   res.status(200).json({ files });
 });
};

export default handler;
` ` `
```

This API route reads the contents of the `uploads` directory and responds with a list of filenames.

In summary, handling file uploads in Next.js involves setting up a user interface for file selection, processing the file uploads on the server, and managing file storage. By leveraging Next.js API routes and libraries such as `formidable`, you can build a robust file upload system that supports various types of file handling and storage needs.

Upon receiving the file upload request, the server-side processing becomes critical for managing and storing the uploaded files. In a Next.js application, server-side logic for file handling is often implemented using API routes. These routes provide an interface between the client and the server, allowing you to process the uploaded files and handle any necessary operations.

To process file uploads on the server, you will need to set up an API route that can handle multipart form data. This is where the file is received and processed. Next.js API routes are built using Node.js, and you can use middleware libraries like `multer` to facilitate file handling. `Multer` is a middleware for handling `multipart/form-data`, which is used for uploading files.

Here's how you can set up an API route to handle file uploads using `multer`:

1. Install `multer`: Begin by installing `multer` in your Next.js project. Run the following command in your project directory:

```bash
npm install multer
```

2. Create an API Route: Next, create an API route to handle the file upload. In your `pages/api` directory, create a file named `upload.js` (or any other name you prefer). This file will define your API route for handling uploads.

```javascript
import nextConnect from 'next-connect';
import multer from 'multer';

// Configure multer storage
const upload  multer({
  storage: multer.diskStorage({
    destination: './public/uploads', // Directory to save uploaded files
    filename: (req, file, cb) > cb(null, file.originalname),
  }),
});

// Initialize nextConnect
const handler  nextConnect();

handler.use(upload.single('file')) // Handle single file upload
  .post((req, res) > {
        res.status(200).json({ message: 'File uploaded successfully' });
```

```
});

export default handler;
```
` ` `

In this setup, `multer` is configured to save files to the `public/uploads` directory. The `nextConnect` library helps to integrate `multer` with Next.js API routes, enabling easier handling of middleware. The `upload.single('file')` middleware specifies that a single file upload is expected, with `file` being the name attribute used in the form.

3. File Storage and Retrieval: Once the file is processed, it's essential to manage how and where the files are stored. In the example above, files are saved to the `public/uploads` directory. This directory should be created if it does not already exist.

For production environments, you may want to use cloud storage solutions such as AWS S3, Google Cloud Storage, or similar services. These solutions offer scalability and reliability for handling large volumes of files. To integrate cloud storage, you would use the respective SDK for your chosen service and update the API route to upload files directly to the cloud storage instead of saving them locally.

4. Error Handling and Validation: It's also crucial to handle errors and validate uploaded files to ensure that the application behaves correctly and securely. This includes checking file types, sizes, and handling any errors during the upload process. You can implement additional validation in your API route before saving the file.

For example, to check the file size and type, you might modify the `multer` configuration as follows:

```javascript
const upload multer({
limits: { fileSize: 5 1024 1024 }, // 5 MB limit
```

```
 fileFilter: (req, file, cb) > {
  const allowedTypes ['image/jpeg', 'image/png', 'image/gif'];
  if (allowedTypes.includes(file.mimetype)) {
   cb(null, true);
  } else {
   cb(new Error('Invalid file type'), false);
  }
 },
 storage: multer.diskStorage({
  destination: './public/uploads',
  filename: (req, file, cb) > cb(null, file.originalname),
 }),
});
` ` `
```

Here, `limits` specifies a maximum file size, and `fileFilter` ensures only specific file types are accepted. Handling errors and providing user feedback is essential for a robust file upload process.

By implementing these practices, you create a file upload system that not only meets the basic functional requirements but also ensures a smooth, reliable, and secure experience for users. Customizing the file upload handling to fit your application's specific needs and leveraging cloud storage solutions for scalability can further enhance the robustness of your file upload functionality.

Once the file is uploaded and saved to the server, the next step is to manage its storage and retrieval effectively. Efficient file storage practices are essential to ensure that your application remains scalable and performs well. Depending on the needs of your application, you might choose to store files locally on the server, on a cloud storage service, or in a distributed file system. Each method has its own advantages and considerations.

Local Storage

Storing files locally on the server is the simplest approach. This method involves saving the files directly to a directory on your server. While this can be effective for small-scale applications, it may not scale well as your application grows. Local storage is limited by the server's disk capacity and may introduce challenges in load balancing and disaster recovery. To manage local storage effectively, you should implement regular backup procedures and consider using a robust file naming strategy to avoid conflicts.

Cloud Storage

For scalable and reliable file storage, many applications opt for cloud storage solutions. Providers such as Amazon S3, Google Cloud Storage, and Microsoft Azure Blob Storage offer scalable storage that can handle large volumes of data with high availability. These services also provide features like automated backups, data replication, and access control, which can greatly enhance the resilience of your application.

To integrate cloud storage with your Next.js application, you will typically use the provider's SDK or API to upload and manage files. Here's an example of how you might handle file uploads to Amazon S3 using the AWS SDK:

1. Install AWS SDK: First, install the AWS SDK for JavaScript:

```bash
npm install aws-sdk
```

2. Configure AWS SDK: Set up your AWS credentials and configure the SDK in your Next.js API route:

```javascript
import AWS from 'aws-sdk';
import nextConnect from 'next-connect';
import multer from 'multer';
```

```
import multerS3 from 'multer-s3';

// Configure AWS SDK
AWS.config.update({
  accessKeyId: process.env.AWS_ACCESS_KEY_ID,
  secretAccessKey: process.env.AWS_SECRET_ACCESS_KEY,
  region: process.env.AWS_REGION,
});

const s3  new AWS.S3();

// Configure multer-s3
const upload  multer({
  storage: multerS3({
    s3: s3,
    bucket: process.env.AWS_S3_BUCKET,
    acl: 'public-read',
    key: (req, file, cb) > cb(null, file.originalname),
  }),
});

const handler  nextConnect();

handler.use(upload.single('file'))
  .post((req, res) > {
            res.status(200).json({ message: 'File uploaded
successfully' });
  });

export default handler;
```

In this example, `multer-s3` is used to integrate `multer` with S3, allowing files to be directly uploaded to an S3 bucket. The `accessKeyId`, `secretAccessKey`, and `region` are set up via environment variables, which is a best practice for keeping sensitive credentials secure.

File Retrieval and Management

Retrieving files from your chosen storage solution requires implementing functionality to access and serve the files as needed. For local storage, this might involve serving static files directly or providing an endpoint to download the files. For cloud storage, you will need to use the provider's API to generate pre-signed URLs or directly serve files via the API.

For instance, if you are using S3, you can generate a pre-signed URL that allows users to access a file for a limited time. This is useful for controlled access and download links. Here is an example of how to generate a pre-signed URL using the AWS SDK:

```javascript
const handler nextConnect();

handler.get((req, res) > {
  const { key } req.query; // File key from request query

  const params {
    Bucket: process.env.AWS_S3_BUCKET,
    Key: key,
    Expires: 60, // URL expiration time in seconds
  };

  s3.getSignedUrl('getObject', params, (err, url) > {
    if (err) {
      return res.status(500).json({ error: 'Error generating URL' });
    }
    res.status(200).json({ url });
  });
});

export default handler;
```

This API route generates a pre-signed URL for a file specified by its key, allowing users to download it directly from S3 without exposing your credentials.

Security Considerations

When handling file uploads, security is a critical concern. Always validate file types and sizes on both the client and server sides to prevent malicious file uploads. Implement access controls and ensure that sensitive data is not exposed through file uploads. For cloud storage solutions, configure permissions and access policies to safeguard your files and manage who can upload or access them.

By carefully managing file uploads and storage, you ensure that your Next.js application can handle media efficiently and securely, providing a robust user experience while maintaining performance and scalability.

CHAPTER 36:
BUILDING
CUSTOM APIS

Next.js provides an efficient way to build custom APIs directly within your application through its API routes feature. This chapter delves into the process of creating and managing these custom API routes, exploring how to handle various HTTP methods, manage request and response data, and integrate APIs with frontend components to create a cohesive and dynamic user experience.

To begin with, Next.js API routes allow you to build server-side endpoints that can be used to handle requests and responses directly within your Next.js application. These routes are essentially functions that reside in the `pages/api` directory. Each file within this directory corresponds to a specific API endpoint. For example, a file named `pages/api/user.js` would create an API endpoint accessible at `/api/user`.

Creating an API route involves defining a handler function that processes HTTP requests. This function receives a request object and a response object, and it typically performs actions such as querying a database, processing form data, or interacting with external APIs. The handler function then sends a response back to the client.

Here's a basic example of an API route that handles a GET request:

```javascript
// pages/api/hello.js
export default function handler(req, res) {
  res.status(200).json({ message: 'Hello, world!' });
}
```

In this example, the `handler` function sends a JSON response with a status code of 200, indicating a successful request. This endpoint can be accessed from the frontend using the `fetch` API or any other HTTP client library.

Handling different HTTP methods is a critical aspect of working with API routes. You can use conditional logic within your handler function to differentiate between GET, POST, PUT, DELETE, and other HTTP methods. For instance, if you need to handle POST requests to create a new resource, you can extend your handler function as follows:

```javascript
// pages/api/users.js
export default function handler(req, res) {
  switch (req.method) {
    case 'GET':
      // Logic to handle GET requests
      res.status(200).json({ users: ['Alice', 'Bob'] });
      break;
    case 'POST':
      // Logic to handle POST requests
      const user  req.body;
      // Save the user to the database
      res.status(201).json({ message: 'User created', user });
      break;
    default:
      res.setHeader('Allow', ['GET', 'POST']);
      res.status(405).end(`Method ${req.method} Not Allowed`);
```

```
    break;
  }
}
` ` `
```

In this example, the `handler` function uses a `switch` statement to handle GET and POST requests differently. For GET requests, it sends a list of users, while for POST requests, it processes the incoming data and responds with a confirmation message. If the HTTP method is not supported, the function returns a 405 Method Not Allowed status.

When working with request data, such as form submissions or JSON payloads, you need to handle data parsing and validation. Next.js automatically parses JSON payloads sent with POST requests, so you can access this data using `req.body`. For more complex parsing requirements, such as handling `multipart/form-data`, you might need additional middleware or libraries.

For instance, to handle file uploads, you could use middleware like `multer` to process `multipart/form-data`. This involves setting up the middleware in your API route and configuring it to store uploaded files:

```javascript
// pages/api/upload.js
import multer from 'multer';
import nextConnect from 'next-connect';

const upload  multer({ dest: 'uploads/' });
const handler  nextConnect();

handler.use(upload.single('file')).post((req, res) > {
  res.status(200).json({ file: req.file });
});

export default handler;
```

In this example, the `multer` middleware is configured to save uploaded files to the `uploads/` directory. The `nextConnect` library is used to integrate the middleware with the API route, allowing you to handle file uploads and respond with information about the uploaded file.

Integrating your API routes with frontend components is a straightforward process. You can use standard HTTP methods to interact with these routes from your React components. For example, using the `fetch` API, you can make a request to your custom API route and handle the response:

```javascript
// components/UserList.js
import { useEffect, useState } from 'react';

function UserList() {
 const [users, setUsers] useState([]);

  useEffect(() > {
  async function fetchUsers() {
   const response await fetch('/api/users');
   const data await response.json();
   setUsers(data.users);
  }

   fetchUsers();
 }, []);

  return (
  <ul>
   {users.map((user) > (
    <li key{user}>{user}</li>
   ))}
  </ul>
 );
}
```

```
export default UserList;
```
```

In this component, the `useEffect` hook fetches user data from the `/api/users` endpoint when the component mounts. The data is then used to render a list of users. This integration allows you to build dynamic and responsive user interfaces that interact seamlessly with your backend logic.

By leveraging Next.js API routes, you can build powerful and efficient APIs directly within your application. This approach simplifies the development process by keeping both frontend and backend code in the same codebase, promoting a unified development experience.

To effectively manage request and response data within Next.js API routes, you must understand how to work with the request object (`req`) and the response object (`res`). The `req` object contains information about the incoming request, such as headers, query parameters, and body data, while the `res` object is used to construct and send the response back to the client.

When dealing with request data, you can access query parameters through `req.query`, which holds parameters passed in the URL, and body data through `req.body`, which contains data sent in the body of POST or PUT requests. Parsing this data is essential for performing operations such as saving information to a database or processing user input.

For instance, if you are building an API endpoint that handles user registration, you might want to extract user details from the request body. Here is an example of how you could manage this:

```javascript
// pages/api/register.js
import { connectToDatabase } from '../../lib/mongodb';
```
```

```
export default async function handler(req, res) {
 if (req.method 'POST') {
  const { name, email } req.body;

  if (!name || !email) {
     return res.status(400).json({ error: 'Name and email are
required' });
  }

  try {
   const { db } await connectToDatabase();
   const result  await db.collection('users').insertOne({ name,
email });
   res.status(201).json(result.ops[0]);
  } catch (error) {
   res.status(500).json({ error: 'Failed to register user' });
  }
 } else {
  res.setHeader('Allow', ['POST']);
  res.status(405).end(`Method ${req.method} Not Allowed`);
 }
}
```

In this example, the handler function first checks if the request method is POST. It then extracts the user's name and email from `req.body` and performs validation. If validation passes, the handler interacts with a database to insert the new user. Errors are handled appropriately with response status codes and messages.

Integrating custom APIs with frontend components in a Next.js application involves making HTTP requests to these API routes from your React components. This can be accomplished using built-in methods like `fetch` or third-party libraries such as Axios. Handling these requests properly ensures smooth interaction between the frontend and backend of your application.

For example, to interact with the registration API created above, you could create a form in your React component and submit user data via a POST request:

```javascript
// components/RegisterForm.js
import { useState } from 'react';

export default function RegisterForm() {
 const [name, setName] useState('');
 const [email, setEmail] useState('');
 const [error, setError] useState(null);

  const handleSubmit async (event) > {
  event.preventDefault();
  setError(null);

   try {
   const response await fetch('/api/register', {
    method: 'POST',
    headers: {
     'Content-Type': 'application/json',
    },
    body: JSON.stringify({ name, email }),
   });

    if (!response.ok) {
    throw new Error('Network response was not ok');
   }

    const data await response.json();
   console.log('User registered:', data);
  } catch (error) {
   setError(error.message);
  }
 };
```

```
  return (
  <form onSubmit{handleSubmit}>
    <label>
    Name:
            <input type"text" value{name} onChange{(e) >
setName(e.target.value)} />
    </label>
    <label>
    Email:
            <input type"email" value{email} onChange{(e) >
setEmail(e.target.value)} />
    </label>
    <button type"submit">Register</button>
    {error && <p>Error: {error}</p>}
    </form>
  );
}
` ` `
```

In this React component, `handleSubmit` makes a POST request to the `/api/register` endpoint with the form data. Error handling is implemented to manage and display any issues that arise during the request.

Another important aspect of API development is ensuring that the API is secure and performs efficiently. This involves implementing proper validation, handling authentication and authorization, and optimizing performance. Security best practices include validating and sanitizing input data to prevent malicious attacks, using HTTPS to encrypt data transmission, and employing rate limiting to mitigate abuse.

Moreover, you can enhance performance by optimizing database queries, caching responses, and ensuring that your API routes are efficient and scalable. Tools like caching libraries, database indexing, and serverless functions can contribute significantly to the overall performance of your API.

In summary, building custom APIs in Next.js involves creating API routes within the `pages/api` directory, handling various HTTP methods, managing request and response data, and integrating these APIs with frontend components. Proper implementation and security measures are crucial for developing robust and efficient APIs that enhance the functionality and user experience of your application.

Integrating custom APIs with your frontend components in Next.js involves leveraging HTTP request methods to communicate between the client and server. This integration ensures that your frontend can interact with the API routes you've defined, allowing you to fetch, submit, and manipulate data dynamically. The `fetch` API is commonly used for this purpose, but you can also utilize libraries such as Axios for a more feature-rich experience.

To demonstrate integration, consider a scenario where you want to fetch a list of users from an API endpoint and display it in a component. You would use the `fetch` function to make a request to your API route and then manage the response data within your React component.

Here's a basic example of how you might achieve this:

```javascript
// pages/users.js
import { useState, useEffect } from 'react';

export default function Users() {
  const [users, setUsers] useState([]);
  const [error, setError] useState(null);

  useEffect(() > {
  async function fetchUsers() {
   try {
```

```
    const response  await fetch('/api/users');
    if (!response.ok) {
      throw new Error('Network response was not ok');
    }
    const data  await response.json();
    setUsers(data);
  } catch (error) {
    setError(error.message);
  }
}

  fetchUsers();
}, []);

if (error) return <div>Error: {error}</div>;
if (!users.length) return <div>Loading...</div>;

return (
 <ul>
  {users.map(user > (
   <li key{user._id}>{user.name}</li>
  ))}
 </ul>
);
}
` ` `
```

In this example, the `Users` component uses the `useEffect` hook to fetch data from the `/api/users` endpoint when the component mounts. The response is processed and the user data is stored in the component's state using `setUsers`. Error handling is incorporated to manage any issues that arise during the fetch operation.

Additionally, Next.js allows for more sophisticated integration through server-side rendering (SSR) and static site generation (SSG) which can be combined with custom APIs. For instance, if you want to pre-fetch data at build time and serve it statically, you can use `getStaticProps`. Conversely, if you need data fetched on each request, `getServerSideProps` can be utilized.

Here is an example of using `getStaticProps` to fetch data from an API during build time:

```javascript
// pages/static-users.js
import { useState, useEffect } from 'react';

export default function StaticUsers({ initialUsers }) {
 const [users, setUsers] useState(initialUsers);

  useEffect(() > {
  // Example for client-side fetch if needed
 }, []);

  return (
  <ul>
   {users.map(user > (
    <li key{user._id}>{user.name}</li>
   ))}
  </ul>
 );
}

export async function getStaticProps() {
 try {
   const response  await fetch('https://your-api-url.com/api/users');
  const initialUsers  await response.json();

   return {
   props: {
    initialUsers,
   },
   revalidate: 10, // In seconds
  };
```

```javascript
  } catch (error) {
   return {
    props: {
     initialUsers: [],
    },
   };
  }
}
```

In this code snippet, `getStaticProps` fetches user data at build time, and the result is passed to the component as props. This approach is beneficial for SEO and performance as it allows the page to be served with pre-rendered data.

On the other hand, `getServerSideProps` can be used to fetch data on every request, which is useful for applications where the data is highly dynamic and changes frequently. Here's an example of using `getServerSideProps`:

```javascript
// pages/server-users.js
export default function ServerUsers({ users }) {
 return (
  <ul>
   {users.map(user > (
    <li key{user._id}>{user.name}</li>
   ))}
  </ul>
 );
}

export async function getServerSideProps() {
 try {
   const response  await fetch('https://your-api-url.com/api/users');
   const users  await response.json();
```

```
  return {
  props: {
   users,
   },
  };
 } catch (error) {
  return {
  props: {
   users: [],
   },
  };
 }
}
` ` `
```

In this case, `getServerSideProps` ensures that the latest data is fetched on each request, providing up-to-date information.

Overall, building custom APIs in Next.js offers a streamlined way to handle server-side logic and data management directly within your application. By effectively integrating these APIs with frontend components, you can create dynamic and responsive web applications that leverage the full capabilities of both server-side and client-side rendering. Whether using `fetch`, Axios, or Next.js data-fetching methods, understanding how to manage and integrate custom APIs is crucial for developing robust and interactive web applications.

CHAPTER 37: LEVERAGING TYPESCRIPT FOR TYPE SAFETY

In the evolving landscape of modern web development, ensuring code quality and reducing bugs are paramount concerns. TypeScript, a statically typed superset of JavaScript, provides a robust solution for enhancing code reliability and maintainability by introducing type safety. This chapter explores how to integrate TypeScript into Next.js projects, focusing on configuration, type definitions, and leveraging TypeScript features to enrich the development workflow.

Integrating TypeScript into a Next.js application begins with the initial setup, which is relatively straightforward. Next.js supports TypeScript out of the box, facilitating a seamless configuration process. To get started, you need to install TypeScript and the necessary type definitions for React and Node.js. This can be done using npm or yarn with the following commands:

```bash
npm install --save-dev typescript @types/react @types/node
```

or

```bash
yarn add --dev typescript @types/react @types/node
```

Once the packages are installed, you can initiate TypeScript configuration by creating a `tsconfig.json` file. Running the `next dev` command in a Next.js project with TypeScript installed will automatically generate a default `tsconfig.json` file if one does not already exist. This configuration file is crucial as it dictates how TypeScript compiles your code, specifying compiler options, including module resolution and type checking settings.

With TypeScript installed and configured, the next step is to start using it in your project. TypeScript's core feature is its type system, which allows you to define and enforce the structure of your data. For instance, you can define types or interfaces to represent complex data structures, ensuring that the data conforms to expected shapes. This feature is particularly useful when dealing with props and state in React components.

Consider a scenario where you have a component that receives props. In JavaScript, you might pass props without explicit type checking, which can lead to runtime errors. In TypeScript, you can define a type for the props, enhancing code safety. Here's an example of a simple React component written in TypeScript:

```typescript
// components/UserProfile.tsx
import React from 'react';

interface UserProfileProps {
  name: string;
  age: number;
  email?: string; // Optional property
```

```
}
const UserProfile: React.FC<UserProfileProps> ({ name, age,
email }) > {
 return (
  <div>
   <h1>{name}</h1>
   <p>Age: {age}</p>
   {email && <p>Email: {email}</p>}
  </div>
 );
};

export default UserProfile;
```

In this example, the `UserProfileProps` interface defines the structure of the props expected by the `UserProfile` component. The `name` and `age` fields are required, while `email` is optional. This type definition ensures that only the correct types of data can be passed to the component, and any deviation from this structure will be flagged by TypeScript during development.

TypeScript also enhances error handling by catching type-related errors at compile time, thus preventing potential bugs from making it to production. For instance, if you attempt to pass a string where a number is expected, TypeScript will generate a compile-time error:

```typescript
<UserProfile name"John Doe" age"thirty" />
```

Here, TypeScript will report an error because `age` is expected to be a number, not a string.

Furthermore, TypeScript's powerful type inference capabilities can simplify your development process. When you use TypeScript, the compiler can often infer the type of a variable based on its initial value, reducing the need for explicit type annotations. This can make your codebase cleaner and more concise.

In addition to basic type annotations, TypeScript supports advanced features such as union types, intersection types, and generics, which allow for more flexible and reusable code. Generics, for instance, enable you to create functions and components that work with various types while maintaining type safety. Consider the following example of a generic function that works with different types of data:

```typescript
function identity<T>(arg: T): T {
  return arg;
}

const num identity(42); // num is of type number
const str identity("Hello"); // str is of type string
```

In this function, `T` is a generic type parameter that represents any type. The `identity` function returns a value of the same type that is passed in, ensuring that the type is preserved throughout the function.

TypeScript also integrates seamlessly with popular development tools and editors, such as Visual Studio Code, providing real-time feedback, auto-completion, and refactoring support. These features significantly enhance the development experience by catching errors early and providing useful suggestions.

In summary, integrating TypeScript into your Next.js projects offers substantial benefits in terms of type safety and code quality. By defining types, leveraging TypeScript's advanced features, and using its powerful development tools, you can create more reliable and maintainable applications. The setup process is straightforward, and once in place, TypeScript can greatly improve both the development workflow and the end-user experience.

With the foundational setup of TypeScript in place, the focus now shifts to leveraging its features to enhance code quality and maintainability within Next.js applications. One of the key benefits of TypeScript is its ability to catch type errors during development, long before runtime. This feature is particularly valuable in a large codebase, where managing the interactions between various components can be complex.

TypeScript's type system includes several constructs, such as interfaces, types, and enums, which can be used to define and enforce data structures. Interfaces and types allow developers to define the shape of objects, function signatures, and class structures, ensuring that the data being handled conforms to expected patterns. For example, in a Next.js application, you might define an interface to represent user data fetched from an API. This interface would specify the types of each property, helping to prevent issues that might arise from unexpected data formats.

Consider an interface for user data:

```typescript
// types/User.ts
export interface User {
  id: number;
  name: string;
  email: string;
  isActive: boolean;
}
```

This `User` interface can be used throughout the application to type-check data related to users. For instance, when fetching user data from an API, you can use this interface to ensure that the data returned matches the expected structure:

```typescript
// pages/api/users.ts
import { User } from '../../types/User';

export async function fetchUser(userId: number): Promise<User> {
  const response await fetch(`/api/users/${userId}`);
  const data: User await response.json();
  return data;
}
```

By typing the response data as `User`, TypeScript will ensure that the structure of the received data adheres to the `User` interface, catching any discrepancies at compile-time.

Another crucial aspect of TypeScript is its support for generic types. Generics allow you to create reusable components and functions that can work with a variety of data types while still providing strong type safety. In Next.js applications, generics can be particularly useful in scenarios involving data fetching or handling different types of components.

For example, a generic hook for fetching data might look like this:

```typescript
// hooks/useFetch.ts
import { useState, useEffect } from 'react';

export function useFetch<T>(url: string): [T | null, boolean, any] {
  const [data, setData] useState<T | null>(null);
  const [loading, setLoading] useState(true);
  const [error, setError] useState<any>(null);
```

```
useEffect(() > {
 async function fetchData() {
  try {
   const response  await fetch(url);
   const result: T  await response.json();
   setData(result);
  } catch (err) {
   setError(err);
  } finally {
   setLoading(false);
  }
 }

  fetchData();
}, [url]);

 return [data, loading, error];
}
` ` `
```

In this hook, the generic type `` `T` `` allows the hook to be used with different types of data, providing type safety while still being flexible. You can use this hook to fetch user data, posts, or any other type of resource, with TypeScript ensuring that the data returned conforms to the expected type.

Additionally, TypeScript enhances the development experience through its powerful tooling. IDEs with TypeScript support, such as Visual Studio Code, offer features like auto-completion, inline documentation, and real-time type checking, which can significantly speed up development and reduce errors. TypeScript's type inference also aids in this process by automatically deducing types based on the code, reducing the need for explicit type annotations in many cases.

Furthermore, TypeScript's strict mode provides additional safety by enabling more rigorous type checking. Activating strict mode in the `tsconfig.json` file can help catch potential issues early:

```json
{
 "compilerOptions": {
  "strict": true,
  // other options
 }
}
```

Strict mode enforces stricter type checks and requires explicit handling of null and undefined values, improving the robustness of your codebase.

As you integrate TypeScript into your Next.js projects, it is important to continuously refine and update your type definitions to reflect changes in your application's data structures and logic. Regularly reviewing and updating your types ensures that they remain accurate and effective in catching type-related issues.

In summary, TypeScript offers a range of features that enhance type safety and code quality in Next.js applications. By defining types and interfaces, leveraging generics, and utilizing TypeScript's tooling and strict mode, developers can build more reliable and maintainable applications. Integrating TypeScript into your development workflow not only helps prevent bugs but also improves the overall development experience by providing clear and actionable feedback throughout the coding process.

With TypeScript's power to enhance code quality and reliability firmly established, the next step involves effectively integrating TypeScript with Next.js's advanced features. One area where TypeScript can significantly improve development is in the management of Next.js's data fetching methods, such as `getStaticProps`, `getServerSideProps`, and `getStaticPaths`. These methods are pivotal in Next.js for pre-rendering pages with dynamic data. TypeScript can enforce types on the data returned from these methods, ensuring that your components receive and process the expected data formats.

For instance, when using `getStaticProps` to fetch data at build time, you can define the type of the returned data to enhance type safety. Here's how you might define a type for the props that will be passed to a page component:

```typescript
// pages/index.tsx
import { GetStaticProps } from 'next';

interface Props {
  posts: Post[];
}

const HomePage: React.FC<Props> ({ posts }) > {
  return (
    <div>
     <h1>Blog Posts</h1>
     <ul>
      {posts.map(post > (
       <li key{post.id}>{post.title}</li>
      ))}
     </ul>
    </div>
  );
};

export const getStaticProps: GetStaticProps<Props> async () >
{
  const res  await fetch('https://api.example.com/posts');
  const posts: Post[]  await res.json();
```

```
  return {
  props: {
   posts,
  },
 };
};
```

export default HomePage;
` ` `

In this example, `Props` defines the structure of the data expected by the `HomePage` component. TypeScript ensures that the `getStaticProps` function returns the correct shape of data, and that the `HomePage` component properly receives and handles this data.

Handling forms and user input is another area where TypeScript shines. By defining types for form data and validation schemas, you can catch potential issues early. For instance, if you're building a form to submit user data, you can define the types for form fields and use them to validate the data before sending it to your API.

Consider a form component where you define types for form fields:

```typescript
// components/UserForm.tsx
import { useState } from 'react';

interface FormData {
  name: string;
  email: string;
}

const UserForm: React.FC () > {
  const [formData, setFormData] useState<FormData>({ name: ", email: " });
```

```
const          handleChange                  (event:
React.ChangeEvent<HTMLInputElement>) > {
  const { name, value } event.target;
  setFormData(prevData > ({ ...prevData, [name]: value }));
};

const         handleSubmit          async     (event:
React.FormEvent<HTMLFormElement>) > {
  event.preventDefault();

  // Perform validation if necessary
  if (!formData.name || !formData.email) {
    console.error('All fields are required.');
    return;
  }

  // Submit form data
  await fetch('/api/submit', {
    method: 'POST',
    headers: { 'Content-Type': 'application/json' },
    body: JSON.stringify(formData),
  });
};
  return (
   <form onSubmit{handleSubmit}>
    <label>
     Name:
        <input type"text" name"name" value{formData.name}
onChange{handleChange} />
    </label>
    <label>
     Email:
        <input type"email" name"email" value{formData.email}
onChange{handleChange} />
```

```
    </label>
    <button type"submit">Submit</button>
    </form>
  );
};
export default UserForm;
```
` ` `

Here, `FormData` is used to type-check the form state and handle changes. TypeScript ensures that the form data conforms to the expected structure, which minimizes the risk of errors when handling user input.

Lastly, integrating TypeScript with Next.js's dynamic routing can further solidify type safety. For instance, if you are working with dynamic routes, TypeScript can be used to ensure that parameters and query strings are correctly typed. This is crucial for preventing runtime errors due to incorrect data types or missing parameters.

Consider a dynamic route component that fetches data based on a route parameter:

```typescript
// pages/posts/[id].tsx
import { GetServerSideProps } from 'next';

interface Post {
  id: number;
  title: string;
  content: string;
}

interface Props {
  post: Post;
}

const PostPage: React.FC<Props> ({ post }) > {
```

```
  return (
   <div>
    <h1>{post.title}</h1>
    <p>{post.content}</p>
   </div>
  );
};

export const getServerSideProps: GetServerSideProps<Props>
async (context) > {
 const { id } context.query;

  if (typeof id ! 'string') {
  return { notFound: true };
 }

  const res  await fetch(`https://api.example.com/posts/${id}
`);
  const post: Post  await res.json();

  return {
  props: {
   post,
  },
 };
};

export default PostPage;
```

In this example, the `id` parameter is checked and typed, ensuring that only valid data is used to fetch the post. This type enforcement helps prevent common errors related to dynamic routing and data fetching.

Through the effective use of TypeScript in these various aspects of Next.js development, developers can significantly enhance the robustness and reliability of their applications, leading to a more stable and maintainable codebase.

CHAPTER 38: IMPLEMENTING SERVER-SIDE RENDERING (SSR)

Server-Side Rendering (SSR) is a critical technique for improving web performance and search engine optimization (SEO) by rendering web pages on the server before they are sent to the client. This process allows for faster page loads and better indexing by search engines, as the fully rendered HTML is available when the page is requested. In this chapter, we will explore the fundamentals of SSR in the context of Next.js, delving into its setup, data fetching strategies, and optimization techniques.

To begin with, understanding the core principle of SSR is essential. Unlike client-side rendering, where JavaScript executes in the browser to render the page, SSR involves rendering the HTML on the server. This means that when a user requests a page, the server processes the request, generates the HTML, and sends the fully rendered page to the client. This approach results in a quicker time-to-content, which can significantly enhance user experience, especially on slower networks or devices.

Next.js simplifies the implementation of SSR through its built-in data fetching methods. The primary method used for SSR is `getServerSideProps`, which enables you to fetch data server-side on each request. This method is invoked on the server for every request to the page, allowing dynamic data to be fetched and included in the HTML sent to the client. This is particularly useful for pages that require up-to-date data or personalized content.

To illustrate, consider a Next.js page that displays user profiles. Using `getServerSideProps`, you can fetch user data directly on the server before rendering the page. Here is a basic example:

```typescript
// pages/profile/[id].tsx
import { GetServerSideProps } from 'next';

interface ProfileProps {
 user: {
  id: string;
  name: string;
  email: string;
 };
}

const ProfilePage: React.FC<ProfileProps> ({ user }) > {
 return (
  <div>
   <h1>{user.name}'s Profile</h1>
   <p>Email: {user.email}</p>
  </div>
 );
};

export const getServerSideProps:
GetServerSideProps<ProfileProps> async (context) > {
 const { id } context.params!;
 const res  await fetch(`https://api.example.com/users/${id}
`);
```

```
const user  await res.json();

 return {
 props: {
  user,
 },
 };
};

export default ProfilePage;
` ` `
```

In this example, `getServerSideProps` fetches user data based on the user ID obtained from the URL parameters. This data is then passed to the `ProfilePage` component as props, ensuring that the HTML sent to the client includes the user information.

However, while SSR offers significant benefits, it also introduces some challenges. One of the primary concerns is the performance impact on the server, as each request involves rendering the page and fetching data. Therefore, optimizing server-rendered pages is crucial to maintain scalability and efficiency.

Caching strategies are an effective way to mitigate performance issues with SSR. By caching rendered pages or the data used to generate them, you can reduce the load on your server and improve response times. Various caching techniques can be employed, such as HTTP caching, server-side caching with tools like Redis, or even static generation for frequently requested pages. Implementing these strategies can help balance the benefits of SSR with the need for server efficiency.

In addition to caching, optimizing data fetching is essential. When using `getServerSideProps`, consider minimizing the amount of data fetched or making use of conditional requests.

For instance, if the data for a page doesn't change frequently, it may be more efficient to use static generation or incremental static regeneration (ISR) instead. ISR allows you to update static pages in the background without rebuilding the entire site, offering a middle ground between static and server-side rendering.

Furthermore, you should be mindful of the code executed on the server. Reducing the complexity of server-side logic can help speed up the rendering process. Ensure that any heavy computations or long-running processes are optimized or handled asynchronously, to avoid slowing down the response time.

Lastly, integrating SSR with client-side interactivity requires careful consideration. While SSR provides a fully rendered HTML page, client-side JavaScript can still enhance user interactions and update the UI dynamically. It's important to ensure that client-side rendering and server-side rendering work harmoniously, without introducing conflicts or inconsistencies.

In summary, Server-Side Rendering in Next.js offers significant advantages for performance and SEO by delivering fully rendered pages from the server. Through the use of `getServerSideProps`, effective caching, and optimization strategies, you can harness the power of SSR while maintaining a scalable and efficient application. As with any rendering strategy, balancing performance with functionality is key to delivering a seamless user experience.

To effectively implement Server-Side Rendering (SSR) in Next.js, it is crucial to understand its interaction with data fetching and page optimization. Beyond the foundational method of `getServerSideProps`, Next.js offers additional strategies and tools to further refine server-side rendered applications.

First, consider the importance of managing data fetching efficiently. When using `getServerSideProps`, the function is executed on every page request, which may result in performance bottlenecks if the data fetching is not optimized. To mitigate this, it's advisable to employ caching mechanisms, both on the server and client side, to reduce redundant data fetching. For instance, server-side caching can store responses to frequent queries, decreasing the load on your data sources and speeding up the response time for subsequent requests. Similarly, client-side caching can reduce the need for re-fetching data on the client, enhancing the overall user experience.

Moreover, integrating APIs efficiently is another aspect of optimizing SSR. Using asynchronous functions to fetch data ensures that the server can handle multiple requests concurrently, thus improving throughput and responsiveness. It is also beneficial to use lightweight data-fetching libraries that support server-side operations, such as Axios or the Fetch API, tailored to fit the asynchronous nature of SSR.

An integral part of optimizing server-rendered pages is understanding how to handle and render dynamic content. SSR allows for dynamic content to be fetched and rendered on the server, which is particularly advantageous for pages with user-specific data or frequently changing information. By leveraging server-side data fetching methods, you ensure that users receive the most up-to-date content without waiting for client-side JavaScript to render the page.

However, SSR introduces its own set of challenges, including managing server load and ensuring efficient data handling. It is essential to balance the benefits of SSR with the potential costs of increased server workload. Techniques such as incremental static regeneration (ISR), which allows pages to be updated incrementally without rebuilding the entire site, can complement SSR by offering a hybrid approach. ISR combines the benefits of static generation with the flexibility of SSR, providing updated content while maintaining performance efficiency.

Additionally, optimizing the performance of SSR involves carefully managing how data is rendered and how the application responds to various user interactions. Utilizing tools like Next.js's built-in performance monitoring can help identify and address performance bottlenecks. For example, monitoring server response times and page load metrics provides insights into how effectively the server handles requests and where improvements may be necessary.

In terms of deployment, it's crucial to consider how SSR fits within your hosting environment. Platforms like Vercel, which is specifically designed for Next.js, offer seamless support for SSR and static site generation, providing built-in optimizations and scalability. When deploying on other platforms, ensure that your server infrastructure can handle the increased demands of SSR, including sufficient server resources and efficient request handling.

Security is another important consideration when implementing SSR. Since server-side rendering involves executing code on the server, it is vital to ensure that your application is protected from common security threats. Implementing robust validation and sanitization of input data helps prevent attacks such as SQL injection or cross-site scripting (XSS). Additionally, secure data handling practices, such as encrypting sensitive information and using secure protocols for data transmission, are essential for safeguarding user data and maintaining trust.

As you continue to work with SSR in Next.js, keep in mind that the goal is to enhance the user experience by delivering fast, dynamic, and secure web pages. Balancing performance, data management, and security considerations will help you leverage the full potential of SSR while addressing the inherent challenges of server-side rendering.

By integrating these strategies into your Next.js projects, you can build applications that not only perform well but also offer a superior user experience. SSR, when executed effectively, provides a powerful tool for creating fast, SEO-friendly web pages that meet modern web standards and user expectations.

When implementing Server-Side Rendering (SSR) in Next.js, one of the key aspects to focus on is the efficient management of server resources and response times. To optimize server-rendered pages, careful attention must be given to how server-side code interacts with both the application and the database.

An important consideration is how to manage server load during peak traffic periods. With SSR, each request necessitates a server-side render, which can strain server resources if not managed properly. Load balancing techniques can be employed to distribute incoming requests across multiple servers, thus ensuring that no single server becomes a bottleneck. Additionally, leveraging serverless architectures or cloud-based services, which automatically scale based on demand, can also enhance the performance and reliability of SSR implementations. These solutions allow the application to handle increased traffic without compromising response times or server stability.

Another critical element is optimizing the data-fetching process. When `getServerSideProps` is used to fetch data, the function executes on each request, which can be costly in terms of performance if not optimized. To address this, data-fetching strategies such as pagination, filtering, and batching should be employed. Pagination helps limit the amount of data retrieved in each request, while filtering and batching can reduce the volume of data processed at any given time. These techniques can alleviate the load on the server and improve overall response times.

Caching is another powerful tool for enhancing the performance of SSR. By implementing server-side caching, responses to frequent requests can be stored temporarily, thus avoiding the need for redundant data fetching and processing. Caching strategies can include in-memory caching for fast access, as well as more persistent solutions such as Redis or Memcached. On the client side, caching data in local storage or using service workers to manage cache can further reduce the need for repeated data fetches, providing a smoother experience for users.

Furthermore, optimizing the rendering process itself is crucial for maintaining performance. Techniques such as code splitting, where only the necessary JavaScript is sent to the client, can significantly reduce the time required for initial page loads. Next.js supports automatic code splitting out of the box, but additional optimization can be achieved through manual code splitting based on the application's needs. This approach ensures that users receive only the essential code for the current page, which improves both loading times and overall performance.

Additionally, optimizing images and other media resources is essential for fast server-side rendering. Images should be compressed and resized appropriately to balance quality and load times. Tools like Next.js's built-in `Image` component provide automatic optimization for images, ensuring that they are served in the most efficient format and size for each user. This not only enhances performance but also contributes to a better user experience.

It is also important to handle error scenarios gracefully within the SSR context. Implementing robust error handling and fallback mechanisms ensures that users receive informative messages or alternative content if something goes wrong during server-side rendering. This includes setting up custom error pages for common HTTP errors such as 404 Not Found or 500 Internal Server Error. By providing clear and user-friendly error messages, you can maintain a positive user experience even in the face of server-side issues.

Finally, thorough testing is indispensable for optimizing SSR implementations. Performance testing tools can simulate different traffic loads and measure server response times to identify potential bottlenecks. End-to-end testing frameworks can validate that server-side rendering functions correctly across various scenarios, ensuring that both data fetching and rendering processes are robust and reliable.

In conclusion, implementing Server-Side Rendering (SSR) in Next.js involves a multifaceted approach to optimize performance and enhance user experience. By focusing on efficient data fetching, server resource management, caching strategies, rendering optimization, and robust error handling, developers can harness the full potential of SSR to deliver fast, dynamic, and SEO-friendly web applications.

CHAPTER 39: MANAGING STATIC SITE GENERATION (SSG)

Static Site Generation (SSG) offers a robust approach to pre-rendering web pages at build time, contrasting with Server-Side Rendering (SSR) which generates pages on-the-fly per request. SSG in Next.js enables the generation of static content that can be served quickly and efficiently, significantly enhancing load times and overall user experience. This chapter delves into the practical implementation of SSG, highlighting the advantages and techniques involved, and explores how to utilize `getStaticProps` and `getStaticPaths` to streamline the generation of static pages.

The fundamental benefit of SSG is its ability to pre-render pages at build time, creating static HTML files that are served to users quickly. This process reduces the server's workload during user requests, as the static files are readily available, thus improving performance and scalability. For content that doesn't change frequently or doesn't require real-time updates, SSG provides an ideal solution, allowing pages to be generated once and served efficiently across multiple requests.

To implement SSG in Next.js, developers use the `getStaticProps` function, which allows for data fetching at build time. This function runs during the build process, enabling the generation of static pages with dynamic content. By returning an object with a `props` key, `getStaticProps` provides the necessary data to render the page statically. For example, if a blog page needs to display a list of articles, `getStaticProps` can fetch the articles from a CMS or database and pass them to the page component as props. The result is a fully-rendered HTML page that can be quickly served to users without additional server processing on each request.

Another key function in the SSG process is `getStaticPaths`, which is used in conjunction with `getStaticProps` to generate dynamic routes. When dealing with pages that depend on dynamic routes, such as product pages or blog posts, `getStaticPaths` determines which paths should be pre-rendered at build time. This function returns an object with a `paths` key, containing an array of path parameters, and a `fallback` key that specifies what should happen if a user navigates to a path not yet generated. By providing the paths, `getStaticPaths` ensures that Next.js knows which dynamic pages need to be pre-rendered, while `getStaticProps` fills in the dynamic data for each page.

One of the advantages of SSG is the ability to utilize incremental static regeneration (ISR), which allows pages to be regenerated after the build process without requiring a complete rebuild of the entire site. ISR provides flexibility for handling dynamic content that changes over time, such as news articles or product listings. By specifying a `revalidate` period in `getStaticProps`, developers can set an interval at which the static page will be re-generated. This ensures that users receive updated content while maintaining the performance benefits of static generation.

In practice, setting up SSG involves defining `getStaticProps` and `getStaticPaths` within the page components. For instance, consider a Next.js project with a blog. To implement

SSG for blog posts, `getStaticProps` would be used to fetch the post data from a CMS or a database. The function might look something like this:

```javascript
export async function getStaticProps({ params }) {
   const res   await fetch(`https://api.example.com/posts/${params.id}`);
  const post  await res.json();

  return {
  props: { post },
  revalidate: 60, // Re-generate the page at most once every 60 seconds
  };
}
```

In conjunction with this, `getStaticPaths` would be used to specify which blog post pages should be pre-rendered:

```javascript
export async function getStaticPaths() {
  const res  await fetch('https://api.example.com/posts');
  const posts  await res.json();

  const paths posts.map(post > ({
  params: { id: post.id.toString() },
  }));

  return { paths, fallback: 'blocking' };
}
```

The `fallback` option in `getStaticPaths` can be set to `'blocking'`, `'false'`, or `'true'`, depending on how you want to handle paths that are not pre-rendered. Setting it to `'blocking'` ensures that users will see the generated page only after it has been created, while `'true'` allows for incremental generation, and `'false'` results in a 404 page for unknown paths.

By leveraging SSG, developers can achieve significant performance improvements and provide a better user experience. Static pages are served quickly and efficiently, minimizing server load and enhancing scalability. Additionally, combining SSG with ISR allows for dynamic content updates while retaining the benefits of static generation. As a result, Next.js provides a versatile approach to rendering web pages that can be tailored to meet various needs, from highly dynamic content to more static, information-rich pages.

The application of Static Site Generation (SSG) in Next.js extends beyond basic use cases, offering sophisticated methods for handling various content types and optimizing performance. By leveraging `getStaticProps` and `getStaticPaths`, developers can effectively manage content generation, cater to dynamic routes, and ensure an efficient, scalable web application.

When utilizing `getStaticProps`, it's essential to understand its role in the build process. This function is executed at build time, fetching necessary data and pre-rendering the page as static HTML. This approach contrasts with client-side fetching, where data is retrieved dynamically, often leading to delays and additional load on the client-side. In scenarios where data changes infrequently, such as product catalogs or blog posts, `getStaticProps` ensures that the data is readily available at the time of the request, enhancing the user's experience by delivering fast-loading pages.

The function `getStaticProps` accepts an object with a `props` key, which is passed to the page component as props. This process allows developers to use static generation while still incorporating dynamic content. For instance, an e-commerce site could use `getStaticProps` to fetch product details and generate static pages for each product, ensuring that each product page is served with pre-rendered content. The data fetching logic inside `getStaticProps` could involve querying a CMS, a database, or even an API, which then populates the static pages with up-to-date information during the build process.

On the other hand, `getStaticPaths` is crucial for managing dynamic routes, especially when dealing with pages that require unique URLs based on data. For example, if you have a blog with individual posts, each with its own URL, `getStaticPaths` helps in generating these paths at build time. This function returns an object containing `paths`, which is an array of path parameters required to generate static pages, and `fallback`, which determines the behavior for paths not generated at build time.

The `fallback` key can be set to `false`, `true`, or `'blocking'`, each affecting how Next.js handles new or missing pages. Setting `fallback` to `false` means that only the paths specified in `getStaticPaths` will be pre-rendered. Any requests to other paths will result in a 404 error. This approach is straightforward and ensures that users can only access pages that were generated during the build. Conversely, setting `fallback` to `true` allows Next.js to serve a static shell while new pages are being generated in the background. Once the new page is generated, it will be cached and served for future requests. This option is useful for content that is frequently updated or where new paths might be added after the initial build. Finally, setting `fallback` to `'blocking'` means that Next.js will wait until the new page is generated before serving it to the user. This ensures that users only see fully rendered pages, though it might introduce some delay.

Handling data fetching and page generation efficiently is key to optimizing the performance of an application using SSG. It's vital to balance between static and dynamic content based on the nature of the website and user requirements. For instance, static content like marketing pages, documentation, and blog posts benefit greatly from SSG, offering fast load times and improved SEO. On the other hand, frequently changing data or personalized content may be better suited to SSR or client-side rendering, where content can be fetched and rendered dynamically.

Moreover, Next.js provides additional features to further enhance SSG performance. Incremental Static Regeneration (ISR) is one such feature, allowing developers to update static content without rebuilding the entire site. ISR enables pages to be regenerated in the background while serving stale content to users until the new page is ready. This approach helps maintain high performance while accommodating updates and changes.

In conclusion, managing Static Site Generation (SSG) in Next.js involves a thorough understanding of its capabilities and configurations. By utilizing `getStaticProps` and `getStaticPaths`, developers can efficiently pre-render pages at build time, manage dynamic routes, and optimize performance. Understanding the nuances of SSG and leveraging advanced features like Incremental Static Regeneration ensures that web applications remain fast, scalable, and responsive to both static and dynamic content needs.

When managing Static Site Generation (SSG) in Next.js, developers must also consider strategies for maintaining and updating static content. Since SSG generates pages at build time, any changes in the data source after the initial build will not be reflected in the static pages until the next build occurs. This characteristic presents both an advantage and a challenge: while static pages are delivered quickly to users, they may become outdated if not properly managed.

To address this issue, developers can use a combination of incremental static regeneration and deployment strategies. Incremental Static Regeneration (ISR) allows pages to be updated in the background without requiring a full rebuild of the site. With ISR, developers can specify a revalidation period for each page, indicating how often the page should be regenerated. For instance, setting a revalidation period of 60 seconds means that after 60 seconds, the next request to the page will trigger a regeneration if the page has changed, while subsequent requests will still serve the pre-rendered version.

This approach enables websites to maintain up-to-date content while still benefiting from the performance advantages of static generation. ISR is particularly useful for content that changes frequently but does not require real-time updates, such as news articles or product listings. By configuring ISR in Next.js, developers can balance between static content delivery and timely updates, ensuring that users see the latest information without compromising performance.

Another important aspect of managing SSG is handling large-scale data and content updates. For websites with extensive content or frequent updates, a full rebuild of the site can become time-consuming and resource-intensive. In such cases, using tools like build caching and partial builds can help mitigate these challenges. Build caching allows developers to reuse previously built pages or assets, reducing the time required for subsequent builds. Additionally, implementing partial builds, where only specific parts of the site are rebuilt, can further optimize the build process and improve overall efficiency.

Furthermore, integrating a headless CMS or an external

data source with SSG can streamline content management and updates. Headless CMS platforms, such as Contentful or Sanity, provide a user-friendly interface for managing content while allowing Next.js to fetch data during the build process. By connecting a headless CMS with `getStaticProps` and `getStaticPaths`, developers can automate content updates and ensure that the site remains current with minimal manual intervention.

Despite its many advantages, SSG may not be suitable for all scenarios. Applications that require real-time data or highly personalized content might benefit more from server-side rendering or client-side fetching methods. For example, user dashboards or applications with dynamic data interactions may not align well with the static nature of SSG, where data is pre-rendered and does not change until the next build.

In such cases, Next.js provides flexibility through its support for multiple rendering methods. Developers can combine SSG with server-side rendering (SSR) and client-side fetching to create a hybrid approach that leverages the strengths of each method. For instance, static pages can be used for general content and routes, while SSR or client-side fetching can handle user-specific data or real-time interactions.

Overall, managing Static Site Generation in Next.js involves understanding the trade-offs between performance and data freshness, utilizing incremental static regeneration, optimizing build processes, and integrating content management solutions. By carefully implementing these techniques and considering the specific needs of the application, developers can create efficient, scalable web applications that deliver high performance and a positive user experience.

CHAPTER 40: IMPLEMENTING AUTHENTICATION AND AUTHORIZATION

In the rapidly evolving landscape of web development, securing applications against unauthorized access and ensuring that users are who they claim to be are fundamental responsibilities. In this chapter, we will explore the critical concepts of authentication and authorization in the context of Next.js applications. These concepts are pivotal in safeguarding user data and managing access to different parts of an application. We will delve into various methods of implementing these security features, including JSON Web Tokens (JWT), OAuth, and integration with third-party identity providers.

Authentication is the process of verifying the identity of a user. It ensures that the user is indeed who they claim to be. Authorization, on the other hand, involves determining what an authenticated user is allowed to do. Both processes are essential for maintaining the security and integrity of web applications. In Next.js, implementing these features requires a thoughtful approach, considering both security best practices and the specific capabilities of the framework.

To begin with, JSON Web Tokens (JWT) are a popular method for implementing authentication in web applications. JWTs are compact, URL-safe tokens that represent claims to be transferred between two parties. In a Next.js application, JWTs are used to securely transmit user credentials between the client and server. The token contains encoded JSON objects, including a header, payload, and signature, which can be used to verify the authenticity of the token.

The process of using JWTs typically involves generating a token upon user login, which is then stored in a secure manner on the client side, such as in an HTTP-only cookie. This token is sent with subsequent requests to authenticate the user and ensure they have access to protected resources. On the server side, the token is verified and decoded to extract user information and validate the user's identity. The advantages of JWTs include their stateless nature, allowing for scalable and distributed systems, and their flexibility in containing custom claims for various application needs.

OAuth is another method used for managing authentication and authorization, especially when integrating with third-party services. OAuth allows users to grant third-party applications limited access to their resources without exposing their credentials. This is achieved through the issuance of access tokens by an authorization server. In a Next.js application, implementing OAuth typically involves integrating with identity providers such as Google, Facebook, or GitHub. The OAuth flow involves redirecting the user to the provider's authorization server, where they authenticate and grant access. The provider then redirects the user back to the application with an authorization code, which is exchanged for an access token.

Integrating OAuth into a Next.js application requires setting up appropriate endpoints for handling the OAuth flow, such as authorization and token endpoints. Additionally, the application must manage the storage and use of access tokens, ensuring they are securely handled and used to access protected resources. OAuth provides a robust mechanism for integrating with external identity providers and is particularly useful for applications that need to leverage existing user accounts from popular services.

Third-party identity providers offer another avenue for authentication, simplifying the login process by leveraging established services like Google, Facebook, or GitHub. These providers handle the complexities of user authentication, allowing developers to focus on other aspects of application development. To integrate with third-party identity providers in a Next.js application, developers typically use libraries and packages designed for this purpose. For example, the NextAuth.js library provides a comprehensive solution for adding authentication to Next.js applications, supporting various providers and authentication methods out of the box.

When implementing authentication and authorization in a Next.js application, it is essential to consider best practices for security. For instance, securing JWTs involves ensuring they are transmitted over HTTPS, using secure storage mechanisms on the client side, and implementing proper token expiration and renewal strategies. Similarly, OAuth implementations should follow best practices for securing authorization codes and access tokens, including using secure redirect URIs and validating tokens properly.

In summary, implementing authentication and authorization in Next.js applications involves a range of techniques and considerations. Whether using JWTs, OAuth, or integrating with third-party identity providers, developers must ensure that user data is protected and access is managed effectively. By following best practices and leveraging the tools and libraries available, developers can build secure and reliable applications that meet the needs of modern web users.

through a series of redirects and user interactions, culminating in the issuance of an authorization code that is exchanged for an access token. This access token is then used to authenticate API requests on behalf of the user. In the context of a Next.js application, OAuth integration typically involves setting up an authorization flow that includes configuring client credentials, defining scopes, and handling tokens securely. The use of OAuth provides a streamlined and secure approach for users to log in using their existing accounts with other services, enhancing user experience while maintaining robust security.

Integrating third-party identity providers into a Next.js application can further simplify the authentication process and enhance security. Providers such as Google, Facebook, and GitHub offer authentication services that leverage their own security infrastructure. When integrating these services, it is essential to handle tokens and user data with care, ensuring that any sensitive information is stored and transmitted securely. Third-party identity providers often support OAuth, making the integration process more straightforward.

One common approach to integrating third-party identity providers in Next.js is through the use of libraries and frameworks designed to streamline the process. For instance, NextAuth.js is a popular authentication library for Next.js applications that supports a range of authentication methods, including OAuth and email sign-ins. NextAuth.js abstracts much of the complexity involved in setting up authentication flows, providing a configurable and extensible solution for managing user sessions and integrating with various identity providers.

When implementing authentication and authorization, it is crucial to ensure that user data is protected and that access controls are properly enforced. This involves securing sensitive information both at rest and in transit. For example, when storing tokens on the client side, it is advisable to use secure, HTTP-only cookies to mitigate the risk of cross-site scripting (XSS) attacks. Additionally, implementing secure storage practices for tokens and user credentials on the server side helps to prevent unauthorized access and data breaches.

Furthermore, it is important to manage user sessions effectively to provide a seamless experience while maintaining security. Session management involves tracking user activity and ensuring that access rights are appropriately enforced throughout the user's interaction with the application. This may include setting up mechanisms for session expiration, token refresh, and logout functionality. Proper session management helps to mitigate risks associated with session hijacking and ensures that users have a consistent experience while using the application.

To enhance the security of authentication and authorization mechanisms, it is also essential to consider additional security measures such as multi-factor authentication (MFA). MFA adds an extra layer of security by requiring users to provide additional verification factors beyond their primary credentials. This could include something the user knows (such as a password), something the user has (such as a mobile device), or something the user is (such as biometric data). Implementing MFA can significantly increase the security of user accounts and reduce the likelihood of unauthorized access.

In addition to these practices, regular security audits and updates are crucial for maintaining the integrity of authentication and authorization systems. Security threats and vulnerabilities are continually evolving, and it is essential to stay informed about the latest developments in security best practices. Regularly reviewing and updating authentication and authorization mechanisms helps to address emerging threats and ensure that the application remains secure.

Overall, implementing robust authentication and authorization systems in Next.js applications involves a combination of understanding core security concepts, leveraging appropriate technologies and libraries, and adhering to best practices for securing user data and managing access. By carefully designing and implementing these systems, developers can create secure and reliable applications that protect user information and provide a seamless experience for authenticated users.

to implement additional layers of security, such as multi-factor authentication (MFA). MFA requires users to provide multiple forms of verification before gaining access, significantly enhancing security beyond the traditional username and password combination. For Next.js applications, integrating MFA typically involves adding support for additional verification methods, such as SMS codes or authentication apps. This can be achieved by leveraging third-party services that provide MFA functionality or by developing custom solutions that integrate with existing authentication workflows.

Another critical aspect of securing authentication and authorization processes is protecting against common vulnerabilities and attacks. One such vulnerability is Cross-Site Request Forgery (CSRF), which can occur when malicious websites trick users into performing actions on a site where they are authenticated. To mitigate CSRF attacks, it is essential to use anti-CSRF tokens and ensure that state-changing requests are protected by these tokens. In Next.js applications, this often involves including anti-CSRF tokens in forms and validating them server-side to confirm their authenticity.

Similarly, protecting against Cross-Site Scripting (XSS) attacks involves ensuring that user input is properly sanitized and that potentially dangerous content is not executed within the application. Implementing strict Content Security Policies (CSP) and using secure coding practices help to reduce the risk of XSS vulnerabilities. For instance, escaping user input and avoiding the use of `innerHTML` or other methods that directly inject HTML content into the DOM can prevent malicious scripts from executing.

Another important consideration is ensuring that sensitive data is transmitted securely. This is typically achieved through the use of HTTPS, which encrypts data transmitted between the client and server, protecting it from interception and eavesdropping. Configuring your Next.js application to enforce HTTPS for all communications is a fundamental step in securing user data and maintaining the integrity of authentication and authorization processes.

In addition to these security practices, monitoring and logging play a crucial role in maintaining the security of authentication and authorization systems. By implementing robust logging mechanisms, you can track authentication attempts, authorization decisions, and any anomalies or suspicious activities. This information can be invaluable for detecting and responding to potential security incidents. In a Next.js application, logging can be integrated with various monitoring tools and services to provide real-time insights and alerts.

Regular security audits and updates are also essential for maintaining the security of your application. As new vulnerabilities and threats emerge, it is important to stay informed about the latest security best practices and updates for the technologies you are using. This includes keeping dependencies up-to-date, applying security patches, and reviewing your authentication and authorization implementation to ensure it adheres to current security standards.

In summary, implementing authentication and authorization in Next.js applications requires a comprehensive approach that encompasses various methods and best practices. By leveraging techniques such as JWT, OAuth, and third-party identity providers, and by incorporating additional security measures like MFA, anti-CSRF protections, and HTTPS, you can create a secure environment for managing user access and protecting sensitive data. Effective session management, vulnerability mitigation, and ongoing monitoring further enhance the robustness of your authentication and authorization systems. As security is an ever-evolving field, staying informed and proactive in applying best practices is crucial for maintaining the integrity and security of your applications.

CHAPTER 41:
SETTING UP
CONTINUOUS
INTEGRATION AND
DEPLOYMENT

In the realm of modern software development, Continuous Integration (CI) and Continuous Deployment (CD) have become indispensable practices. These methodologies streamline and automate the processes of building, testing, and deploying applications, thus enhancing development efficiency and ensuring consistent delivery of high-quality software. In this chapter, we will explore how to establish CI/CD pipelines specifically for Next.js projects, focusing on automating various stages of the development workflow, from code integration to deployment in different environments.

Continuous Integration (CI) is the practice of frequently merging code changes from multiple contributors into a shared repository. This process is supported by automated build and test systems that validate the codebase with each integration. The primary goal of CI is to detect integration issues early and ensure that new code does not introduce bugs or conflicts. For Next.js applications, setting up a CI pipeline involves configuring automation tools to handle tasks such as code linting, unit testing, and integration testing.

The first step in setting up a CI pipeline for a Next.js project is selecting a CI tool that fits your needs. Popular CI tools include Jenkins, CircleCI, GitHub Actions, and GitLab CI. These tools provide the infrastructure necessary to automate the build and testing processes. Once a tool is chosen, you will need to create a configuration file that defines the steps to be executed during the CI process. For instance, in GitHub Actions, this involves creating a `.github/workflows` directory and adding YAML configuration files that specify the workflow steps.

In the CI configuration, you will typically define jobs that include installing dependencies, running linting tools, executing unit tests, and performing integration tests. For a Next.js project, this might involve commands such as `npm install` to install project dependencies, `npm run lint` to check for code style issues, and `npm test` to run automated tests. Additionally, you may include steps to build the application and ensure that the build artifacts are generated correctly.

Once the CI pipeline is in place, it is crucial to focus on Continuous Deployment (CD), which extends the principles of CI by automating the deployment of applications to various environments, such as staging, production, or test environments. The goal of CD is to deliver changes to end-users quickly and reliably, with minimal manual intervention. Setting up CD for a Next.js project involves configuring deployment pipelines that automatically deploy the application whenever code changes are merged into specific branches or when new builds are generated.

To implement CD, you will need to define deployment jobs in your CI/CD configuration that handle the process of deploying your application to the target environment. This typically includes steps such as building the application for production, uploading build artifacts to a hosting service, and performing deployment verification checks. For Next.js applications, common deployment platforms include Vercel, Netlify, and AWS. Each platform offers specific integration options and deployment configurations.

For example, if using Vercel, the deployment process can be simplified by connecting your repository to Vercel's platform, which automatically triggers deployments based on changes to your repository. Vercel handles the build and deployment processes internally, providing seamless integration with Next.js applications. Similarly, if deploying to Netlify, you can configure your CI/CD pipeline to push build artifacts to Netlify's platform, where they will be deployed automatically.

In addition to configuring deployment steps, it is also important to incorporate deployment verification into your CD pipeline. This might involve running end-to-end tests or smoke tests to ensure that the deployed application is functioning correctly. Automated deployment verification helps to catch issues early and ensures that the application remains stable and reliable after each deployment.

Effective monitoring and alerting are also essential components of a robust CI/CD pipeline. By integrating monitoring tools and services, you can track the health of your application, monitor deployment performance, and receive alerts for any issues that arise. This proactive approach allows you to address potential problems promptly and maintain a high level of service quality for end-users.

In summary, setting up Continuous Integration and Continuous Deployment pipelines for Next.js projects involves configuring automation tools to handle code integration, testing, and deployment processes. By implementing CI/CD practices, you can streamline your development workflow, improve code quality, and deliver updates to users more efficiently. As you proceed with setting up your CI/CD pipelines, consider the specific requirements of your Next.js application and the deployment platforms you are using to tailor the configuration to your needs.

involves configuring deployment pipelines that automatically take the output of successful builds and push it to the target environments. In the context of Next.js, this means setting up workflows to deploy your application to platforms such as Vercel, Netlify, or custom servers.

To establish a CD pipeline, begin by defining the environments to which your application will be deployed. Common environments include development, staging, and production. Each environment may have different configurations and deployment requirements. For instance, the production environment typically requires a higher level of stability and performance, while staging might be used for final testing before a production release.

For deploying Next.js applications, many developers opt for platforms like Vercel or Netlify, which offer seamless integration with modern CI/CD workflows. Both platforms provide native support for deploying Next.js applications and include features for automatic builds and deployments. Setting up a deployment pipeline on these platforms usually involves connecting your repository to the service, configuring build settings, and specifying deployment triggers.

When using Vercel, you can link your GitHub, GitLab, or Bitbucket repository directly to your Vercel project. Vercel automatically detects changes pushed to your repository, triggers builds, and deploys the latest version of your application. In the Vercel dashboard, you can manage environment variables, view build logs, and monitor deployments. Vercel also supports custom domains and provides a global Content Delivery Network (CDN) to enhance the performance of your application.

Netlify offers similar capabilities for deploying Next.js applications. By connecting your Git repository to Netlify, you can enable automatic builds and deployments. Netlify also provides a simple configuration file, `netlify.toml`, where you can specify build commands, environment variables, and deployment settings. Netlify's interface allows you to manage deploy previews, rollbacks, and site settings, making it a versatile choice for continuous deployment.

For custom server setups, where you might be deploying to traditional cloud providers or self-hosted environments, configuring a CD pipeline often involves more manual setup. In these cases, you would use CI tools to build and test your application, and then employ deployment scripts or tools like Docker to deploy your application to the desired server. This could include setting up SSH access, configuring deployment scripts, and ensuring that your server is correctly configured to handle the Next.js application.

When creating a custom deployment script, consider automating tasks such as stopping the current application, pulling the latest code, building the application, and starting the new version. This process can be managed through shell scripts or deployment automation tools like Ansible or Terraform. Additionally, you may integrate these scripts into your CI/CD pipeline to ensure that deployments are executed automatically following successful builds.

As part of the CD process, monitoring and managing deployments are crucial for maintaining application reliability. Implementing monitoring tools and services can help you track the performance and health of your deployed applications. Services like Datadog, New Relic, and Sentry provide insights into application performance, errors, and user interactions, allowing you to respond proactively to issues that arise in production.

In addition to monitoring, setting up alerts and notifications can help you stay informed about the status of your deployments. Most CI/CD platforms and deployment tools offer integrations with communication channels such as Slack, email, or SMS, enabling you to receive updates about build statuses, deployment successes, or failures. This immediate feedback helps ensure that any issues are addressed promptly, minimizing downtime and maintaining a smooth user experience.

Ultimately, establishing a robust CI/CD pipeline for Next.js projects involves careful planning and configuration to automate the build, test, and deployment processes. By leveraging CI tools to validate code changes and CD tools to deploy applications, you can achieve a more efficient development workflow, improve code quality, and accelerate the delivery of new features and fixes. The combination of automated testing, seamless deployments, and effective monitoring ensures that your Next.js applications are consistently delivered with high reliability and performance.

Beyond basic deployment, enhancing your CI/CD pipeline involves addressing aspects such as rollback strategies, security practices, and monitoring. Implementing robust rollback strategies is critical for ensuring that you can revert to a previous stable state in case of deployment issues. Most CI/CD platforms provide built-in mechanisms for rolling back deployments. For instance, platforms like Vercel and Netlify allow you to easily revert to previous versions of your application through their dashboards. If you are deploying to custom servers, you might need to implement your own rollback procedures, such as maintaining backup snapshots of your application or using versioned deployments.

Security is another vital consideration when setting up CI/CD pipelines. Ensuring the security of your deployment process involves safeguarding sensitive data such as API keys, secrets, and environment variables. Using environment variables is a common practice to manage sensitive information securely. Most CI/CD platforms provide mechanisms for securely storing and managing these variables. In addition, applying the principle of least privilege when configuring access permissions for your CI/CD systems can help mitigate potential security risks. Regularly reviewing and updating access controls and security configurations is essential to maintaining a secure deployment pipeline.

Monitoring and observability are crucial for maintaining the health of your application after deployment. Effective monitoring involves tracking application performance, user interactions, and error rates. Many CI/CD platforms integrate with monitoring and logging services, providing insights into your application's behavior and performance. For instance, integrating tools like Sentry or LogRocket with your Next.js application can help capture and analyze errors and user feedback. Monitoring services can alert you to issues in real-time, enabling prompt responses and reducing downtime.

Furthermore, implementing automated tests within your CI/CD pipeline ensures that code changes do not introduce new issues. Automated testing should cover various aspects of your application, including unit tests, integration tests, and end-to-end tests. For Next.js applications, you might use testing frameworks such as Jest for unit testing and testing-library/react for component testing. Integrating these tests into your CI pipeline ensures that any issues are detected early in the development process, contributing to the overall quality and stability of your application.

As you set up and refine your CI/CD pipeline, continuous improvement is key. Regularly reviewing and optimizing your pipeline can lead to increased efficiency and effectiveness. This includes evaluating the performance of your builds and deployments, identifying and addressing bottlenecks, and incorporating feedback from stakeholders. Adapting your pipeline to evolving project needs and technologies ensures that it remains aligned with best practices and continues to meet the demands of modern development workflows.

In summary, setting up Continuous Integration and Continuous Deployment pipelines for Next.js projects involves a series of well-defined steps that enhance the development and deployment process. By automating testing, building, and deployment processes, you streamline workflows, reduce manual intervention, and increase the reliability of your releases. Implementing best practices in rollback strategies, security, monitoring, and automated testing further strengthens your CI/CD pipeline, contributing to a more robust and efficient development lifecycle. As you navigate these practices, remember that the ultimate goal is to deliver high-quality software consistently while adapting to the ever-changing landscape of technology and user expectations.

CHAPTER 42:
USING NEXT.JS
WITH SERVERLESS
FUNCTIONS

In contemporary web development, serverless functions offer a streamlined approach to handling backend operations while benefiting from automatic scaling and reduced server management. This chapter delves into how to integrate serverless functions with Next.js, exploring deployment strategies, management of serverless environments, and leveraging these functions to handle backend logic effectively.

Serverless computing abstracts away the complexities of managing servers, allowing developers to focus on writing code rather than dealing with infrastructure concerns. Serverless functions, also known as Function-as-a-Service (FaaS), run in response to specific events or triggers and scale automatically based on demand. Integrating serverless functions with Next.js enables developers to create dynamic and responsive applications without the overhead of managing server infrastructure.

The integration of serverless functions with Next.js begins with understanding how to deploy these functions and manage their environments. Next.js provides built-in support for API routes, which can be utilized to create serverless functions. These API routes are defined in the `pages/api` directory of a Next.js project. Each file in this directory corresponds to a serverless function that can handle HTTP requests and responses. For example, a file named `hello.js` in the `pages/api` directory would expose an endpoint `/api/hello`, which can be used to execute the function defined within.

Deploying serverless functions in a Next.js application often involves leveraging cloud platforms that offer serverless infrastructure. Popular platforms include Vercel, AWS Lambda, and Netlify Functions. Each of these platforms has its own approach to deploying and managing serverless functions. Vercel, for instance, seamlessly integrates with Next.js and provides automatic deployment of API routes as serverless functions. When you deploy your Next.js application to Vercel, the platform automatically handles the deployment and scaling of API routes without requiring additional configuration.

For AWS Lambda, serverless functions can be integrated with Next.js by utilizing the serverless framework or AWS SAM (Serverless Application Model). The serverless framework simplifies the deployment process by providing configuration files that define the functions, their triggers, and deployment settings. AWS SAM offers a similar approach with its own configuration options. Both tools facilitate the deployment of serverless functions to AWS Lambda and enable you to manage their lifecycle, including updates and scaling.

Netlify Functions offer another option for deploying serverless functions with Next.js. Netlify provides a simple configuration for defining serverless functions in the `netlify/functions` directory. Deploying to Netlify involves linking your repository to Netlify, where the platform automatically detects and deploys functions alongside your Next.js application. Netlify Functions support various programming languages and frameworks, making it a versatile choice for serverless deployments.

Managing serverless environments requires attention to various factors, including function performance, security, and cost. Performance optimization involves understanding how serverless functions execute and ensuring that they are designed to handle requests efficiently. This might include optimizing code execution times, minimizing cold start durations, and managing dependencies effectively.

Security is another critical aspect of managing serverless environments. Serverless functions often handle sensitive data and interact with various services. Implementing proper authentication and authorization mechanisms, such as API keys or OAuth tokens, helps ensure that functions are accessed securely. Additionally, securing data in transit and at rest, as well as regularly updating dependencies to address vulnerabilities, are important practices for maintaining a secure serverless environment.

Cost management is also essential when working with serverless functions. Most serverless platforms charge based on the number of function invocations, execution time, and resource usage. Understanding the pricing model of your chosen platform and monitoring function usage can help you optimize costs. Implementing best practices such as optimizing function performance and minimizing unnecessary invocations can contribute to more efficient cost management.

Leveraging serverless functions with Next.js allows for a modular and scalable approach to handling backend logic. By utilizing API routes within Next.js, you can create endpoints that interact with databases, external services, or perform other backend operations. This integration simplifies the development process by providing a unified framework for both frontend and backend functionality.

In summary, integrating serverless functions with Next.js offers a powerful solution for managing backend operations while benefiting from automatic scaling and reduced infrastructure management. By understanding deployment strategies, managing serverless environments, and optimizing performance, developers can harness the full potential of serverless computing to build dynamic and scalable applications. As serverless technologies continue to evolve, staying informed about best practices and emerging trends will ensure that you can effectively utilize these technologies to meet your development needs.

for integrating serverless functions with Next.js, particularly through Netlify. Netlify Functions are designed to handle server-side logic and integrate seamlessly with Next.js applications. To use Netlify Functions, you would typically place your function code in a `netlify/functions` directory within your project. Each function file represents a serverless function that can be invoked through HTTP requests. Netlify automatically packages and deploys these functions when you push your code, making it easy to manage and scale your backend logic.

Managing serverless environments involves understanding the nuances of function execution and lifecycle management. Serverless functions are ephemeral by nature, meaning they are created and destroyed as needed. This dynamic nature requires a shift in how you handle state and data. Unlike traditional server-based applications, serverless functions do not maintain persistent connections or states between executions. This can impact how you design your backend logic and handle data persistence.

For state management, serverless functions often rely on external services such as databases or caching systems. For instance, if your function requires access to user data or session information, you might use a managed database service like Amazon DynamoDB, Google Cloud Firestore, or a SQL database hosted on a cloud provider. Similarly, you can utilize caching solutions like Redis to store frequently accessed data and reduce the load on your serverless functions.

Another important aspect of managing serverless environments is handling function execution times and cold starts. Serverless functions are subject to cold start latency, which occurs when a function is invoked after being idle for a period. This latency can affect the response times of your application. To mitigate cold start issues, you can optimize your function code to reduce initialization time and use techniques such as provisioned concurrency in AWS Lambda to keep functions warm and reduce latency.

In terms of security, serverless functions should be designed with best practices in mind. This includes managing access control, securing sensitive data, and ensuring that your functions are not vulnerable to common security threats. When deploying serverless functions, it is crucial to configure appropriate permissions and access controls. For instance, you should use IAM roles in AWS to grant functions only the permissions they need, minimizing the risk of unauthorized access.

Securing sensitive data involves encrypting information both in transit and at rest. Most cloud providers offer built-in encryption features that can be enabled for your serverless functions. Additionally, environment variables should be used to manage sensitive credentials and secrets, and these variables should be handled securely within your function code.

Logging and monitoring are also essential for effective management of serverless functions. Since serverless functions can be triggered by various events and have transient lifecycles, having robust logging mechanisms helps in troubleshooting and performance monitoring. Cloud providers typically offer logging services that integrate with serverless functions, such as AWS CloudWatch Logs or Google Cloud Logging. These services enable you to track function invocations, monitor performance metrics, and identify issues in real-time.

When using serverless functions with Next.js, it's important to design your application architecture to leverage the benefits of serverless computing while addressing its limitations. This includes creating stateless functions, managing external dependencies effectively, and optimizing function performance to ensure a seamless user experience. By integrating serverless functions thoughtfully, you can enhance the scalability and flexibility of your Next.js application, ultimately delivering a more robust and efficient solution.

variables used by serverless functions should be handled with care to ensure that sensitive information is not exposed. Most serverless platforms provide mechanisms for securely storing and managing environment variables, which can be utilized to store API keys, database credentials, and other confidential data. It is essential to avoid hardcoding such information into your function code or version control systems.

Monitoring and debugging serverless functions is another critical aspect of managing serverless environments. Due to their distributed and ephemeral nature, traditional debugging techniques may not be directly applicable. Instead, leveraging logging and monitoring tools is crucial. Cloud providers typically offer integrated logging services, such as AWS CloudWatch or Google Cloud Logging, which capture function execution logs and performance metrics. These logs can be invaluable for diagnosing issues and understanding how functions perform under various conditions.

Implementing comprehensive logging within your serverless functions helps track execution flow, identify errors, and measure performance. It is advisable to use structured logging formats that facilitate easier parsing and analysis of log data. By integrating your serverless functions with monitoring tools, you can gain insights into metrics such as execution duration, error rates, and resource usage. This information can guide optimizations and ensure that functions are operating efficiently.

Additionally, managing dependencies and optimizing function performance is essential for maintaining an efficient serverless architecture. Serverless functions typically have constraints on execution time, memory usage, and package size. To adhere to these constraints, it is crucial to minimize the size of dependencies and optimize code execution. Techniques such as code splitting, lazy loading, and efficient use of libraries can help reduce function size and improve performance.

As you develop and deploy serverless functions with Next.js, it is beneficial to adopt practices that align with the serverless paradigm. This includes designing functions to be stateless and focusing on single-purpose tasks. By keeping functions small and focused, you can enhance their scalability and maintainability. Additionally, considering the cost implications of serverless functions is important, as billing is typically based on the number of invocations and execution time. Efficient function design and optimization can help manage costs and avoid unnecessary expenses.

In summary, integrating serverless functions with Next.js applications provides a powerful approach to handling backend logic while benefiting from automatic scaling and reduced infrastructure management. Deploying functions through platforms like Vercel, AWS Lambda, or Netlify

Functions offers flexibility and scalability. Managing serverless environments requires careful consideration of state management, security, monitoring, and performance optimization. By following best practices and leveraging the capabilities of serverless platforms, you can build robust and efficient applications that capitalize on the advantages of serverless architecture.

CHAPTER 43:
BUILDING SCALABLE
ARCHITECTURES

In the realm of modern web applications, scalability is a fundamental requirement for accommodating growing user bases and increasing amounts of data. As applications evolve, their ability to handle higher volumes of traffic and data without degradation in performance becomes critical. This chapter explores strategies for building scalable architectures with Next.js, focusing on performance optimization, server load management, and designing systems capable of scaling effectively.

Scalability involves the ability of a system to maintain or improve its performance as it encounters increased load. In the context of Next.js, this entails addressing both the front-end and back-end aspects of the application to ensure a seamless experience for users, even under significant load.

One of the primary strategies for enhancing scalability is optimizing performance at various levels of the application stack. For Next.js applications, performance optimization begins with optimizing the rendering process. Next.js offers several features that contribute to performance, such as server-side rendering (SSR) and static site generation (SSG). By choosing the appropriate rendering method based on the use case, you can significantly reduce load times and improve user experience.

Server-side rendering, which generates HTML on the server before sending it to the client, can be beneficial for dynamic content that requires real-time data. This method reduces the time required for the client to render the page and provides a faster initial load. However, it may introduce additional server load, especially under high traffic conditions. On the other hand, static site generation pre-renders pages at build time, delivering static HTML that can be served quickly to users. This approach is highly efficient for content that does not change frequently and can significantly reduce server load and response times.

In addition to rendering optimizations, efficient data fetching and caching strategies play a crucial role in performance. For data that changes infrequently, implementing caching mechanisms can reduce the number of server requests and speed up response times. Next.js supports various caching strategies, including caching static assets, API responses, and server-side rendered pages. Utilizing Content Delivery Networks (CDNs) to cache and deliver static assets can further enhance performance by reducing latency and improving load times for users globally.

Managing server load is another critical aspect of building scalable architectures. As traffic increases, the server must be able to handle the additional load without compromising performance. One approach to managing server load is horizontal scaling, which involves adding more server instances to distribute the load. This can be achieved through cloud providers that offer auto-scaling capabilities, such as AWS Elastic Beanstalk or Google Cloud App Engine. These platforms automatically adjust the number of instances based on traffic patterns, ensuring that your application can handle spikes in demand.

Load balancing is also a key component of managing server load. Load balancers distribute incoming traffic across multiple server instances, preventing any single server from becoming overwhelmed. Implementing a load balancer in front of your Next.js application ensures that traffic is evenly distributed and that no single instance bears the brunt of the load. This helps to maintain high availability and reliability for your application.

Designing systems to handle increased traffic and data requires a thoughtful approach to architecture and data management. One effective strategy is to use microservices or modular architecture, where different components of the application are designed as independent services. This approach allows you to scale individual services based on their specific needs, rather than scaling the entire application. Microservices can also improve maintainability and reduce the impact of changes on the overall system.

In the context of data management, implementing efficient data storage and retrieval mechanisms is essential for handling large volumes of data. Databases play a crucial role in this aspect, and choosing the right database solution is key to scalability. For example, relational databases like PostgreSQL offer strong consistency and powerful querying capabilities, while NoSQL databases like MongoDB or DynamoDB provide flexibility and scalability for unstructured data.

Additionally, data partitioning and sharding can be employed to manage large datasets by distributing data across multiple database instances. This approach helps to improve performance and ensure that no single database instance becomes a bottleneck.

In summary, building scalable architectures with Next.js involves optimizing performance through efficient rendering and caching, managing server load through horizontal scaling and load balancing, and designing systems that can handle increased traffic and data through modular architecture and effective data management. By implementing these strategies, you can ensure that your Next.js application remains performant and reliable as it grows, providing a seamless experience for users even under the most demanding conditions.

involves adding more instances of your application servers to distribute the load. This approach can be achieved through cloud-based services that offer auto-scaling capabilities, such as AWS Elastic Beanstalk, Google Cloud App Engine, or Azure App Services. These platforms can automatically adjust the number of running instances based on the current load, ensuring that your application remains responsive even during traffic spikes.

In addition to horizontal scaling, employing load balancers is essential for managing and distributing traffic across multiple server instances. Load balancers ensure that incoming requests are evenly distributed, preventing any single server from becoming a bottleneck. Cloud providers often offer integrated load balancing solutions, which can be configured to work seamlessly with auto-scaling features. For instance, AWS Elastic Load Balancing and Google Cloud Load Balancing provide robust options for managing traffic and maintaining application performance.

When designing scalable architectures, it is also important to consider database scalability. As the volume of data grows, the database can become a significant performance bottleneck. To address this, various database scaling strategies can be employed. Sharding, for instance, involves partitioning data across multiple database instances, allowing each instance to handle a portion of the data. This approach can improve performance by distributing the load and reducing the pressure on any single database server.

Another strategy is to use managed database services that offer automatic scaling features. Cloud providers such as Amazon RDS, Google Cloud SQL, and Azure SQL Database provide managed database solutions with built-in scaling capabilities. These services can automatically adjust the database resources based on the workload, ensuring that your database can handle increased traffic and data volume efficiently.

Caching is another critical aspect of scaling databases. By caching frequently accessed data, you can reduce the number of queries sent to the database and improve response times. Implementing caching solutions such as Redis or Memcached can enhance performance by storing and quickly retrieving data that does not change frequently.

Designing a system that can handle increased traffic and data also involves implementing robust monitoring and alerting mechanisms. Monitoring tools provide insights into the performance of your application, servers, and databases, allowing you to identify and address issues before they impact users. Cloud providers often offer integrated monitoring solutions, such as AWS CloudWatch, Google Cloud Monitoring, and Azure Monitor, which can track metrics like CPU usage, memory consumption, and response times.

Setting up alerts based on predefined thresholds can help you respond proactively to potential issues. For example, you might configure alerts to notify you when server CPU usage exceeds a certain percentage or when response times exceed acceptable limits. By staying informed about the health of your application, you can take timely action to address performance issues and maintain a high level of service.

Incorporating resilience and fault tolerance into your architecture is also crucial for scalability. Ensuring that your system can withstand failures and continue to operate effectively is essential for maintaining service availability. Strategies such as implementing redundancy, using failover mechanisms, and designing for graceful degradation can help your application remain functional even in the event of failures.

Redundancy involves deploying multiple instances of critical components to ensure that if one instance fails, others can continue to operate. Failover mechanisms automatically switch to backup instances or systems in case of primary component failures, minimizing downtime and service disruptions. Designing for graceful degradation means that your application can continue to provide limited functionality even if certain components experience issues.

In summary, building scalable architectures with Next.js requires a multifaceted approach that encompasses performance optimization, server load management, and effective data handling strategies. By leveraging Next.js's built-in features for rendering and data fetching, employing horizontal scaling and load balancing techniques, and implementing robust monitoring and caching solutions, you can create an architecture that handles increased traffic and data efficiently. Designing with resilience and fault tolerance in mind further ensures that your application remains reliable and responsive as it scales.

ensures that you can proactively address potential issues and maintain application performance. Effective monitoring and alerting can help you detect anomalies, performance degradation, or resource constraints early, allowing for timely interventions.

In addition to monitoring, implementing a robust disaster recovery and backup strategy is crucial for maintaining system reliability. As your application scales, ensuring that data and critical components are protected against failures or outages becomes essential. Regularly scheduled backups of your data and configuration settings, along with tested recovery procedures, can mitigate the risk of data loss and reduce downtime in the event of a failure.

Another key consideration in building scalable architectures is designing for fault tolerance and high availability. Fault tolerance involves designing your system to continue operating correctly even in the presence of failures. This can be achieved through redundancy, such as deploying multiple instances of critical components across different regions or availability zones. High availability ensures that your application remains accessible and responsive by distributing resources and balancing the load effectively.

Incorporating resilience patterns, such as circuit breakers and retries, can further enhance fault tolerance. Circuit breakers prevent your system from making requests to a failing service, allowing it to recover and avoid cascading failures. Retry mechanisms can handle transient issues by retrying operations a specified number of times before failing. These patterns contribute to a more robust and resilient architecture.

As applications scale, managing configuration and deployment also becomes more complex. Implementing Infrastructure as Code (IaC) practices allows you to define and manage your infrastructure using code, enabling automated and consistent provisioning of resources. Tools such as Terraform, AWS CloudFormation, or Google Cloud Deployment Manager facilitate the management of infrastructure components, configurations, and deployments. IaC enhances reproducibility, reduces manual errors, and supports version control for infrastructure changes.

Lastly, as you build scalable architectures with Next.js, adopting a microservices architecture can be a valuable strategy. Microservices involve breaking down your application into smaller, independently deployable services that communicate through well-defined APIs. This approach allows for greater flexibility, scalability, and isolation of components. Each microservice can be scaled independently based on its specific requirements, leading to more efficient resource utilization and better overall performance.

Implementing a microservices architecture requires careful consideration of inter-service communication, data consistency, and service discovery. Service meshes and API gateways can facilitate communication between microservices, manage traffic routing, and provide additional features such as load balancing and security.

In summary, building scalable architectures with Next.js involves a multifaceted approach, encompassing performance optimization, effective management of server load, and designing systems capable of handling increased traffic and data. By leveraging advanced strategies such as horizontal scaling, caching, database scaling, and adopting best practices for monitoring, fault tolerance, and deployment, you can create a robust and scalable application capable of meeting the demands of a growing user base.

CHAPTER 44: FUTURE TRENDS AND ADVANCED TECHNIQUES

As web development continues to evolve, staying abreast of future trends and advanced techniques is crucial for leveraging the full potential of Next.js and creating cutting-edge applications. This chapter explores emerging technologies, evolving best practices, and potential enhancements that are poised to shape the future of web development and the Next.js ecosystem.

One of the most significant trends in web development is the rise of edge computing. Edge computing refers to the practice of processing data closer to the source of data generation, rather than relying on centralized data centers. This approach reduces latency, improves performance, and enhances user experience by delivering content and services faster. With Next.js, edge computing can be leveraged through platforms that offer edge functions and global content delivery networks (CDNs). By deploying Next.js applications to edge servers, developers can achieve faster response times and provide a more responsive user experience across diverse geographical locations.

Another trend gaining traction is the adoption of server-side components and hybrid rendering models. Next.js has been at the forefront of supporting hybrid rendering through its static site generation (SSG) and server-side rendering (SSR) capabilities. The evolution towards more granular server-side components, which combine the benefits of SSR with client-side interactivity, is likely to be a key area of advancement. These components can be rendered on the server and then hydrated on the client, enabling highly dynamic and performant applications that benefit from both server and client-side rendering.

The integration of artificial intelligence (AI) and machine learning (ML) into web applications is also a burgeoning trend. AI and ML can enhance user experiences through personalized content, intelligent recommendations, and advanced analytics. In the context of Next.js, integrating AI and ML involves incorporating APIs and services that provide predictive analytics, natural language processing, and image recognition. These capabilities can be integrated into Next.js applications to deliver more tailored and engaging user experiences.

GraphQL continues to gain momentum as an alternative to traditional REST APIs. Its ability to allow clients to request only the data they need and its strong typing system make it a powerful tool for managing complex data interactions. Next.js's support for GraphQL can be further enhanced by exploring advanced features such as schema stitching, federated schemas, and real-time subscriptions. These advancements enable developers to build more efficient and flexible data fetching strategies, improving both performance and developer productivity.

Progressive Web Apps (PWAs) represent another significant trend. PWAs combine the best of web and mobile applications, offering offline capabilities, push notifications, and a native app-like experience. Next.js is well-suited for building PWAs due to its support for service workers, caching strategies, and responsive design. As the web continues to embrace mobile-first approaches, integrating PWA features into Next.js applications will become increasingly important for delivering high-quality user experiences across devices.

The adoption of web components is also likely to impact the future of web development. Web components are a set of standards that allow developers to create reusable and encapsulated elements that can be used across different frameworks and libraries. Next.js's architecture can benefit from the integration of web components by enabling more modular and maintainable application structures. As web components gain traction, Next.js applications may see increased adoption of this technology to enhance reusability and interoperability.

Another area of advancement is the evolution of build tools and development environments. As web applications become more complex, the need for efficient build processes and development workflows grows. Innovations in build tools, such as improvements in bundling, tree shaking, and incremental builds, are expected to enhance the development experience and optimize performance. Next.js's integration with modern build tools and practices, such as Rust-based build systems and advanced code splitting techniques, will likely contribute to faster builds and more efficient development cycles.

Additionally, the rise of decentralized technologies and blockchain is starting to influence web development. Decentralized applications (dApps) and smart contracts offer new ways to build secure and transparent systems. While still an emerging field, integrating blockchain technology with Next.js could enable developers to create decentralized features, such as secure transactions and digital asset management, within their applications.

As we look to the future of web development with Next.js, it is clear that advancements in edge computing, server-side rendering, AI and ML integration, GraphQL, PWAs, web components, build tools, and decentralized technologies will play a significant role in shaping the next generation of web applications. By staying informed and adapting to these trends, developers can continue to push the boundaries of what is possible with Next.js and deliver innovative and high-performing applications that meet the evolving needs of users and the industry.

As the landscape of web development continues to advance, the integration of advanced techniques and technologies becomes increasingly relevant. One noteworthy development is the growing emphasis on API-first design and microservices architecture. API-first design ensures that APIs are treated as first-class citizens in the development process, enabling more modular and scalable systems. This approach allows for the seamless integration of various services and applications, which is particularly beneficial in a microservices architecture where different services communicate through well-defined APIs. Next.js applications can benefit from this by using API-first principles to build robust, flexible backends that can evolve independently from the front-end.

The adoption of WebAssembly (Wasm) is another promising trend. WebAssembly enables developers to run code written in languages other than JavaScript at near-native speed in the browser. This technology opens up new possibilities for performance optimization and advanced functionality within Next.js applications. By leveraging WebAssembly, developers can integrate high-performance computing tasks, such as image processing or complex calculations, directly into the client-side experience without relying on server-side execution. This can enhance the capabilities of Next.js applications, providing a more responsive and feature-rich user experience.

Additionally, the rise of headless CMS (Content Management Systems) offers a new paradigm for content management and delivery. Headless CMS platforms decouple the content management interface from the presentation layer, allowing content to be managed independently and delivered via APIs. This approach aligns well with Next.js's capabilities, as it enables developers to build dynamic, content-driven applications with greater flexibility. By integrating headless CMS solutions, such as Strapi or Contentful, with Next.js, developers can create applications that are both scalable and easy to manage.

The proliferation of Jamstack architecture represents another significant shift in web development. Jamstack, which stands for JavaScript, APIs, and Markup, emphasizes a decoupled architecture where the front-end is built separately from the back-end services. Next.js is well-suited for Jamstack projects due to its support for static site generation and server-side rendering. Embracing Jamstack principles can lead to faster load times, improved security, and a more scalable application infrastructure.

In terms of user experience, the focus on progressive web apps (PWAs) continues to grow. PWAs combine the best aspects of web and mobile applications, offering offline capabilities, push notifications, and improved performance. Next.js applications can be enhanced with PWA features through service workers and manifests, providing users with a more engaging and app-like experience. By adopting PWA techniques, developers can ensure that their Next.js applications perform well across various devices and network conditions.

Another advanced technique gaining traction is the use of static rendering and incremental static regeneration (ISR). Static rendering, which involves pre-rendering pages at build time, can significantly improve performance and SEO. Incremental static regeneration extends this concept by allowing static pages to be updated incrementally as new data becomes available. This technique provides a balance between static site benefits and dynamic content needs, making it ideal for applications that require frequent updates while maintaining high performance.

The ongoing development of Next.js itself is likely to introduce new features and enhancements that align with these trends. Keeping up with the latest releases and updates will be essential for leveraging emerging technologies and techniques effectively. As the framework evolves, it is expected to incorporate improvements in areas such as serverless functions, edge computing, and developer experience, further enhancing its capabilities and relevance in the modern web development landscape.

As we look towards the future, the ability to adapt to new technologies and methodologies will be key to staying competitive in web development. Embracing advanced techniques and trends, such as those discussed, will enable developers to build more scalable, performant, and user-centric applications with Next.js. By integrating these innovations into their projects, developers can ensure that their applications remain at the forefront of web development, meeting the ever-evolving needs of users and leveraging the latest advancements in technology.

Progressive web apps (PWAs) continue to gain traction as a means to deliver high-quality user experiences that bridge the gap between web and native applications. PWAs leverage service workers to enable offline functionality and enhance performance through caching strategies. With Next.js, developers can integrate PWA features by configuring service workers and manifest files to ensure that applications are reliable, fast, and engaging even in low-network conditions.

This integration enhances user retention and accessibility, making applications more resilient and versatile across various devices.

Furthermore, the evolution of user interface (UI) and user experience (UX) design reflects a growing trend towards more immersive and interactive web applications. Techniques such as augmented reality (AR) and virtual reality (VR) are becoming increasingly accessible, and their incorporation into web applications can provide users with novel and engaging experiences. While integrating AR and VR into Next.js applications requires careful consideration of performance and compatibility, the potential to create unique and interactive user experiences offers significant advantages.

Another noteworthy advancement is the increasing focus on developer experience (DX). As the complexity of web applications grows, the tools and practices that support developers in creating, testing, and maintaining applications become crucial. Improved development workflows, enhanced debugging tools, and streamlined deployment processes contribute to a more efficient and enjoyable developer experience. Next.js has made strides in this area by offering built-in features for hot reloading, automatic code splitting, and optimized build processes. Continued improvements in DX will likely include more sophisticated development environments, better integration with other tools and platforms, and enhanced support for collaborative development practices.

In addition to these technological advancements, evolving best practices for security and privacy are critical in the context of modern web development. With increasing concerns over data protection and privacy, implementing robust security measures becomes essential. Next.js provides various mechanisms to enhance security, including support for secure headers, content security policies, and secure data handling practices. As security threats continue to evolve, staying informed about the latest best practices and emerging security standards will be crucial for safeguarding user data and maintaining trust.

Finally, the future of web development with Next.js will be shaped by the continued evolution of the underlying technologies and ecosystems. The ongoing advancements in JavaScript, improvements in serverless architectures, and innovations in cloud computing will influence how Next.js applications are built and deployed. Keeping abreast of these changes and adapting to new technologies will be essential for leveraging the full potential of Next.js and ensuring that applications remain at the forefront of performance, scalability, and user experience.

In conclusion, the landscape of web development is characterized by rapid technological advancements and evolving best practices. Next.js, with its flexibility and powerful features, is well-positioned to embrace these changes and drive the development of innovative and scalable applications. By staying informed about emerging technologies, integrating advanced techniques, and adhering to evolving best practices, developers can build Next.js applications that are not only current but also future-proof, ensuring they continue to meet the demands of an ever-changing digital world.